Microsoft Dynamics NAV 2009 Programming Cookbook

Build better business applications with NAV

Over 110 simple but incredibly effective recipes for taking control of Microsoft Dynamics NAV 2009

Matt Traxinger

Husen, best of luck in your NAV career.

Matt

[PACKT] enterprise

PUBLISHING

professional expertise distilled

BIRMINGHAM - MUMBAI

Microsoft Dynamics NAV 2009 Programming Cookbook
Build better business applications with NAV

First published: October 2010

Production Reference: 141010

Published by Packt Publishing Ltd.
32 Lincoln Road
Olton
Birmingham, B27 6PA, UK.

ISBN 978-1-849680-94-3

www.packtpub.com

Cover Image by Sandeep Babu (sandyjb@gmail.com)

Credits

Author
Matt Traxinger

Reviewer
David Roys

Acquisition Editor
Rashmi Phadnis

Development Editor
Mayuri Kokate

Technical Editor
Alina Lewis

Indexer
Rekha Nair

Editorial Team Leader
Gagandeep Singh

Project Team Leader
Priya Mukherji

Project Coordinator
Sneha Harkut

Proofreader
Lesley Harrison

Graphics
Geetanjali Sawant

Production Coordinator
Arvindkumar Gupta

Cover Work
Arvindkumar Gupta

About the author

Matt Traxinger graduated from the Georgia Institute of Technology in 2005 with a B.S. in Computer Science, specializing in Human Computer Interaction and Cognitive Science. After college, he took a job as an add-on developer using a language he was unfamiliar with and for a product he had never heard of: Navision. It turned out to be a great decision.

In the years following, Matt learned all areas of the product and earned Microsoft Certified Business Solutions Professional certifications in both technical and functional areas of NAV. He continues to stay current with new releases of the product and is certified in multiple areas for versions 4.0, 5.0, and 2009.

Currently, Matt works in Norcross, GA, for Canvas Systems—one of the largest resellers of new and refurbished computer equipment—as an in-house NAV Developer and Business Analyst. He supports multiple offices in the United States as well as locations in the United Kingdom and the Netherlands.

In his spare time you can find him on the online communities `Mibuso.com` and `DynamicsUser.net` under the name MattTrax, helping others learn more about the Dynamics NAV software.

I would like to thank my mom, Norma, not just for buying me my first computer, but for everything that I cannot put into words. Your decisions have put me down the path I am on and I would not trade it for anything.

Thank you to my sister, Alex. Your hard work inspires me. I could not imagine having a better sister than you.

For my wife, Kim. Watching you chase your dreams for the past six years has motivated me to keep going after mine. Thank you for everything you do for me.

Finally, thank you to Mibuso and the Millenium Club. Without your help over the past five years, my knowledge of NAV would be nowhere near what it is today.

About the reviewer

David Roys is a Microsoft Most Valuable Professional (MVP) for the Microsoft Dynamics NAV product and is a co-author of the first book on NAV 2009 – *Implementing Microsoft Dynamics NAV 2009* – which was published by *Packt Publishing* in December 2008.

He works for Intergen Ltd., a bunch of fun-loving, incredibly smart people who are guided by the BHAG (Big Hairy Audacious Goal): "Everyone, every day is touched positively by the things we do". To learn more about Intergen and to read their blog, visit www.intergen.co.nz.

David created www.teachmenav.com, a website that allows readers to access programming samples that accompany the book he wrote with Vjeko Babić and regularly blogs on the subject of NAV at http://www.teachmenav.com/blogs/dave/default.aspx.

> I would like to thank Matt for giving me the opportunity to make my comments on the early drafts of his book. He has taught me many things along the way and I am sure there is something in this book for everyone.

Table of Contents

Preface

Microsoft Dynamics NAV 2009 is a business management solution that helps simplify and streamline highly specialized business processes such as finance, manufacturing, customer relationship management, supply chains, analytics, and electronic commerce for small and medium-sized enterprises. ERP systems like NAV thus become the center of a company's day-to-day operations. When you learn to program in an environment like this, it opens up doors to many other exciting areas such as .NET programming, SQL Server, and Web Services.

Microsoft Dynamics NAV 2009 Programming Cookbook will take you through interesting topics that span a wide range of areas such as integrating the NAV system with other software applications like Microsoft Office, creating reports to present information from multiple areas of the system, and so on. You will not only learn the basics of NAV programming, but you will also be exposed to the technologies that surround the NAV system such as .NET programming, SQL Server, and Web Services.

The first half of the cookbook will help programmers using NAV for the first time by walking them through the building blocks of writing code and creating objects such as tables, forms, and reports.

The second half focuses on using the technologies surrounding NAV to build better solutions. You will learn how to write .NET code that works with the NAV system and how to integrate the system with other software applications such as Microsoft Office or even custom programs. You will also discover some of the features of the RoleTailored client including creating pages and custom add-ins.

What this book covers

Chapter 1, Strings, Dates, and Other Data Types, covers the processes involved in working with most common, simple data types. You will learn how to convert data into different data types as well as some of the basic NAV functions that can be used to control the data stored in those variables. Each recipe is accompanied by base NAV code so that you can see how these building blocks are used to create the full application.

Chapter 2, General Development, focuses on the traditional code structures native to most programming languages. These structures include loops, conditional statements, functions, and so on. You will also learn some commands that are found exclusively in C/AL including ones that allow you to create your own progress bars and how to reference dynamic data.

Chapter 3, Working with Tables and Records, discusses the many things that can be done with the database in NAV. You will learn how to create table structures to hold business data, such as fields and keys, and how to filter that data to return only what you wish to see. Additionally, you will find out how to retrieve data from other companies and rollback any data changes that may have been committed to the database.

Chapter 4, Designing Forms, shows you how to create displays that will allow your users to interact with the data. You will learn how to create several different types of forms including matrixes and wizards and to customize its look and feel.

Chapter 5, Report Design, focuses on displaying data from multiple sources to your users. You will learn how to group data and display totals, and create reports that only process data. There are also recipes that will teach you how to make reports look more professional with tools such as watermarks and page counts.

Chapter 6, Diagnosing Code Problems, explains how to use built-in NAV tools such as Debugger and Client Monitor to find problems in your code. You will also learn techniques for structuring your code so that you can bypass any errors that might occur.

Chapter 7, Roles and Security, covers setting up user roles and permissions. You will learn several methods that will let you interact with the NAV security system and different ways to restrict user access to data such as field-level security and overriding the Zoom window. Integration with Active Directory is also discussed.

Chapter 8, Leveraging Microsoft Office, describes different methods to integrate with the Microsoft Office suite of products. These include Word, Excel, InfoPath, Communicator (instant messenger), and Visio. Many of these recipes require you to build .NET automation classes that will be used within the NAV client.

Chapter 9, OS Interaction, focuses on different ways to integrate with the Windows operating system. There are several recipes to replace deprecated functions from versions prior to NAV 2009. You will learn how to search the file system as well as how to directly query the system registry.

Chapter 10, Integration, explains different methods by which NAV can interact with outside applications. You will learn how to exchange flat files with Dataports and XMLports, write your own .NET classes which can be used in NAV, and access data directly from other systems. The new Web Services features in NAV 2009 are also discussed.

Chapter 11, Working with SQL Server, provides an introduction to the SQL Server environment. There recipes will help you understand SIFT (Sum Index Field Technology), to use SQL Views as data in NAV, and to call NAV code from a SQL Job.

Chapter 12, The RoleTailored Client, covers many of the new features found in NAV 2009. You will learn the basics of creating pages, Role Centers, and report layouts. In addition, you will learn how to write your own .NET add-in to display data from outside sources directly in the NAV client.

What you need for this book

Used in the recipes: NAV 2009 SP1, Visual Studio 2008, SQL Server 2008.

Most recipes will work with: NAV 5.0, Visual Studio 2005, SQL Server 2005.

Who this book is for

If you are a junior/entry level NAV developer then the first half of the book is designed primarily for you. You may or may not have any programming experience. This book focuses on the basics of NAV programming. It would be best if you have gone through a brief introduction to the NAV client.

If you are a mid-level NAV developer, you will find the second half more useful. These chapters explain how to think outside the NAV box when building solutions. Senior developers will find these recipes useful too.

Conventions

In this book, you will find a number of styles of text that distinguish between different kinds of information. Here are some examples of these styles, and an explanation of their meaning.

Code words in text are shown as follows: "The `sp_who` command queries the `sys.sysprocesses` system table in SQL."

A block of code is set as follows:

```
Window.OPEN('Customer No: #1###################');
Window.INPUT(1, CustomerNo);
Window.CLOSE;

IF Customer.GET(CustomerNo) THEN
  MESSAGE('Customer Name: %1', Customer.Name)
ELSE
  MESSAGE('No customer found!');
```

Any command-line input or output is written as follows:

```
"Path to Application Server\nassql" debug, appservername="NAS",
servername="Your Server Name", database="Your Database
Name",company="Your Company Name", startupparameter="NEP-", object-
cache=32000, nettype=tcp
```

New terms and **important words** are shown in bold. Words that you see on the screen, in menus or dialog boxes for example, appear in the text like this: "From the NAV client menu, click on **Tools | Debugger | Code Coverage**."

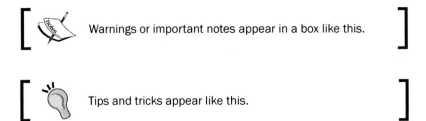

Warnings or important notes appear in a box like this.

Tips and tricks appear like this.

Reader feedback

Feedback from our readers is always welcome. Let us know what you think about this book—what you liked or may have disliked. Reader feedback is important for us to develop titles that you really get the most out of.

To send us general feedback, simply send an e-mail to feedback@packtpub.com, and mention the book title via the subject of your message.

If there is a book that you need and would like to see us publish, please send us a note in the **SUGGEST A TITLE** form on www.packtpub.com or e-mail suggest@packtpub.com.

If there is a topic that you have expertise in and you are interested in either writing or contributing to a book, see our author guide on www.packtpub.com/authors.

Customer support

Now that you are the proud owner of a Packt book, we have a number of things to help you to get the most from your purchase.

Downloading the example code for this book

You can download the example code files for all Packt books you have purchased from your account at http://www.PacktPub.com. If you purchased this book elsewhere, you can visit http://www.PacktPub.com/support and register to have the files e-mailed directly to you.

Errata

Although we have taken every care to ensure the accuracy of our content, mistakes do happen. If you find a mistake in one of our books—maybe a mistake in the text or the code—we would be grateful if you would report this to us. By doing so, you can save other readers from frustration and help us improve subsequent versions of this book. If you find any errata, please report them by visiting http://www.packtpub.com/support, selecting your book, clicking on the **errata submission form** link, and entering the details of your errata. Once your errata are verified, your submission will be accepted and the errata will be uploaded on our website, or added to any list of existing errata, under the Errata section of that title. Any existing errata can be viewed by selecting your title from http://www.packtpub.com/support.

Piracy

Piracy of copyright material on the Internet is an ongoing problem across all media. At Packt, we take the protection of our copyright and licenses very seriously. If you come across any illegal copies of our works, in any form, on the Internet, please provide us with the location address or website name immediately so that we can pursue a remedy.

Please contact us at copyright@packtpub.com with a link to the suspected pirated material.

We appreciate your help in protecting our authors, and our ability to bring you valuable content.

Questions

You can contact us at questions@packtpub.com if you are having a problem with any aspect of the book, and we will do our best to address it.

1

Strings, Dates, and Other Data Types

In this chapter, we will cover:

- ▶ Retrieving the system date and time
- ▶ Retrieving the work date
- ▶ Determining the day, month, and year from a given date
- ▶ Converting a value to a formatted string
- ▶ Creating an array
- ▶ Creating an Option variable
- ▶ Converting a string to another data type
- ▶ Manipulating string contents
- ▶ Using date formulas to calculate dates

Introduction

Simple data types are building blocks for everything you will program. C/AL contains the same data types that you will find in most other programming languages: Booleans, integers, decimals, dates, and strings. There are of course more than just these five, but majority of your programming will revolve around using these types of variables.

As a developer, your job is to build business logic that will manipulate the data that is input by users. This ensures that the data stored in tables is meaningful. Most of this data will be of one of the following data types. NAV is, after all, a financial system at heart. At its most basic level, it cares about three things: "How much money?" (decimal), "What was it for?" (string), and "When did it happen?" (date).

The recipes you will find in this section may not be the most interesting, but are valuable. The functionality described here is used throughout the system. As such, each example in this chapter is accompanied by actual code from base NAV objects in order to better illustrate how they can be used.

Retrieving the system date and time

There are many instances when it is necessary to obtain the current date and time from the user's system. This recipe will show you how to get that information.

How to do it...

1. Create a new codeunit from **Object Designer**.

2. Write the following code in the OnRun trigger of the codeunit:

   ```
   MESSAGE('Todays Date: %1\Current Time: %2', TODAY, TIME);
   ```

3. Save and close the codeunit.

4. When you run the codeunit you should see a window similar to the following screenshot:

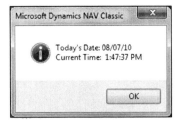

How it works...

The TODAY keyword returns the date from the system clock on the client computer. In Windows, the current system time is usually located at the bottom-right corner of the task bar. The same holds true for the system time which is returned by the TIME keyword.

There's more...

The actual date and time returned depends on which version of the NAV client you are using. In the **RoleTailored client**, the date and time come from the NAV server. In the **Classic client**, the date and time come directly from the client computer and users will be able to manipulate the system clock to their advantage if they need to. An example could be a time clock application where a user can clock in, change the system time to eight hours later, clock out, and change it back to the original time.

You can also retrieve the system date and time, all at once, using the CURRENTDATETIME function. The date and time can be extracted using the DT2DATE and DT2TIME functions respectively.

 For a complete list of date functions, search the C/SIDE Reference Guide under the **Help** menu for date and time functions.

Logging changes and events

The ChangeLog is a base NAV module that allows you to track changes to specific fields in tables. The following code can be found in **Codeunit 423, Change Log Management**, in the InsertLogEntry() method.

```
ChangeLogEntry.INIT;
ChangeLogEntry."Date and Time" := CURRENTDATETIME;
ChangeLogEntry.Time := DT2TIME(ChangeLogEntry."Date and Time");
```

Here, instead of using the WORKDATE function, we use the CURRENTDATETIME function and then extract the time using the DT2TIME function. The system designers could have just done the following setup:

```
ChangeLogEntry.Date := TODAY;
ChangeLogEntry.Time := TIME;
```

The advantage of using CURRENTDATETIME over TODAY and TIME is minimal. CURRENTDATETIME makes one request to the system, while the second method makes two. It is possible that another operation or thread on the client machine could take over between retrieving the date and time from the computer, however, this is very unlikely. The operations could also take place right before and after midnight, generating some very strange data. The requirements for your modification will determine which method is suits best, but generally CURRENTDATETIME is the correct method to use.

See also

- Retrieving the work date
- Determining the day, month, and year from a date
- Converting a value to a formatted string
- Writing your own rollback routine

Retrieving the work date

The work date is an essential part of the NAV system. This recipe will show you how to determine what that date is, as well as when and where you should use it.

Getting ready

1. Click on **Tools | Workdate** from the NAV client.
2. Set the work date to `01/01/2010`.

How to do it...

1. Create a new codeunit from **Object Designer**.
2. Write the following code in the `OnRun` trigger of the codeunit:

   ```
   MESSAGE('Work Date: %1\Todays Date: %2\Current Time: %3',
                           WORKDATE, TODAY, TIME);
   ```

3. Save and close the codeunit.
4. When you run the codeunit you should see a window like the following screenshot:

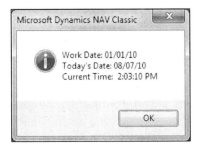

How it works...

The work date is a date internal to the NAV system. This date is returned using the `WORKDATE` keyword. It can be changed at any time by going to **Tools | Work Date**.

There's more...

It is important to understand the difference between the NAV work date and the computer system date. They should be used in specific circumstances. When performing general work in the system, you should almost always use the WORKDATE keyword. In cases where you need to log information and the exact date or time when an action occurred, you should use TODAY and TIME or CURRENTDATETIME.

Populating date fields when a document is created

The following code can be found in table 36, Sales Header, in the InitRecord() method:

```
IF "Document Type" IN ["Document Type"::Order,"Document
                    Type"::Invoice,"Document Type"::Quote] THEN BEGIN
   "Shipment Date" := WORKDATE;
   "Order Date" := WORKDATE;
END;

IF "Document Type" = "Document Type"::"Return Order" THEN
   "Order Date" := WORKDATE;
IF NOT ("Document Type" IN ["Document Type"::"Blanket
      Order","Document Type"::Quote]) AND ("Posting Date" = 0D) THEN
   "Posting Date" := WORKDATE;
IF SalesSetup."Default Posting Date" = SalesSetup."Default
      Posting Date"::"No Date" THEN
   "Posting Date" := 0D;
"Document Date" := WORKDATE;
```

It is common to create and call an InitRecord() method from a table's OnInsert trigger especially for document-style tables. Unlike with the InitValue property for fields in a table, fields here are filled in based on conditional logic. More importantly, validation can be performed to ensure data integrity.

Looking at this snippet of code, we can see that every date is filled in using the WORKDATE keyword, and not using TODAY. This is so that a user can easily create records that are pre-dated or post-dated.

See also

- ▶ Retrieving the system date and time
- ▶ Determining the day, month, and year from a date
- ▶ Converting a value to a formatted string
- ▶ Checking for conditions using an IF statement
- ▶ Using a CASE statement to test multiple conditions

Determining the day, month, and year from a given date

Sometimes it is necessary to retrieve only a part of a date. NAV has built-in functions to do just that. We will show you how to use it in this recipe.

How to do it...

1. Create a new codeunit from **Object Designer**.

2. Add the following global variables:

Name	Type
Day	Integer
Month	Integer
Year	Integer

3. Write the following code in the OnRun trigger of the codeunit:

```
Day := Date2DMY(TODAY, 1);
Month := Date2DMY(TODAY, 2);
Year := Date2DMY(TODAY, 3);
MESSAGE('Day: %1\Month: %2\Year: %3', Day, Month, Year);
```

4. Save and close the codeunit.

5. When you run the codeunit you should see a window like the following screenshot:

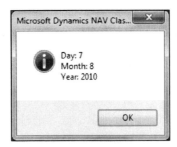

How it works...

The Date2DMY function is a basic feature of NAV. The first parameter is a date variable. This parameter can be retrieved from the system using TODAY or WORKDATE, a hard-coded date such as 01312010D, or a field from a table such as Sales Header or Order Date.

The second parameter is an integer that tells the function which part of the date to return. This number can be 1, 2, or 3 and corresponds to the day, month, and year (DMY) respectively.

There's more...

NAV has a similar function called Date2DWY. It will return the week of the year instead of the month if 2 is passed as the second parameter.

Determining depreciation

Codeunit 5616, Depreciation Calculation, contains functions to calculate depreciation based on start and end dates. In order to correctly calculate these values, you must know some details such as the number of days between two dates and whether or not any of those days is a leap day. It is with these types of operations that date functions like DATE2DMY are extremely useful. Have a look at the function DeprDays365 in this codeunit.

```
StartingYear := DATE2DMY(StartingDate,3);
EndingYear := DATE2DMY(EndingDate,3);
LeapDays := 0;
IF (DATE2DMY(StartingDate,1) = 29) AND
  (DATE2DMY(StartingDate,2) = 2) AND (DATE2DMY(EndingDate,1) = 29)
  AND (DATE2DMY(EndingDate,2) = 2) THEN
  LeapDays := -1;
  ActualYear := StartingYear;
  WHILE ActualYear <= EndingYear DO BEGIN
    LeapDate := (DMY2DATE(28,2,ActualYear) + 1);
    IF DATE2DMY(LeapDate,1) = 29 THEN BEGIN
      IF (LeapDate >= StartingDate) AND (LeapDate <= EndingDate) THEN
        LeapDays := LeapDays + 1;
      END;
      ActualYear := ActualYear + 1;
    END;
    EXIT((EndingDate - StartingDate) + 1 - LeapDays);
```

See also

  ▸ Retrieving the system date and time

  ▸ Retrieving the work date

  ▸ Converting a value to a formatted string

  ▸ Repeating code using a loop

  ▸ Checking for conditions using an IF statement

Converting a value to a formatted string

There will be many occasions when you will need to display information in a certain way or display multiple variable types on a single line. The FORMAT function will help you change almost any data type into a string that can be manipulated in any way you see fit.

How to do it...

1. Create a new codeunit from **Object Designer**.
2. Add the following global variables:

Name	Type	Length
FormattedDate	Text	30

3. Add the following code to the OnRun trigger:

```
FormattedDate := FORMAT(TODAY, 0, '<Month Text> <Day,2>,
                                    <Year4>');

MESSAGE('Today is %1', FormattedDate);
```

4. Save and close the codeunit.
5. When you run the codeunit you should see a window similar to the following :

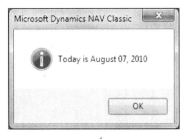

How it works...

The FORMAT function takes one to three parameters. The first parameter is required and can be of almost any type: date, time, integer, decimal, and so on. This parameter is returned as a string.

The second parameter is the length of the string to be returned. A default zero means that the entire string will be returned. A positive number tells the function to return a string of *exactly* that length, and a negative number returns a string no larger than that length.

There are two options for the third and final parameter. One is a number, representing a predefined format you want to use for the string and the other is a literal string. In the example, we used the actual format string. The text contained in brackets (< >) will be parsed and replaced with the data in the first parameter.

There's more...

There are many predefined formats for dates. The examples listed in the following table are taken from the C/SIDE Reference Guide in the **Help** menu of the NAV client. Search for "Format Property" to find more information.

Date	Format	Example
`<Closing><Day,2>-<Month,2>-<Year>`	0	05-04-03
`<Closing><Day,2>-<Month,2>-<Year>`	1	05-04-03
`<Day,2><Month,2><Year><Closing>D`	2	050403D
`<Closing><Year>-<Month,2>-<Day,2>`	3	03-04-05
`<Closing><Day>. <Month Text> <Year4>`	4	5. April 2003
`<Closing><Day,2><Month,2><Year>`	5	050403
`<Closing><Year><Month,2><Day,2>`	6	030405
`<Day,2><Filler Character,` `>. <Month Text,3> <Year4>`	7	5. Apr 2003
`XML format`	9	2003-04-05

Creating filters using other variable types

You will often need to create filters on dates or other simple data types. Usually these filters are not just for a single value. For example, a date filter for all values between January 1st, 2010 and January 31st, 2010 would look like `010110..013110`. Because ".." is a string, and you cannot concatenate it with two date variables. Instead, you will have to convert those dates into strings and then place the filters together.

Take the `CreateAccountingDateFilter` function from **codeunit 358**, **DateFilter-Calc**. It creates date filters based on accounting periods for the exact scenario we are describing.

```
AccountingPeriod.RESET;
IF FiscalYear THEN
  AccountingPeriod.SETRANGE("New Fiscal Year",TRUE);
  AccountingPeriod."Starting Date" := Date;
  AccountingPeriod.FIND('=<>');
  IF AccountingPeriod."Starting Date" > Date THEN
    NextStep := NextStep - 1;
  IF NextStep <> 0 THEN
    IF AccountingPeriod.NEXT(NextStep) <> NextStep THEN BEGIN
      IF NextStep < 0 THEN
```

```
        Filter := '..' + FORMAT(
                 AccountingPeriod."Starting Date" - 1)
    ELSE
        Filter := FORMAT(AccountingPeriod."Starting Date") +
                            '..' + FORMAT(12319999D);

        Name := '...';
        EXIT;
END;
StartDate := AccountingPeriod."Starting Date";
IF FiscalYear THEN
  Name := STRSUBSTNO(Text000,FORMAT(DATE2DMY(StartDate,3)))
ELSE
  Name := AccountingPeriod.Name;
IF AccountingPeriod.NEXT <> 0 THEN
  Filter := FORMAT(StartDate) + '..' +
            FORMAT(AccountingPeriod."Starting Date" - 1)
ELSE BEGIN
  Filter := FORMAT(StartDate) + '..' + FORMAT(12319999D);
  Name := Name + '...';
END;
```

See also

▶ Retrieving the system date and time

▶ Retrieving the work date

▶ Determining the day, month, and year from a given date

▶ Converting a string to another data type

▶ Checking for conditions using an `IF` statement

▶ Using advanced filtering

▶ Retrieving data using `FIND`

Creating an array

Creating multiple variables to store related information can be time consuming. It leads to more code and hence, more work. Using an array to store related and similar type of information can speed up development and lead to much more manageable code. This recipe will show you how to create and access array elements.

How to do it...

1. Create a new codeunit in **Object Designer**.

2. Add the following global variables:

Name	Type
i	Integer
IntArray	Integer

3. With the cursor on that variable, click on **View | Properties** (*Shift + F4*).

4. Set the following property:

Property	Value
Dimensions	10

5. In the OnRun trigger add the following code:

```
FOR i := 1 TO ARRAYLEN(IntArray) DO BEGIN
  IntArray[i] := i;
  MESSAGE('IntArray[%1] = %2', i, IntArray[i]);
END;
```

6. When you run the codeunit you will see ten windows, one after the other, similar to the following screenshot:

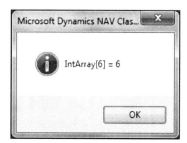

How it works...

An array is a single variable that holds multiple values. The values are accessed using an integer index. The index is passed within square brackets ([]).

There's more...

NAV provides several functions to work with arrays. ARRAYLEN returns the number of dimensions of the array. COPYARRAY will copy all of the values from one array into a new array variable. For a complete list of functions, search the C/SIDE Reference Guide under the **Help** menu for "Array Functions".

Creating an address using the format address codeunit

Open **codeunit 365, Format Address**. Notice the first function, `FormatAddr`, has a parameter which is an array. This is the basic function that all of the address formats use. It is rather long, so we will discuss only a few parts of it here.

This first section determines how the address should be presented based on the country of the user. Variables are initialized depending on which line of the address should certain information appear. The variables will be the indexes of our array.

```
CASE Country."Contact Address Format" OF
  Country."Contact Address Format"::First:
  BEGIN
    NameLineNo := 2;
    Name2LineNo := 3;
    ContLineNo := 1;
    AddrLineNo := 4;
    Addr2LineNo := 5;
    PostCodeCityLineNo := 6;
    CountyLineNo := 7;
    CountryLineNo := 8;
  END;
```

Then we will fill in the array values in the following manner:

```
AddrArray[NameLineNo]  := Name;
AddrArray[Name2LineNo] := Name2;
AddrArray[AddrLineNo]  := Addr;
AddrArray[Addr2LineNo] := Addr2;
```

Scroll down and take a look at all the other functions. You'll see that they all take in an array as the first parameter. It is always a text array of length 90 with 8 dimensions. These are the functions you will call when you want to format an address. To use this codeunit correctly, you will need to create an empty array with the specifications listed before and pass it to the correct function. Your array will be populated with the appropriately formatted address data.

See also

▸   Manipulating string contents

▸   Using a CASE statement to test multiple conditions

Creating an Option variable

If you need to force the user to select a value from a pre-defined list then an Option is the way to go. This recipe explains how to create an Option variable and access each of its values.

How to do it...

1. Create a new codeunit from **Object Designer**.

2. Add the following global variables:

Name	Type
ColorOption	Option

3. Set the following property on the variable:

Property	Value
OptionString	None,Red,Green,Blue

4. Add the following code to the OnRun trigger of your codeunit:

```
ColorOption := ColorOption::Red;
CASE ColorOption OF
  ColorOption::None: MESSAGE('No Color Selected');
  ColorOption::Red: MESSAGE('Red');
  ColorOption::Green: MESSAGE('Green');
  ColorOption::Blue: MESSAGE('Blue');
END;
```

5. When you run the codeunit you should see a window similar to the following screenshot:

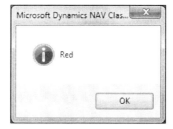

How it works...

An **Option** is a field or variable that stores one value from a selectable list. In a form, this list will appear as a drop-down from which the user can select a value. The list of options is stored as a comma-separated string in the `OptionString` property.

These values are accessed using the `variable_name::option_name` syntax. The first line of the example assigns one of the possible values (Red) to the variable. Then we use a `CASE` statement to determine which of the values was selected.

There's more...

You can also access possible options in other ways. In a database, an Option is stored as an integer. Each Option corresponds to a specific number, starting with the number 1. In this case None=1, Red=2, Green=3, and Blue=4. You could write this code to perform the safe actions:

```
ColorOption := ColorOption::"1";
CASE ColorOption OF
  ColorOption::None: MESSAGE('No Color Selected');
  ColorOption::Red: MESSAGE('Red');
  ColorOption::Green: MESSAGE('Green');
  ColorOption::Blue: MESSAGE('Blue');
END;
```

To reduce your development time, you can also use a shorthand notation to access the Option values. Again, the following code is exactly the same as that above:

```
ColorOption := ColorOption::R;
CASE ColorOption OF
  ColorOption::None: MESSAGE('No Color Selected');
  ColorOption::Red: MESSAGE('Red');
  ColorOption::Green: MESSAGE('Green');
  ColorOption::Blue: MESSAGE('Blue');
END;
```

When you close, save, and reopen the codeunit, the Option values will automatically be filled in for you. That is, both of these examples will look exactly like the first example once it has been saved and reopened. It is always best to write the code exactly as you want it to appear.

Using Options in documents

Option fields are prevalent throughout the NAV system, but most commonly on documents. In NAV, many documents share the same table. For example, sales quotes, orders, invoices, and return orders are all based on the Sales Header table. In order to distinguish between the types, there is an Option field called Document Type. Design table 36, Sales Header, to see the available options for this field.

Now, design **codeunit 80**, **Sales-Post**. Examine the OnRun trigger. Early in the function, you will see the following code:

```
CASE "Document Type" OF
  "Document Type"::Order:
  Receive := FALSE;
  "Document Type"::Invoice:
  BEGIN
    Ship := TRUE;
    Invoice := TRUE;
    Receive := FALSE;
  END;
  "Document Type"::"Return Order":
  Ship := FALSE;
  "Document Type"::"Credit Memo":
  BEGIN
    Ship := FALSE;
    Invoice := TRUE;
    Receive := TRUE;
  END;
END;
```

This is a common example of how Options are used in NAV. You can scroll through the codeunit to find more examples.

See also

▸ Using a CASE statement to test multiple conditions

Converting a string to another data type

Sometimes a string representation isn't enough. In order to perform certain actions, you need your data to be in a certain format. This recipe will show you how to change that data into a format that you can use.

How to do it...

1. Create a new codeunit from **Object Designer**.

2. Add the following global variables:

Name	Type	Length
DateText	Text	30
DateValue	Date	

3. Write the following code in the OnRun trigger:

```
DateText := '01/01/2010';
EVALUATE(DateValue, DateText);
MESSAGE('Date: %1', DateValue);
```

4. Save and close the codeunit.

5. When you run the codeunit you should see a window similar to the following screenshot:

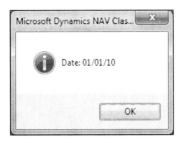

How it works...

The EVALUATE() function takes in two parameters. The first is a variable of the type that you want your value to be converted into. This could be date, time, boolean, integer, or any other simple data type. This parameter is passed by reference, meaning that the result of the function is stored in that variable. There is no need to do a manual assign using the := syntax.

The second parameter is the string which you need to convert. This text is usually stored in a field or variable, but can also be hard coded.

For a list of all of the functions related to text variables, search for "Text Data Type" in the C/SIDE Reference Guide under the **Help** menu.

There's more...

EVALUATE() returns a boolean value when executed. If the conversion is successful, it returns TRUE or 1; otherwise, it returns FALSE or 0. If the function returns FALSE, an error will be generated. If you wish to display the standard system error, you can leave the code as it is, but if you want to handle the error yourself, you must make the following changes:

```
DateText := '01/01/2010';
IF NOT EVALUATE(DateValue, DateText) THEN
  ERROR('Custom Error Message');
MESSAGE('Date: %1', DateValue);
```

Incrementing a number series

Number series are used throughout the NAV system. Every document has a unique identifier that is usually retrieved from the **No. Series** table. This table keeps a track of the last number used so that it knows what the next number should be.

However, this identifier is not just a number. A purchase order, for example, might have an identifier of PO123456, which means that it is actually a string. As you can't add a number to a string, you will have to figure out what the number part is, convert it to an actual number, and then increment it. This code from the `IncrementNoText()` function in **codeunit 396**, **NoSeriesManagement**, does exactly that. As this code calls several other functions, it may be beneficial for you to look through the entire codeunit.

```
GetIntegerPos(No,StartPos,EndPos);
EVALUATE(DecimalNo,COPYSTR(No,StartPos,EndPos - StartPos + 1));
NewNo := FORMAT(DecimalNo + IncrementByNo,0,1);
ReplaceNoText(No,NewNo,0,StartPos,EndPos);
```

See also

▸ Converting a value to a formatted string

▸ Checking for conditions using an `IF` statement

▸ Passing parameters by reference

Manipulating string contents

It can be very useful to parse a string and retrieve certain values. This recipe will show you how to examine the contents of a string and manipulate that data.

How to do it...

1. Create a new codeunit from **Object Designer**.

2. Add a function called `RemoveNonNumeric()`. It should return a text variable named `NewString`.

3. The function should take in the following parameter:

Name	Type	Length
String	Text	30

4. Add the following global variable:

Name	Type
I	Integer

5. Add the following global variables:

Name	Type	Length
OldPhoneNumber	Text	30
NewPhoneNumber	Text	30

6. Add the following code to the `RemoveNonNumeric()` function:

```
FOR i := 1 TO STRLEN(String) DO BEGIN
  IF String[i] IN ['0', '1', '2', '3', '4', '5', '6', '7', '8',
                                                          '9'] THEN
    NewString := NewString + FORMAT(String[i]);
END;
```

7. Add the following code to the `OnRun` trigger:

```
OldPhoneNumber := '(404) 555-1234';
NewPhoneNumber := RemoveNonNumeric(OldPhoneNumber);
MESSAGE('Old Phone Number: %1\New Phone Number: %2',
          OldPhoneNumber, NewPhoneNumber);
```

8. When you run the codeunit you will see a window similar to the following screenshot:

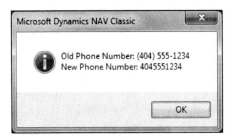

How it works...

A string is actually an array of characters. The same array syntax will be used to access the individual characters of the string.

We start with a FOR loop that begins at the first character, with index 1, and goes until we reach the end of our string. This is determined using the STRLEN() function which stands for STRing LENgth. As the first index is 1 the last index will be N, or the number of characters in the string.

Next, we access the character at that index using square brackets. If the character is a number, meaning we want to keep it because it is numeric, we add it to our resulting string.

 We can only add strings to other strings so we must convert this character using the FORMAT() function. If the character is not a number, we ignore it.

There's more...

NAV comes with plenty of built-in string manipulation functions to remove characters, return substrings, find characters within string, and many more. A search in the C/SIDE Reference Guide from the NAV client help menu for string functions will give you a complete list.

Parsing strings has several uses in NAV. Some easy-to-implement examples include checking/converting a phone number to a proper format based on country code, properly capitalizing names, and removing illegal characters.

Linking records with strings

Using the **Object Designer** run table 6508, **Value Entry Relation**. You should see a column named **Source RowId** that contains some strange looking text. A careful examination reveals that these are not as strange as they appear. It is simply a string containing six values, each separated by a semicolon and enclosed within quotes. For example: "123";"0";"123456";"";"0";"10000".

In a typical installation involving shipments and receipts, the value of the current inventory is adjusted every time an item comes in or goes out of stock. This amount is stored in the Value Entry table. In order to know which document created which value entry, a subsidiary table was created: Value Entry Relation. In this basic scenario, the first field refers to the table that the value entry came from. The most common are: 113 for shipments and 123 for receipts. The third value stores the document number and the sixth contains the line number. Take a look at the function DecomposeRowID() in **codeunit 6500, Item Tracking Management**.

```
FOR ArrayIndex := 1 TO 6 DO
  StrArray[ArrayIndex] := '';
Len := STRLEN(IDtext);
Pos := 1;
ArrayIndex := 1;
WHILE NOT (Pos > Len) DO BEGIN
  Char := COPYSTR(IDtext,Pos,1);
  IF (Char = '"') THEN BEGIN
    Write := FALSE;
    Count += 1;
  END ELSE BEGIN
    IF Count = 0 THEN
      Write := TRUE
```

```
    ELSE BEGIN
      IF Count MOD 2 = 1 THEN BEGIN
        Next := (Char = ';');
        Count -= 1;
      END ELSE
        IF NoWriteSinceLastNext AND (Char = ';') THEN BEGIN
          Count -= 2;
          Next := TRUE;
        END;
        Count /= 2;
        WHILE Count > 0 DO BEGIN
          StrArray[ArrayIndex] += '"';
          Count -= 1;
        END;
        Write := NOT Next;
    END;
    NoWriteSinceLastNext := Next;
  END;
  IF Next THEN BEGIN
    ArrayIndex += 1;
    Next := FALSE;
  END;
  IF Write THEN
    StrArray[ArrayIndex] += Char;
    Pos += 1;
  END;
```

This is an amazing example of how you can manipulate strings to your advantage. The code is fairly complex and may take some time to understand, but it can give you a basis to write your own code. You should be able to see the code that looks for semicolons, or field separators, as well as the code that finds quotes, or field identifiers. The code separates out those fields and stores them in a string array for later use.

See also

- ► Converting a value to a formatted string
- ► Creating an array
- ► Repeating code using a loop
- ► Checking for conditions using an IF statement

Using date formulas to calculate dates

Date formulas allow you to determine a new date based on a reference date. This recipe will show you how to use the built-in NAV function called CALCDATE to calculate them.

How to do it...

1. Create a new codeunit from **Object Designer**.

2. Add the following global variable:

Name	Type
CalculatedDate	Date

3. In the OnRun trigger write the following code:

```
CalculatedDate := CALCDATE('CM+1D', 01012010D);
MESSAGE('Calculated Date: %1', CalculatedDate);
```

4. Save and close the codeunit.

5. When you run the codeunit you should see a window like the following screenshot:

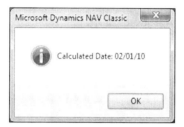

How it works...

The CALCDATE() function takes in two parameters, a calculation formula and a starting date. The calculation formula is a string that tells the function how to calculate the new date. The second parameter tells the function which date it should start with. A new date is returned by this function, so the value must be assigned to a variable using standard := syntax.

There's more...

The following units can be used in the calculation formula:

Unit	Description
D	Day
WD	Weekday
W	Week
M	Month
Q	Quarter
Y	Year

These units may be different depending on what language your version of NAV is running under.

You have two options for the number to place before the unit. This can either be a standard number ranging between 1 and 9, or the letter C, which stands for Current. These units can be added and subtracted to determine a new date based on any starting date.

Calculation formulas can become very complex. The best way to fully understand them is to write your own formulas to see the results. Start out with basic formulas like 1M+2W-1D and move on to more complex ones like –CY+2Q-1W.

Calculating reminder terms using date formulas

NAV has the ability to issue a reminder whenever a customer goes past due on their balance. These reminders are issued at specific times based on date formulas entered by the user during setup.

Look at the `MakeReminder()` method in **codeunit 392, Reminder-Make**. This function has a large amount of code so only a small section is shown here. The date formula is stored in a field called **Grace Period** and is used to determine if those many days have passed since the due date of the document.

```
IF (CALCDATE(ReminderLevel."Grace Period",ReminderDueDate) <
   ReminderHeaderReq."Document Date") AND
      ((LineLevel <= ReminderTerms."Max. No. of Reminders") OR
      (ReminderTerms."Max. No. of Reminders" = 0))
THEN BEGIN
```

See also

▶   Retrieving the system date and time

▶   Retrieving the work date

▶   Determining the day, month, and year from a given date

▶   Checking for conditions using an `IF` statement

2
General Development

In this chapter, we will cover:

- ▸ Repeating code using a loop
- ▸ Displaying a Progress Bar
- ▸ Checking for conditions using an IF statement
- ▸ Using a CASE statement to test multiple conditions
- ▸ Creating a function
- ▸ Passing parameters by reference
- ▸ Referencing dynamic tables and fields
- ▸ Using recursion

Introduction

Generally developers are not the ones who generate data for their company. Programmers are not employees entering sales orders or new contacts into the system. As a developer, you give users the ability to enter that data, but your main job is to build business logic to manipulate data for the company's benefit.

C/AL, the development language for NAV, is similar to other languages out there. It provides similar commands and functions that other programming languages do. It may not have all of the libraries that .NET does, but C/AL provides all the necessary functions to control data in any way you see fit. The development environment, C/SIDE, is also not very attractive. It does not have all the bells and whistles of Visual Studio, but it has everything you need to get your job done easily. There will be times when you will have to think a little harder about your solution and take a little longer to plan it out, but there is no problem that cannot be solved within NAV.

If you have programmed in other languages you will notice obvious similarities in syntax. It's the logic behind the program, and not the way you code it that makes the difference. After all, there are so many ways to assign values to variables, check for conditions, and create functions. These basic commands and functions are building blocks for any program world. NAV is no different. Once you've mastered the nuts and bolts, you can begin to put them together to perform any function your company needs. This chapter will serve as a brief introduction to these parts, but for a more in-depth study you can read "*Programming Microsoft Dynamics NAV 2009*" by *David Studebaker* or "*Implementing Microsoft Dynamics NAV 2009*" by *David Roys* and *Vjekoslav Babic.*

Repeating code using a loop

Looping is an essential part of dealing with records in NAV. Using a FOR loop is a common way to iterate over multiple lines of code. This recipe will show you how to construct a FOR loop and use it.

How to do it...

1. Create a new codeunit from **Object Designer**.

2. Add the following global variables:

Name	Type
n	Integer
i	Integer
Factorial	Integer

3. Add the following code to the OnRun trigger of the codeunit:

    ```
    Factorial := 1;
    n := 4;
    FOR i := 1 TO n DO
      Factorial := Factorial * i;

    MESSAGE('Factorial of %1 = %2', n, Factorial);
    ```

4. Save and close the codeunit.

5. When you run the codeunit you will see a window similar to the following screenshot:

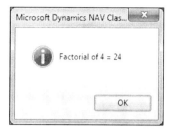

How it works...

A FOR loop has four parts: a counter, a starting value, the step to be taken, and an ending value. In this code, our counter variable is "i". The starting value is 1 and the ending value is "n", which in this case has been assigned to the value 4.

Each time the loop iterates, the value of "i" is increased by one (the step). The code indented under the FOR loop will be executed four times. It is exactly the same as:

```
Factorial := Factorial * 1;
Factorial := Factorial * 2;
Factorial := Factorial * 3;
Factorial := Factorial * 4;
```

If you want to use a step other than one or negative one you will need to use a WHILE loop or REPEAT..UNTIL loop.

There's more...

You can also use a FOR loop by decreasing the counter. To do this, instead of a TO you use DOWNTO. The structure for this type of loop is as follows:

```
Factorial := 1;
n := 4;
FOR i := n DOWNTO 1 DO
  Factorial := Factorial * i;

MESSAGE('Factorial of %1 = %2', n, Factorial);
```

Using a WHILE loop

A WHILE loop is similar to a FOR loop. The main difference is that you have to take control of the counter.

```
Factorial := 1;
n := 4;
i := 1;
WHILE i <= n DO BEGIN
  Factorial := Factorial * i;
  i += 1;
END;

MESSAGE('Factorial of %1 = %2', n, Factorial);
```

First we have to initialize our starting value, which is accomplished by the third line i := 1.

Then in the WHILE line, we have to give a stop condition. As long as i <= n (4), we want the statements to execute.

Finally, we have added the i += 1; command to the code inside our loop. A FOR loop does this behind the scenes, but a WHILE loop doesn't. Here we can increment our counter by any value we want. This basic line is perhaps the most important. Without it we will never reach our stop condition and be stuck in an infinite loop.

Using a REPEAT..UNTIL loop

If you have programmed in other languages you know this loop by another name: DO..WHILE. The difference between this type of loop and a standard WHILE loop is that the code is guaranteed to execute at least once. You will use this type of loop often to go access records through tables.

```
Factorial := 1;
n := 4;
i := 1;
REPEAT
  Factorial := Factorial * i;
  i += 1;
UNTIL i > n;

MESSAGE('Factorial of %1 = %2', n, Factorial);
```

See also

- ▶ Creating an array
- ▶ Using recursion
- ▶ Retrieving data using FIND
- ▶ Marking records for future use

Displaying a Progress Bar

There's nothing more frustrating for a user than wondering if the system is done with processing something or not. Displaying an indicator to show the user the system's progress, is an easy way to make the system more user-friendly.

How to do it...

1. Create a new codeunit from **Object Designer**.

2. Add the following global variables:

Name	Type
ProgressBar	Dialog
AmountProcessed	Integer
AmountToProcess	Integer
PercentComplete	Integer

3. Add the following code to the OnRun trigger of your Codeunit:

```
AmountToProcess := 50000;

ProgressBar.OPEN('@1@@@@@@@@@@@@@@@@@@@@@@@@');
REPEAT
  AmountProcessed += 1;
  PercentComplete := ROUND(AmountProcessed / AmountToProcess *
                                                   10000, 1);
  ProgressBar.UPDATE(1, PercentComplete);
UNTIL AmountProcessed = AmountToProcess;
```

4. Save and close the codeunit.

5. When you run the codeunit you will see a progress bar like this:

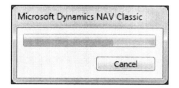

How it works...

In order to track the progress of something, you need to know two things: how much you have to do and how much you have already done. We create two variables for this data, `AmountToProcess` and `AmountProcessed`. In our code shown in step 3, we have set the `AmountToProcess` equal to 50,000. Depending on the speed of your computer, this may make the progress bar advance either too quickly or too slowly. You might need to adjust it.

Basic information such as this is displayed to the user using what is called a **Dialog**. The dialog is given a string as an input parameter. The @ sign tells it to display as a progress indicator and the 1 identifies the indicator for later updates. The rest of the @ signs specify the length of the progress bar.

The minimum and maximum values for the progress bar are not 0 and 100 as you might expect. Instead, they are 0 and 10,000 respectively. This is why we multiply by 10,000 when we are calculating our `PercentComplete` value. As the percentage is an integer, we must also round up our result to the nearest digit.

There's more...

Updating the screen dramatically slows down the process. When dealing with so many items to process the percent processed does not change with every item. You can rather update the screen periodically by adding a single line of code:

```
AmountToProcess := 50000;

ProgressBar.OPEN('@1@@@@@@@@@@@@@@@@@@@@@');
REPEAT
  AmountProcessed += 1;
  PercentComplete := ROUND(AmountProcessed / AmountToProcess *
                                              10000, 1);

  IF AmountProcessed MOD 100 = 0 THEN
  ProgressBar.UPDATE(1, PercentComplete);
UNTIL AmountProcessed = AmountToProcess;
```

We have added a conditional statement so that the screen updates only after every 100 items are processed. You should notice a huge decrease in processing if you run the codeunit with this new line.

Processing only reports

A common way to process large amounts of data is to create a "processing only" report. In this situation, your `AmountToProcess` would be the number of records in the table. This would be calculated in the `OnPreDataItem` trigger. You would also open the dialog here. In the `OnAfterGetRecord` trigger, you would update your `AmountProcessed` variable and update the progress bar as necessary.

Some examples of processing only reports in the base system are: number 296, Batch Post Sales Orders, and 299, Delete Invoiced Sales Orders.

See also

▸ Checking for conditions using an `IF` statement

▸ Creating a report to process data

Checking for conditions using an IF statement

Some code should only be executed when certain conditions occur. This recipe will show you how to write code to make that decision.

How to do it...

1. Create a new codeunit from **Object Designer**.

2. Add the following global variables:

Name	Type	Subtype
SalesHeader	Record	Sales Header
RecordsProcessed	Integer	

3. Write the following code in the `OnRun` trigger:

```
IF SalesHeader.FINDSET THEN BEGIN
 REPEAT
  RecordsProcessed += 1;
  UNTIL SalesHeader.NEXT = 0;
  MESSAGE('Processed %1 records.', RecordsProcessed);
END ELSE
  MESSAGE('No records to process.');
```

4. Save and close the codeunit.

5. When you run the codeunit you will see a window like the one shown in the following screenshot:

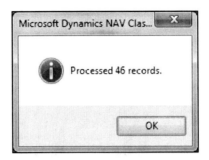

How it works...

In order to execute the code that processes the records, there must be records in the table. That's exactly what the first line does. It tells the code that IF you find some records THEN it should do these actions. In this case, the action is to count the records in the table and display a message to the user.

It could be discouraging for the user to try to process something and have nothing happen, though. That's where the ELSE part comes in. When the condition in the IF statement does not evaluate to true, control falls to the next ELSE statement. So IF we find some records THEN the code must do something OTHERWISE (ELSE) it should do something else. Our "something else" is to inform the user that no records were found. The ELSE part is by no means required, but you should always consider what should happen if the condition is false.

There's more...

IF statements can be chained together to form complex conditionals.

```
IF DATE2DMY(WORKDATE,1) = 1 THEN
  MESSAGE('Monday')
ELSE IF DATE2DMY(WORKDATE,1) = 2 THEN
  MESSAGE('Tuesday')
ELSE IF DATE2DMY(WORKDATE,1) = 3 THEN
  MESSAGE('Wednesday')
ELSE IF DATE2DMY(WORKDATE,1) = 4 THEN
  MESSAGE('Thursday')
ELSE IF DATE2DMY(WORKDATE,1) = 5 THEN
  MESSAGE('Friday')
ELSE
  MESSAGE('Its the weekend!');
```

The next `IF` is simply a new statement inside the `ELSE` clause within the previous `IF` statement.

Generally, if you have more than three possibilities you should not use an `IF` statement, but a `CASE` statement instead. This example simply illustrates the possibilities with conditionals.

Testing multiple conditions

You may need to execute code only when multiple conditions are true. The following syntax can be used to test for conditions in a single statement:

```
IF (condition1) AND (condtion2) THEN
IF (condition1) OR (condition2) THEN
IF (NOT condition1) AND (condition2) THEN
```

The first will only execute when both conditions are true, the second when either of the conditions are true, and the third when the first condition is not true and the second is true. You can combine these operators (AND, OR, NOT) to form very complex conditionals and test as many conditions as necessary.

One thing you need to remember is that the entire clause before the AND or OR has to evaluate to a Boolean value. That means you have to surround your entire condition with parentheses. The following line of code will not work:

```
IF DATE2DMY(WORKDATE,1) >= 5 AND DATE2DMY(WORKDATE,1) <= 6 THEN
```

NAV sees the AND as applying like this: `5 AND DATE2DMY(WORKDATE, 1)`. The 5 doesn't evaluate to a Boolean value and neither does the `DATE2DMY` function. You have to write it like this:

```
IF (DATE2DMY(WORKDATE,1) >= 5) AND (DATE2DMY(WORKDATE,1) <= 6)
    THEN
```

Here, the AND applies to everything in the parentheses, before and after it, each of which evaluates to a boolean value.

See also

> ▸ Using a `CASE` statement to test multiple conditions

Using a CASE statement to test multiple conditions

When you have more than two conditions to test, it can often be beneficial to use a CASE statement for better code readability.

How to do it...

1. Create a new codeunit from **Object Designer**.

2. Add the following global variables:

Name	Type
I	Integer

3. Add the following code to the OnRun trigger of your codeunit:

```
i := 2;

CASE i OF
  1:
    MESSAGE('Your number is %1.', i);
  2:
    MESSAGE('Your number is %1.', i);
  ELSE
    MESSAGE('Your number is not 1 or 2.');
END;
```

4. When you run the codeunit you will see a window like the following screenshot:

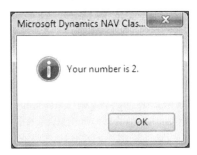

How it works...

A CASE statement compares the value given, in this case "i", to various conditions contained within that statement. Each condition, other than the default ELSE, is followed by a colon. Here it checks if "i" is equal to 1, if "i" is equal to 2, and if "i" is neither 1 nor 2. You would get the same result if you wrote the following code:

```
IF  i  =  1  THEN
    MESSAGE('Your  number  is  %1.',  i)
ELSE  IF  i  =  2  THEN
    MESSAGE('Your  number  is  %1.',  i)
ELSE
    MESSAGE('Your  number  is  not  1  or  2.');
```

There's more...

This example just checks very basic conditions and only conditions where the variable is equal to a specific value. You can do more advanced condition checking like the following example:

```
CASE  TRUE  OF
    i  >  1:
      MESSAGE('i  >  1');
    i  =  1:
      MESSAGE('i  =  1');
    i  <  1:
      MESSAGE('i  <  1');
    ELSE
      MESSAGE('What  kind  of  number  is  this?');
END;
```

Or something like :

```
CASE  TRUE  OF
    i  >  1,  i  <  1:
      MESSAGE('i  is  not  one');
    i  =  1:
      MESSAGE('i  =  1');
    ELSE
      MESSAGE('What  kind  of  number  is  this?');
END;
```

See also

▶   Checking for conditions using an IF statement

Creating a function

Most programs will need to execute code from different NAV objects. This code is contained in functions. This recipe will show you how to create a function and explain what functions are in more detail.

How to do it...

1. Create a new codeunit from **Object Designer**.

2. Add a function called CountToN that takes an integer parameter, n.

3. Add the following local variables

Name	Type
I	Integer

4. Add the following code to your function:

```
FOR i := 1 TO n DO
  MESSAGE('%1', i);
```

5. Add the following code to the OnRun trigger of the codeunit:

```
CountToN(3);
```

6. Save and close the codeunit.

7. When you run the codeunit you will see several windows like the following screenshot:

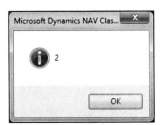

How it works...

By creating a function we can reference multiple lines of code using one easy-to-understand name. Our function is called CountToN and takes an integer "n" as a parameter. This function will display a message box for every number ranging between one and the number that is passed to the function.

There's more...

Proper use of functions is essential to good software development. You will have difficulty finding any objects in NAV that don't contain even a single function.

The main use of functions is to divide complex tasks into manageable chunks of code. This makes debugging a lot easier. Other developers who may add to your code later, will be able to better understand what you were trying to accomplish. By encapsulating code in functions you also reduce the number of places where changes need to be made when you find faulty business logic.

Once written, these functions can then be called from other objects. A great practice is to keep a codeunit with common utility functions in it. You can load this codeunit into any database you happen to be working on and have instant access to your code from any object in the system.

Creating local or private functions

By default, all functions are created as global functions, which means that they can be accessed from any object in the system. Sometimes, though, you may only want a function to be accessed from within the object in which it resides.

It may seem counter-intuitive, but you still define these functions in the same way you define global functions. If you view the properties of the function (*Shift + F4* or click on **View | Properties** from the menu), you will see one called **Local**. Set this property to yes and it will only be available in the current object.

See also

> ▸   Passing parameters by reference

Passing parameters by reference

You may want your function to modify multiple values. As you can't return more than one value from a function (unless you use an array), it can be beneficial to pass your parameters by reference to the function.

How to do it...

1. Create a new codeunit from **Object Designer**.

2. Add the following global variables:

Name	Type	Subtype	Length
CustomerRec	Record	Customer	
OldName	Text		50
NewName	Text		50

3. Add a function called `ChangeCustomerName`.

4. The function should take in the following parameter:

Name	Type	Subtype
Customer	Record	Customer

5. Write the following code in the `ChangeCustomerName` function:

```
Customer.Name := 'Changed Name';
```

6. Add a function called `ChangeCustomerNameRef`.

7. The function should take in the following parameter:

Name	Type	Subtype
Customer	Record	Customer

8. Place a check-mark in the `Var` column for the parameter.

9. Write the following code in the `ChangeCustomerName` function:

```
Customer.Name := 'Changed Name';
```

10. Write the following code in the `OnRun` trigger of your codeunit:

```
IF CustomerRec.FINDFIRST THEN BEGIN
  OldName := CustomerRec.Name;
  ChangeCustomerName(CustomerRec);
  NewName := CustomerRec.Name;
 MESSAGE('Pass by value:\Old Name: %1\New Name: %2', OldName,
                                                     NewName);

  OldName := CustomerRec.Name;
  ChangeCustomerNameRef(CustomerRec);
  NewName := CustomerRec.Name;
  MESSAGE('Pass by reference:\Old Name: %1\New Name: %2',
                                       OldName, NewName);
END;
```

11. Save and close your codeunit.

12. When you run the codeunit, you will see the following two windows:

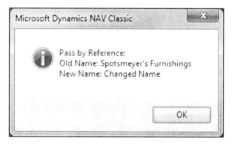

How it works...

The first function, `ChangeCustomerName`, passes the parameter by value, which means that a copy of the variable is created and the function uses that copy. So even though the customer name is changed in the function, only its copy is changed. The original stays the same.

The second function, `ChangeCustomerNameRef`, passes the parameter by reference. When you pass a parameter by reference, the parameter refers to the same location in memory that the actual variable is stored. No copy is made. Any changes made to the parameter will be reflected in the original variable.

There's more...

Reference parameters are common throughout NAV, especially in codeunits. Codeunits such as 12 (General Journal Lines), 80 (Sales), and 90 (Purchases) are all written to work with a specific type of record. This is defined under the `TableNo` property in codeunit properties. When you set a value here, the `OnRun` trigger will automatically have a reference parameter name `Rec` added to it. Any changes made to the `Rec` variable will change the actual value in that record. Also, if you only pass a record by value to a function, you do not get any of the filters applied to the record set.

See also

▶ Creating a function

Referencing dynamic tables and fields

You may, on occasion, need to retrieve data from the system, but not know in advance where that data should come from. NAV accommodates this by allowing you to reference tables and fields dynamically.

How to do it...

1. Create a new codeunit from **Object Designer**.

2. Add a global function, `GetFirstRecord`.

3. The function should take in the following parameter:

Name	Type
TableNo	Integer

4. Add the following local variables:

Name	Type
RecRef	RecordRef
FieldRef	FieldRef

5. Write the following code in your `GetFirstRecord` function:

```
RecRef.OPEN(TableNo);
IF RecRef.FINDFIRST THEN BEGIN
  IF RecRef.FIELDEXIST(1) THEN
  FieldRef[1] := RecRef.FIELDINDEX(1);
 IF RecRef.FIELDEXIST(2) THEN
  FieldRef[2] := RecRef.FIELDINDEX(2);

  IF FieldRef[1].ACTIVE AND FieldRef[2].ACTIVE THEN
  MESSAGE('Table: %1\%2: %3\%4: %5', RecRef.NAME,
          FieldRef[1].NAME, FieldRef[1].VALUE,
          FieldRef[2].NAME, FieldRef[2].VALUE)
  ELSE
    MESSAGE('You cannot retrieve an inactive field.');
END ELSE
  MESSAGE('No records found!');
```

6. Write the following code in your `OnRun` trigger:

```
GetFirstRecord(DATABASE::Customer);
GetFirstRecord(DATABASE::Vendor);
```

7. Save and close your codeunit.

8. When you run the codeunit you will see the following windows:

How it works...

We are creating a function, `GetFirstRecord`, that will return information about the first record found in an unknown table. The `TableNo` parameter will tell the function which table in the database to find the data.

When you don't know the table until runtime, you must use a `RecordRef` variable, which stands for record reference and can refer to any record/table in the database. To point it to the right table, you use the `OPEN` command. Here we tell the `RecordRef` variable to open any table we pass into the function. If a record is found in that table we continue on, otherwise we display the message "No records found!"

To store references to the fields we care about, we have created an array of FieldRef variables called `FieldRef`. In this function, we have hard-coded a lookup for fields one and two, but you could just as easily pass another parameter with the ID of the field you need. If that field exists, we assign its value into our `FieldRef` variable to an appropriate index.

Finally, we have to determine whether the fields are active or in use and available for use by the system. If they were not, we would not have been able to retrieve their values and would instead display a message to the user. But if they are active, we display the name and value of each field using the properties of the same name.

The code in the `OnRun` trigger runs the function with two different tables. The DATABASE::"Table Name" syntax resolves to an integer. You could also pass the actual ID of the tables.

There's more...

Record references act just like their record counterparts. You can use them to insert, modify, or delete records. You can set filters on them and use them to find records. For a complete list of functions and properties, you can use the **Symbol** menu and investigate the C/SIDE Reference Guide from the **Help** menu in the client.

The data migration codeunits in NAV are full of functions that use record and field references. I recommend you start with the functions in **codeunit 8611**, **Migration Management**. This is a great place to see real examples of how this type of code can be used.

See also

- ▶ Checking for conditions using an `IF` statement
- ▶ Writing your own rollback routine

Using recursion

Recursion is not used often in NAV, but the option is available and can shorten your code. **Recursion** is the process by which a function calls itself.

How to do it...

1. Create a new codeunit from **Object Designer**.
2. Add a global function, `Fibonacci`, that returns an integer with no name.
3. The function should take the following parameter:

Name	Type
i	Integer

4. Write the following code in your `Fibonacci` function.

```
IF (i <= 2) THEN
  EXIT(1);
EXIT ( Fibonacci(i-1) + Fibonacci(i-2) );
```

5. Write the following code in your `OnRun` trigger:

    ```
    MESSAGE('Fibonacci(%1) = %2', 4, Fibonacci(4));
    ```

6. When you run the codeunit you will see a window like the one shown in the following screenshot:

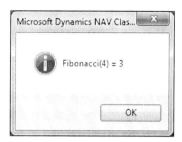

How it works...

The Fibonacci sequence is a series of numbers where the value in a certain position is the sum of the number in the previous two positions.

That is: 1, 1, 2, 3, 5, 8, 13, 21, 34, 55...

A recursive function has two parts. The first is a stopping condition. In our Fibonacci function, the stopping condition is when the variable i is less than or equal to two. In that case, the function will return 1 as the output.

The second part is where the function calls itself with a different parameter. Recursion can be confusing so let's step through the code to get a better understanding. We'll use the following diagram to explain this more clearly:

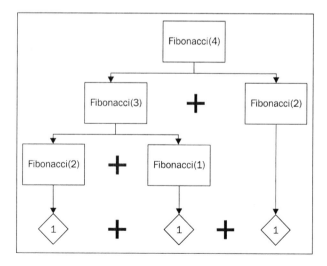

We start by passing the number four as a parameter to our function, which means that the variable i is equal to four. As four is not less than or equal to two, we move to the last line of the function. The function will exit the loop with the value Fibonacci(4 – 1) + Fibonacci(4 – 2), but we don't know what those values are. Now we evaluate each of those function calls separately.

Fibonacci(3) has a parameter that is also not less than two. Again, we move to the last line of the function and exit with Fibonacci(3 – 1) + Fibonacci(3 – 2). This time it gets easier.

Fibonacci(2) exits with the value 1. Fibonacci(1) also exits with the value 1. Hence, Fibonacci(2) = 1 and Fibonacci(1) = 1. Substituting them back in, we know that Fibonacci(3) = Fibonacci(2) + Fibonacci(1) = 1 + 1 = 2.

But we're not done. We still have the original Fibonacci(4 – 2) to evaluate.

Fibonacci(2) = 1. So let's sum it all up.

Fibonacci(4) =[Fibonacci(3)] + [Fibonacci(2)] =

[Fibonacci(2) + Fibonacci(1)] + [Fibonacci(2)] =[1 + 1] + [1] = 3.

There's more...

Recursion can be extremely useful under the right circumstances, most notably performing calculations, processing XML documents with nested nodes, or any sort of tree structure such as a bill of materials. You should be aware, though, that it is not a replacement for loops. Recursion can quickly eat through your available memory. Each function call has to be stored in memory until the entire operation is complete. As a result, there is a limit to the number of recursive calls that can be made.

See also

- ▸ Repeating code using a loop
- ▸ Sharing information using XMLports

3
Working with Tables and Records

In this chapter, we will cover:

- ▶ Creating a table
- ▶ Adding a key to a table
- ▶ Creating transactions to alter data
- ▶ Validating data
- ▶ Retrieving a single record from the database
- ▶ Using advanced filtering
- ▶ Retrieving data using FIND
- ▶ Adding a FlowField to a table
- ▶ Creating a SumIndex field
- ▶ Marking records for future use
- ▶ Clearing filters, keys, and values
- ▶ Using temporary tables to store data
- ▶ Retrieving data from another company
- ▶ Merging records
- ▶ Writing your own rollback routine

Introduction

If the simple data types we reviewed in *Chapter 1, Strings, Dates, and Other Data Types*, are the nuts and bolts of NAV, then records are the assembled parts that make everything work. A **record** is, to put it simply, a collection of related data. Together, this data gives the business a better idea of what is going on with the company. When you view a list of customers, for example, there are certain things you expect to see, which include name, address, phone number, company, and so on. You can view the records in any table by clicking on **Run** from **Object Designer**.

 Be careful, though! You should avoid editing the data in tables directly as it is easy to accidentally change something.

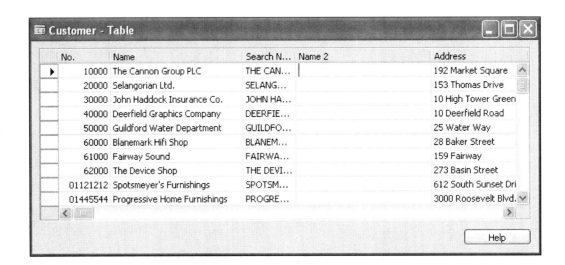

These records are stored in tables. A table acts as a blueprint for the records. It tells NAV what kind of data can be stored in which fields and what should happen when certain actions are performed on data. These blueprints are set up in the **Table Designer**, which is accessed by clicking on **New** or **Design** from the **Object Designer**.

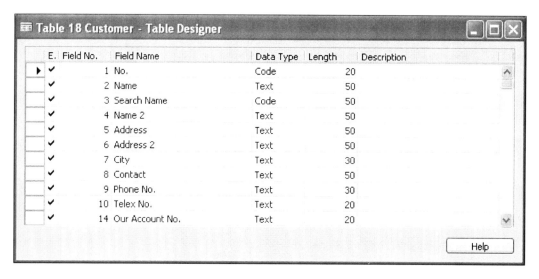

Tables are the foundation of the entire NAV system. Every other object type, that is forms, pages, reports, dataports, XMLports, and codeunits, depend on tables to work. It is critical to understand the basic concepts involved in table design. Although we will not get anywhere near showing you everything that can be done with a table, we will show you what you will need to successfully design and use them. For more information it is recommended that you explore the C/SIDE Reference Guide from the **Help** menu and the Development coursework and training classes.

Creating a table

Tables are the building blocks for all other NAV objects. They store the data that the business needs to access. This recipe will show you how to create a basic table and save it in the system.

How to do it...

1. Create a new table object from **Object Designer**.

2. Add the following fields in the **Table Designer** window:

Field No.	Field Name	Data Type	Length
1	Entry No.	Integer	
2	Document No.	Code	20
3	Description	Text	30
4	Value	Decimal	
5	Posting Date	Date	

3. It should look like the following window:

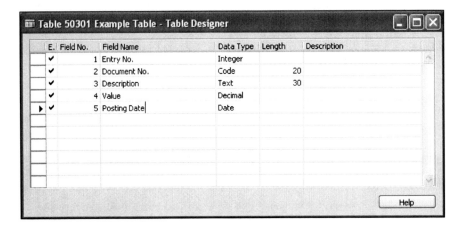

4. Save and close the Table.

How it works...

Each field is just like a variable. These variables, however, are grouped together to form a new type of variable called a `Record`. The field definitions provide the structure for all of the tables, as well as the data in them, inside the system. The data type of your fields can be almost anything. In this example, we have created five fields of the most common types.

There's more...

If you do not specify a key manually, the field you have placed in **Field No. 1** will act as the primary key for your table.

After completing the initial draft of your object, it is a good practice to add a few notes, such as mentioning your initials and a date or a version number in the **Description** column whenever you add a new field. This allows future developers know precisely when the change was made and what other modifications were made. An example description could be "MT 01/01/2010 MOD001".

See also

- ▸ Adding a key to a table
- ▸ Validating data
- ▸ Adding a FlowField to a table
- ▸ Creating a SumIndex field

Adding a key to a table

Keys are used to make sure every record in the table is unique. They are often also referred to as indexes and used to sort your data in ways that are most beneficial to the user.

How to do it...

1. Follow the steps from the _Creating a table_ recipe to create a table.
2. Click on **Design** from **Object Designer** to open the **Table Designer** for that table.
3. Click on **View | Keys** (_Alt + V, K_).
4. On an empty line, add a new key for **Document No.**, **Posting Date**.
5. Your keys should look like the following window:

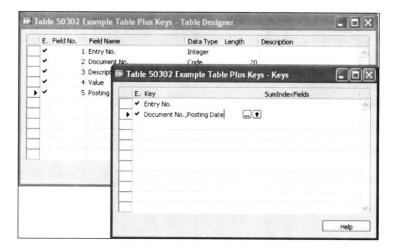

> ► Close the **Keys** window.

> ► Save and close the table.

How it works...

Keys allow you to sort data in a way that will increase your application's performance. There is a trade-off, though. Increased application performance later, costs you some effort earlier.

When we insert data into a table it is automatically sorted based on the primary key of that table, but what about the other keys? The database engine doesn't just magically know how records should be sorted. For every key, the database keeps some sort of information about how the data will be ordered. More number of keys take more time to insert and to track all of that information. This time is usually not noticeable by users, but you should be aware that there is a trade-off. One common technique for database optimization is to remove the keys that are not being used, especially on tables that have a high volume of transactions like Item Ledger Entry or G/L Entry.

See also

> ► Creating a table

> ► Validating data

> ► Adding a FlowField to a table

> ► Creating a SumIndex field

> ► Understanding SIFT tables

Creating transactions to alter data

The purpose of NAV is to help you use business data to improve the way your company operates; that data needs to be saved in the database. This recipe will show you how to add, change, and remove data or records from the tables in the NAV system.

How to do it...

1. Create a new codeunit from **Object Designer**.

2. Add the following global variable:

Name	Type	Subtype
Customer	Record	Customer

3. Add the following code to the `OnRun` trigger of your codeunit:

```
Customer.Name := 'Matt Traxinger';
Customer.INSERT(TRUE);

Customer.SETCURRENTKEY(Name);
Customer.SETRANGE(Name, 'Matt Traxinger');
IF Customer.FINDFIRST THEN BEGIN
  Customer.Name := 'Alex Traxinger';
  Customer.MODIFY;
END;
```

4. Save and close your codeunit.

How it works...

First we fill out the field in our customer record. In this case, it's the **Name** field and we set it to the value **Matt Traxinger**. The next line actually inserts the value into the database.

The first three lines of the next section retrieve the data we just inserted into the database. We then change the name on the record to **Alex Traxinger**, but we still have to save that value. You can't just insert the record because there is already one with the same customer number—Instead you have to modify the existing record.

After running the codeunit you will find a **Customer Card** with the following information:

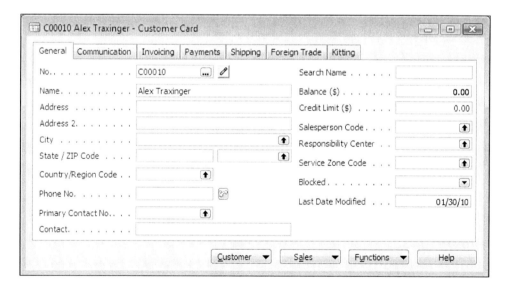

The **No.** field may be different depending on what the next number is currently set to in the customer number series. It is automatically assigned by calling `INSERT(TRUE)`.

There's more...

There are four types of operations you can perform on records in the database. They are insert, modify, delete, and rename. Each does exactly what it sounds like. They add, change, remove, and rename the primary key of the record in question.

Calling code when performing a transaction

Every table has triggers associated with it. They can be viewed by examining the C/AL code when in the **Table Designer** (*F9*). You'll see triggers named `OnInsert`, `OnModify`, `OnDelete`, and `OnRename`, as well as a few others. You can add code in these triggers to check for conditions, fill in other fields, or anything else you might wish to do.

You call this code by passing an optional boolean parameter to the command. By default, this code is not called (`FALSE` is passed), but in the `INSERT` command of our example, we pass the value `TRUE`.

Catching errors when performing a transaction

Insert, modify, delete, and rename, all return a boolean value upon completion of a transaction. When successful, it returns True; when not, it returns False and displays an error message.

It is not always helpful to display this error. Sometimes, you might want to continue with what you were doing. You can trap the error in the following manner:

```
IF Customer.INSERT THEN
// Do Something
IF Customer.MODIFY THEN
// Do Something
```

See also

▶ Checking for conditions using an `IF` statement

▶ Using temporary tables to store data

▶ Merging records

▶ Writing your own rollback routine

▶ Handling runtime errors

Validating data

It is important to make sure that the data being placed into the fields is correct. Many of the checks done to the data can be performed using the field's properties, but in some instances you will need to write code to do very specific data validation. Here we will show you where that code should go and what can be done there.

Getting ready

You will need the customer card from the *Creating transactions to alter data* recipe.

How to do it...

1. Create a new codeunit from **Object Designer**.

2. Add the following global variable:

Name	Type	Subtype
Customer	Record	Customer

3. Add the following code to the OnRun trigger:

```
Customer.SETCURRENTKEY(Name);
Customer.SETRANGE(Name, 'Alex Traxinger');
IF Customer.FINDFIRST THEN BEGIN
  Customer."Search Name" := '';
  Customer.VALIDATE(Name, 'Matt Traxinger');
  Customer.MODIFY;
END;
```

4. Save and close the codeunit.

How it works...

Most of the code in our example is to find and save a record. We're going to look at the following lines:

```
Customer."Search Name" := '';
Customer.VALIDATE(Name, 'Matt Traxinger');
```

First we set the "Search Name" field to be blank. This is so that we know our code will put something in that field and that there wasn't some value already there.

The second line is the one we are more interested in. The **VALIDATE** command can be called on any field in a table. It takes the syntax `Record.VALIDATE(Field, Value)`. So here we are validating the Name field on the customer table with the value 'Matt Traxinger'. Notice how we never fill the "Search Name" field with an actual value. But when we look at the customer card for our record we see:

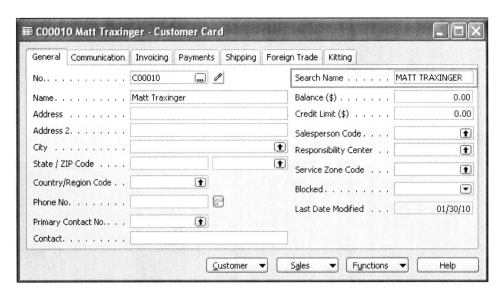

This is because there is some code that was run that you haven't seen yet. Open the **Table Designer** for the **Customer** table (Table 18). Click on field number two, **Name**, and then hit *F9* to view the C/AL code within it. You'll be taken to a function called `Name – OnValidate()`, which contains the following code:

```
IF ("Search Name" = UPPERCASE(xRec.Name)) OR
   ("Search Name" = '') THEN
   "Search Name" := Name;
```

It says that if some condition ends up being true that the "Search Name" field should be filled in with whatever value is in the Name field. That's how it got filled in!

There's more...

Data validation is one of the most important topics in NAV development. Its main purpose is to check that the value is allowed and to automatically fill into other fields.

When the validate function is called on a field, the program first checks the `TableRelation` property of that field. If that is ok, it goes on to execute the code in the `OnValidate` trigger. This trigger is just like any other in NAV. It can have local variables, call other functions, and do everything that you would expect it to.

Remember, though, that the purpose of VALIDATE is to ensure data integrity. This code could be running anywhere, like a NAS server or in a web service, so you don't want to do things such as asking the user for input.

See also

▸ Creating a table

▸ Adding a key to a table

▸ Adding a FlowField to a table

▸ Creating a SumIndex field

Retrieving a single record from the database

It's easy enough to put data into the database, but how do you write code to get it back out? There are several ways and this recipe will discuss the first and easiest.

How to do it...

1. Create a new codeunit from **Object Designer**.

2. Add the following global variable:

Name	Type	Subtype
Customer	Record	Customer

3. Add the following code to the OnRun trigger of your codeunit:

```
Customer.GET('10000');
MESSAGE('No: %1\Name: %2', Customer."No.", Customer.Name);
```

4. Save and close the codeunit.

5. When you run the codeunit you should see a window like the following:

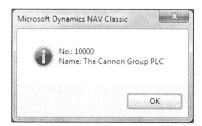

How it works...

The GET command works in conjunction with the primary key of the record. For the customer table, the primary key is **No.**. If you are unsure of the primary key for the table you are using, you can view the keys for the table and check the first entry.

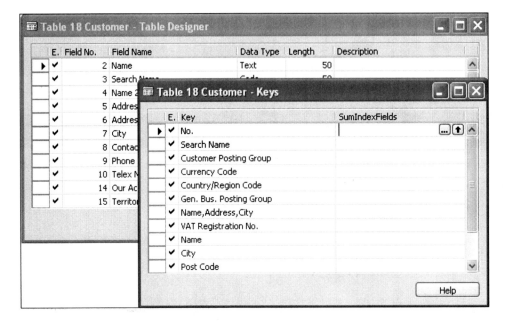

We first tell the database to go to the customer table and GET the record that has a **No.** field equal to 10000. We then display the number and name of the customer to make sure we retrieved the correct entry.

See also

▶ Checking for conditions using an IF statement

▶ Using advanced filtering

▶ Retrieving data using FIND

▶ Clearing filters, keys, and values

Using advanced filtering

When dealing with data you usually do not want to have to look at all of it. Most of the time you have a specific set of data from a table that you want to operate on. In NAV you can set filters on the records so that only the data that you want is returned.

How to do it...

1. Create a new codeunit from **Object Designer**.

2. Create a new function called `CheckForCustomer`. This function should take in the following parameter:

Name	Type	Subtype
Cust	Record	Customer

3. Add the following code to this function:

```
IF Cust.FINDFIRST THEN
    MESSAGE('Found!\No.: %1\Name: %2\Filters: %3', Cust."No.",
                            Cust.Name, Cust.GETFILTER(Name))
ELSE
    MESSAGE('Not Found!\Filters: %1', Cust.GETFILTER(Name));
```

4. Add the following local variable to the `OnRun` trigger:

Name	Type	Subtype
Customer	Record	Customer

5. Add the following code to the `OnRun` trigger of your codeunit:

```
Customer.SETCURRENTKEY(Name);

Customer.SETFILTER(Name, '%1', 'The Cannon Group PLC');
CheckForCustomer(Customer);

Customer.SETFILTER(Name, '%1', 'THE CANNON GROUP PLC);
CheckForCustomer(Customer);

Customer.SETFILTER(Name, '%1', '@THE CANNON GROUP PLC');
CheckForCustomer(Customer);

Customer.SETFILTER(Name, '%1', '*Cannon*');
CheckForCustomer(Customer);
```

6. Save and close the codeunit.

7. When you run the codeunit you will see a window similar to the following screenshot:

How it works...

First we create a function, `CheckForCustomer`, that will look for a filtered record. This is not necessary every time you want to filter, but it makes this codeunit cleaner and easier to understand. This function will display an appropriate message depending on whether or not it finds a record. We have to pass the record parameter by reference instead of passing it by value in order to pass through the filters that have been set. If you try without passing by reference you'll see that the function will always find a record.

Now to the more interesting part: filters. The first function call passes the name of the customer exactly as it appears in the record. Filtering in this method gives us our expected result and returns the record.

The next call is slightly different, but changes the results completely. It is the same name, but everything is capitalized. This does not match any records and the function returns a "Not Found!" message. It doesn't matter if one letters is off, if you add an extra space, or write ", LLC" instead of "LLC". If it doesn't match *exactly* it will not find the record.

Of course that's not very practical and NAV makes accommodations for the user. That's where the at-sign (@) comes in to play. If you add an @ to the beginning of your filter string, as we do in the next call, the filter will ignore capitalization. It doesn't matter if the record you are looking for says Cannon, CANNON, or CaNNoN. They will all fall within the filter if the @ is used.

What about instances where we know that the name has Cannon in it somewhere, but we cannot remember the whole name of the customer? NAV has the ability to handle wild-card filtering as well using the asterisk/star (*). So a filter of "*Cannon" would return anything that ends with Cannon. A filter of "Cannon*" would return everything that starts with the word "Cannon". "*Cannon*" would return anything which contained the text "Cannon".

There's more...

There are many ways to filter your data. From within the C/SIDE Client, click on **Help**, **Microsoft Dynamics NAV Classic Help**. Search for the help topic titled "Field Filters and Table Filters". Microsoft provides wonderful examples of all of the available filtering options, both individually and combined.

See also

- ▸ Creating a function
- ▸ Passing parameters by reference
- ▸ Retrieving a single record from the database
- ▸ Retrieving data using FIND
- ▸ Clearing filters, keys, and values

Retrieving data using FIND

Once you have determined the data that you want to operate on, you must retrieve it from the database. Most of the time the action to be performed must be performed on more than one record. This recipe will show you the best ways to get that data and when certain methods should be used.

How to do it...

1. Create a new codeunit from **Object Manager**.
2. Add the following local variable to the OnRun trigger:

Name	Type	Subtype
Customer	Record	Customer

3. Add the following code to your OnRun trigger:

```
IF Customer.FINDFIRST THEN
  MESSAGE('The first customer in the database is:\No.: %1\Name:
                        %2', Customer."No.", Customer.Name);


IF Customer.FINDLAST THEN
  MESSAGE('The last customer in the database is:\No.: %1\Name:
                        %2', Customer."No.", Customer.Name);


IF Customer.FINDSET THEN BEGIN
  MESSAGE('There are %1 customers in the database',
                        Customer.COUNT);
END;
```

4. Save and close the codeunit.

5. When you run the codeunit you will see windows that look like the following:

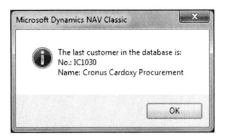

How it works...

There are three types of `FIND` commands, each of which will be discussed. The first two are very similar and do exactly what you would expect. `FINDFIRST` returns the first record in the data set while `FINDLAST` returns the last record. These commands should only be used when you want to retrieve a single record from the database. They have been optimized for this task. If you want to retrieve multiple records and process them individually, you should use the `FINDSET` command.

There's more...

These commands were not introduced until version 5.0 of NAV. Previously, you would use `FIND('-')` for `FINDFIRST` and `FIND('+')` for `FINDLAST`.

See also

- ▶ Repeating code using a loop
- ▶ Checking for conditions using an `IF` statement
- ▶ Retrieving a single record from the database
- ▶ Using advanced filtering
- ▶ Clearing filters, keys, and values

Adding a FlowField to a table

FlowFields are fields that are not actually stored in the database. They are calculated fields that the user can call upon instead of performing the calculation themselves. This recipe will show you how to add a FlowField to your tables.

How to do it...

1. Follow the steps from the *Creating a Table* recipe to create a table.
2. Add the following field to the table:

Field No.	Field Name	Data Type	Length
10	Sell-to Customer No.	Code	20

3. View the **Properties** for this field (*Shift + F4*).
4. Set the following properties:

Property	Value
FieldClass	FlowField
CalcFormula	Lookup("Sales Invoice Header"."Sell-to Customer No." WHERE (No.=FIELD(Document No.)))
Editable	No

5. Close the **Properties** Window.
6. Save and close your table.

How it works...

To start, we create a field like any other field. It should have an ID number, name, and type. In order to make it a FlowField, we have to change the property named `FieldClass`. This tells the system whether or not this is an actual field to be stored in the database (Normal) or a field that should be calculated or used to calculate a value on the fly (FlowField or FlowFilter).

When defining a FlowField you must tell the database how to calculate its value. This is done with the `CalcFormula` property. Our field is a **lookup**, meaning we just want to pull a value from another table that matches some criteria. We also have to tell it which table to pull the value from and which filters should be used to determine the value.

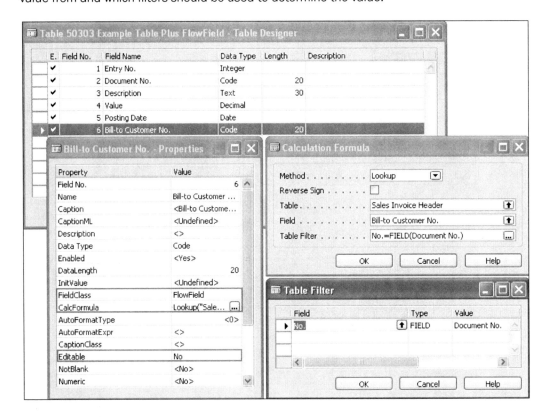

There's more...

A FlowField is not actually stored in the database, which means it can't be used outside the NAV client in other applications. It can't even be used in a SQL procedure. So what exactly is its use?

FlowFields can be used to display related information more easily. A great example is the Cost fields from the Item Ledger Entry table. The actual cost of an item is the sum of all of the associated records from the Value Entry table. You wouldn't want to manually check its value every time you required that information. You also wouldn't want to calculate them using code (this method of calculating and storing in a global variable does not allow you to filter on the values). That's where the FlowField comes in. Not only does it allow you to compile information about related entries, but the database keeps a track of it all for you, allowing for faster reporting and viewing of data.

Determining the value of a FlowField

Remember, the value of a FlowField is not stored in the database. We have to tell the system to calculate the value. Here is a quick example of how to use FlowFields in your own code.

The variable `FlowFieldRec` is a record variable that refers to the table you created in this example. The large conditional block at the start of the code is just to make sure we have data in the table.

```
IF NOT FlowFieldRec.GET(1) THEN BEGIN
  FlowFieldRec."Entry No." := 1;
  FlowFieldRec."Document No." := '103006';
  FlowFieldRec.INSERT;
END;

BeforeValue := FlowFieldRec."Sell-to Customer No.";
FlowFieldRec.CALCFIELDS("Sell-to Customer No.");
AfterValue := FlowFieldRec."Sell-to Customer No.";

MESSAGE('Value before: %1\Value after: %2', BeforeValue, AfterValue);
```

`BeforeValue` and `AfterValue` are code variables. First we assign the uncalculated value to the `BeforeValue` variable. In this case, the value will be an empty string. The next line uses the CALCFIELDS command to tell the system to figure out what the value of that FlowField is. Once it has been calculated, we assign its value to the `AfterValue` variable and display a message like the one shown in the following screenshot:

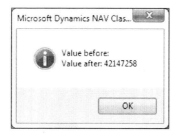

See also

- ▶ Creating a table
- ▶ Adding a key to a table
- ▶ Validating data
- ▶ Creating a SumIndex field
- ▶ Understanding SIFT tables

Creating a SumIndex field

A **SumIndex** is like a running total of certain fields in your table. Instead of calculating these sums manually you can tell NAV to do it for you. Here we'll tell you how to add a SumIndex field to your table and show you how to use it.

How to do it...

1. Follow the steps from *Creating a Table* recipe to create a table.
2. View the keys for the table by clicking **View** | **Keys** from the **Menu**.
3. Add a key for the **Posting Date** and a SumIndexFields for **Value**.
4. Close the **Keys** window.
5. Save and close your table.

How it works...

This recipe, unlike a few others, is very straightforward. By adding fields to list in the SumIndexFields column of a key, you tell the database to keep a track of the totals for those fields for every combination of filters in the key.

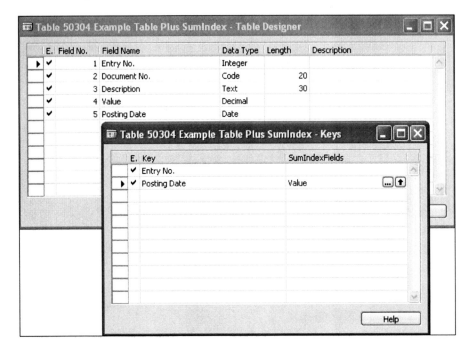

There's more...

Why use SumIndexFields? Why not just calculate these totals manually? The answer is that it is much faster to let the database do it. We won't get into the details behind the scenes regarding SumIndexFields, but will demonstrate how it works using a short example.

Entry No.	Value	Total
1	10	10
2	20	30
3	30	60
4	40	100
5	50	150
6	60	210
7	70	280
8	80	360
9	90	450
10	100	550

In the background, NAV keeps a running total or sum of the values defined as SumIndexFields. If you were to calculate the total manually, you would have to sum up all ten entries individually.

With **SIFT(Sum Index Field Technology)**, NAV can do this with only two entries. Let's try and find the sum of entries four through eight. By manually adding this up we have five entries and the total is 300. SIFT will take the sum of the values up until our first entry (so the total of entries one through three, that is 60) and subtract that from the total of our last entry, number eight, which is equal to 360. 360 – 60 = 300, the same result.

In C/AL code, you will need to use the CALCSUMS function to calculate this value.

For a detailed explanation of how SumIndexFields work with SQL and SIFT Indexes, do take a look at "*The NAV/SQL Performance Guide*" by *Jorg A. Stryk*.

See also

- ▶ Creating a table
- ▶ Adding a key to a table
- ▶ Validating data
- ▶ Adding a FlowField to a table
- ▶ Understanding SIFT tables

Marking records for future use

Sometimes you need to work with records that just don't fall into an easily filterable data set. The most common is when you need Field A to equal one value or Field B to equal some other value. This recipe will show you how to mark the individual records that you need to operate on.

How to do it...

1. Create a new codeunit from **Object Designer**.

2. Add the following global variable:

Name	Type	Subtype
Customer	Record	Customer

3. Add the following code to the OnRun trigger:

```
Customer.SETFILTER(Name, 'C*');
IF Customer.FINDSET THEN
  REPEAT
    Customer.MARK(TRUE);
  UNTIL Customer.NEXT = 0;

Customer.SETRANGE(Name);
Customer.SETRANGE("Location Code", 'YELLOW');
IF Customer.FINDSET THEN
  REPEAT
    Customer.MARK(TRUE);
  UNTIL Customer.NEXT = 0;

Customer.MARKEDONLY(TRUE);
MESSAGE('%1 records marked', Customer.COUNT);
```

4. Save and close the codeunit.

5. When you run this codeunit you will see a message like this one:

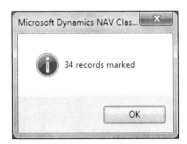

How it works...

Sometimes the records you want to work with don't fit easily into specific filters. One option is to mark the records you need and then perform operations on them. In our simple case, we retrieve records from the database that start with the letter "C" and use the MARK command to mark them for later use. We then do the same thing for all customers that belong to Location Code "YELLOW". In most cases you would have some sort of conditional statement that would determine whether or not to mark the record.

Marking a record is essentially the same as setting a flag on the record. Later, you still need to filter on that flag. That's what the MARKEDONLY function does. Just like the MARK function, it takes in a boolean value that tells the system what to do.

There's more...

You can also mark records from the client using _Ctrl + F1_. When you do this, you'll notice that a small dot is placed to the left of the record as in the following screenshot:

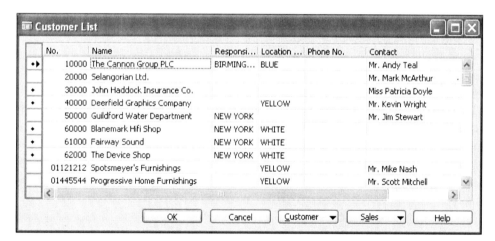

See also

▶ Using advanced filtering
▶ Using temporary tables to store data

Clearing filters, keys, and values

Once you have applied filters to a variable and performed your operations, you may want reuse that variable. Here we will show you how to remove any actions you may have done to it.

How to do it...

1. Create a new codeunit from **Object Designer**.

2. Add the following global variable:

Name	Type	Subtype
Customer	Record	Customer

3. Add the following code to the OnRun trigger of the codeunit:

```
Customer.SETCURRENTKEY(Name);
Customer.SETFILTER(Name, 'Matt');
Customer."No." := 'Num';
Customer.RESET;

MESSAGE('Current Key: %1\Name Filter: %2\Customer No.: %3',
    Customer.CURRENTKEY, Customer.GETFILTER(Name), Customer."No.");

Customer.SETCURRENTKEY(Name);
Customer.SETFILTER(Name, 'Matt');
Customer."No." := 'Num';
CLEAR(Customer);

MESSAGE('Current Key: %1\Name Filter: %2\Customer No.: %3',
    Customer.CURRENTKEY, Customer.GETFILTER(Name), Customer."No.");
```

4. Save and close the codeunit.

5. When you run the codeunit you will see windows like the following:

How it works...

When using a simple variable type, you can set its value to zero or to an empty string whenever you want to reuse them. Record variables are made up of a lot of these simple variable types. You don't need to set each of the fields individually. NAV offers two functions for this, and it is important to understand the differences between them.

The first is the `RESET` function. This will remove any filters you have set on the variable. It will also set the key back to the primary key if you have changed it. It will NOT clear any values from the fields.

The second is the `CLEAR` command. This does everything that `RESET` does, but takes it a step further by clearing individual fields of the record.

In the example code, we set a key, some filters, and the value of a field, then perform each of the functions. The message displayed will show you what gets changed in the record.

See also

- ▸ Retrieving a single record from the database
- ▸ Using advanced filtering
- ▸ Retrieving data using `FIND`

Using temporary tables to store data

Temporary tables can be useful when you need to insert data into a table to perform calculations, but don't want it saved to the database. This recipe will show you how to mark your records as temporary and what to watch out for when you do.

How to do it...

1. Create a new codeunit from **Object Designer**.

2. Add the following global variable:

Name	Type	Subtype
Customer	Record	Customer
TempCustomer	Record	Customer

3. View the properties of the `TempCustomer` variable.

4. Set the following property:

Property	Value
Temporary	Yes

5. Close the **Properties** window.

6. Add the following code to the `OnRun` trigger of the codeunit:

```
MESSAGE('Customer Count: %1\TempCustomer Count: %2',
        Customer.COUNT, TempCustomer.COUNT);
```

7. Save and close the codeunit.

8. When you run the codeunit you will see a window like the one shown in the following screenshot:

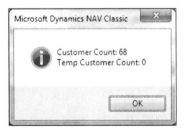

How it works...

Declaring a record variable as temporary is as easy as setting the `Temporary` property to **Yes**. But what is the purpose of setting a temporary table? A temporary table has all the code and properties of a normal table. It functions in exactly the same way. The only difference is that when you perform a transaction (insert, modify, delete, or rename) with a temporary table, the data is not stored in the database. Instead it is held in memory just like any other variable.

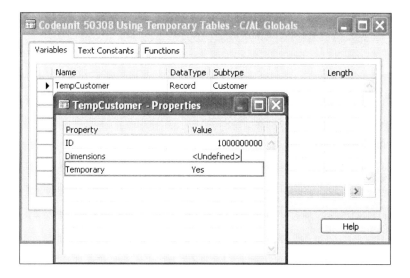

There's more...

It may sound obvious, but when planning to work with a temporary table, don't forget to mark it as Temporary! There's nothing worse than running TempGLEntry.DELETEALL and realizing that all of your real data is gone. This is a perfect example of why you should always do your development in a test system and have a recent backup before performing any changes. Also, if you run a DELETEALL(TRUE) on a temporary record variable, the code that is called in the OnDelete trigger will run with variables that are NOT temporary, which means that actual data will be deleted. Again, be careful!

Storing records to process

Just as you can mark records that have to be processed using the MARK function, you can also create a temporary table to store them. Instead of MARK, the following code can be used:

```
TempCustomer := Customer;
TempCustomer.INSERT;
```

You assign the value of the actual data to a temporary record and the insert into the temporary table. The data will be stored in memory, but not in the database, and you can use it for later operations.

See also

▸ Retrieving a single record from the database

▸ Marking records for future use

▸ Creating a form based on a temporary table

Retrieving data from another company

NAV can hold data for many companies under your corporate umbrella. Many times, users will want consolidated reports that show them data from all of the companies in the system. This recipe will show you how to retrieve that data from anywhere in the system.

Getting ready

Make sure you have at least two companies in your database like Cronus USA and Cronus Canada.

How to do it...

1. Create a new codeunit from **Object Designer**.

2. Add the following global variables:

Name	Type	Subtype
Customer	Record	Customer
Company	Record	Company

3. Add the following code to the OnRun trigger of the codeunit:

```
IF Company.FINDSET THEN
  REPEAT
    Customer.CHANGECOMPANY(Company.Name);
    MESSAGE('Company Name: %1\Customer Count: %2',
               Company.Name,Customer.COUNT);
  UNTIL Company.NEXT = 0;
```

4. Save and close the codeunit.

5. When you run the codeunit you will see a window like the one shown in the following screenshot:

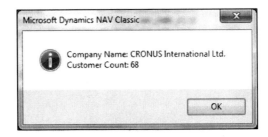

How it works...

In order to get data from another company within NAV, we have to tell it which company we want access to. Records have a built-in function called CHANGECOMPANY. This function takes in a text value that represents the name of the company as a parameter.

In our example, we are going to show the number of customers in every company in NAV. That's why we have the company record variable. Looping through each record in the dataset, we pass the name of the company through the CHANGECOMPANY command and display the customer count. We could just as easily have stored our other company name in a text constant and passed that value instead. In most cases, though, it is good to store the name of the company you want to access in a setup table. This way if the company is renamed, your code will not break.

Remember, just because you are running code on a temporary variable, doesn't mean that the code defined in that object uses temporary variables. For example, you may define a record variable as temporary and call the OnDelete trigger using DELETE(TRUE). If there are record variables in the trigger that are not defined as temporary, they will delete actual data.

See also

- ▸ Retrieving a single record from the database
- ▸ Retrieving data using FIND

Merging records

Many times users will unintentionally enter duplicate data into the system. NAV doesn't offer a built-in way to merge this data, but here we will show you how you can do it yourself.

Getting ready

If you do not have two customer records that you would like to merge together, you must create them. It is best if these customers have some related entries in other tables, for example the Contact or Cust. Ledger Entry tables.

How to do it...

1. Create a new codeunit from **Object Designer**.

2. Add the following global variables:

Name	Type	Subtype	Length
CustToKeep	Record	Customer	
CustToRemove	Record	Customer	
CustNoToKeep	Code		20
CustNoToRemove	Code		20

3. Add the following code to the OnRun trigger of your codeunit:

```
CustNoToKeep := 'C00010';
CustNoToRemove := 'C00020';

CustToKeep.GET(CustNoToKeep);
CustToKeep.DELETE;

CustToRemove.GET(CustNoToRemove);
CustToRemove.RENAME(CustNoToKeep);
```

4. Save and close the codeunit.

How it works...

First, you have to determine the two customer records that you want to merge. The customer number that you want to keep is stored in the CustNoToKeep code variable. The customer number that will be removed from the system is stored in the CustNoToRemove variable.

Now for the part that may seem counter-intuitive at first, we retrieve one customer record from the database using GET and the number in the CustNoToKeep variable and then delete it! It is important that we do a DELETE and not a DELETE(TRUE) in this case. By passing the default value of FALSE to the DELETE command, we only delete this record. This means that any related records, such as customer ledger entries, remain in the database. They just aren't tied to an actual customer anymore.

If that part was confusing, this next set of code will make things clearer. Now we get the customer that we want to remove from the database. Instead of deleting it, we rename it to the customer number that we wanted to keep. So the record we wanted to get rid of is "removed" and it takes the place of the one we are keeping. In this case all of the related records are also renamed, thus merging them with the records that were not removed when we executed our DELETE statement.

The following diagram may help in further illustrating what the records in the database will look like at each step along the way:

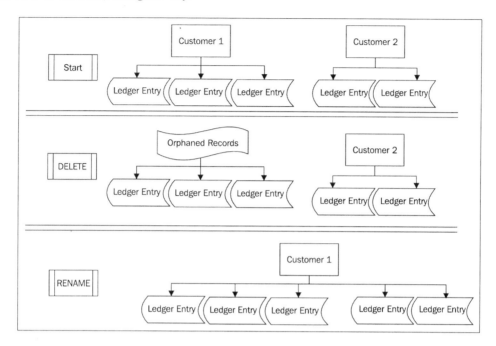

See also

▸   Creating transactions to alter data

Writing your own rollback routine

NAV does some rollback automatically. But if there is a COMMIT statement in the code, only the changes after the COMMIT statement is executed will be reversed by the system. This recipe will show you how to leverage a built-in NAV feature called the Change Log to build your own rollback routine for those cases.

Getting ready

Turn on the **Change Log** for table 36, **Sales Header**.

How to do it...

1. Create a new codeunit from **Object Designer**.

2. Add a function named `FilterRecord` that takes in the following parameters:

Name	Type	Subtype
ChangeLogEntry	Record	Change Log Entry
PrimaryKeyIndex	Integer	
RecRef	RecordRef	

3. Add the following local variables to the function:

Name	Type	Length
FieldRef	FieldRef	
TypeNumber	Decimal	
PrimaryKeyFieldNo	Integer	
PrimaryKeyValue	c	250

4. Add the following code to the function:

```
WITH ChangeLogEntry DO BEGIN
  CASE PrimaryKeyIndex OF
    1: BEGIN
      PrimaryKeyFieldNo := "Primary Key Field 1 No.";
      PrimaryKeyValue := "Primary Key Field 1 Value";
    END;
    2: BEGIN
      PrimaryKeyFieldNo := "Primary Key Field 2 No.";
      PrimaryKeyValue := "Primary Key Field 2 Value";
    END;
    3: BEGIN
      PrimaryKeyFieldNo := "Primary Key Field 3 No.";
      PrimaryKeyValue := "Primary Key Field 3 Value";
    END;
    ELSE EXIT;
  END;

  IF PrimaryKeyFieldNo = 0 THEN
    EXIT;
```

```
IF RecRef.FIELDEXIST(PrimaryKeyFieldNo) THEN BEGIN
  FieldRef := RecRef.FIELD(PrimaryKeyFieldNo);
CASE FORMAT(FieldRef.TYPE) OF
  'Option': BEGIN
  FieldRef.SETRANGE(MatchOptionToInteger(FieldRef.OPTIONSTRING,
                    PrimaryKeyValue));
  END;
  'Code', 'Text': BEGIN
    FieldRef.SETRANGE(PrimaryKeyValue);
  END;
  'Integer', 'Decimal': BEGIN
    EVALUATE(TypeNumber, PrimaryKeyValue);
    FieldRef.SETRANGE(TypeNumber);
  END;
  'Boolean': BEGIN
    IF PrimaryKeyValue = 'No' THEN
      FieldRef.SETRANGE(FALSE)
    ELSE
      FieldRef.SETRANGE(TRUE);
  END;
  END;
END;
END;
```

5. Add a function named `MatchOptionToInteger` with the following parameters:

Name	Type	Length
OptionStringIn	Text	250
Option	Text	250

6. Add the following local variables to the function:

Name	Type	Length
OptionIndex	Integer	
OptionEndPosition	Integer	
OptionValue	Text	250
OptionString	Text	250

7. Set the return value of the function to be an integer.

8. Add the following code to the function:

```
REPEAT
  OptionEndPosition := STRPOS(OptionStringIn, ',');
  IF OptionEndPosition = 0 THEN
    OptionEndPosition := STRLEN(OptionStringIn);
  OptionValue := COPYSTR(OptionStringIn, 1,
                                 OptionEndPosition - 1);

  IF OptionValue = Option THEN
    EXIT(OptionIndex)
  ELSE
    OptionStringIn := COPYSTR(OptionStringIn,
                                 OptionEndPosition + 1);

  OptionIndex += 1;
UNTIL OptionStringIn = '';

EXIT(-1);
```

9. Add a function named `ReverseEntry` with the following parameters:

Name	Type	Subtype
ChangeLogEntry	Record	Change Log Entry

10. Add the following local variables to the function:

Name	Type
RecRef	RecordRef
FieldRef	FieldRef
TypeNumber	Integer

11. Add the following code to the function:

```
WITH ChangeLogEntry DO BEGIN

  RecRef.OPEN("Table No.");
  FilterRecord(ChangeLogEntry, 1, RecRef);
  FilterRecord(ChangeLogEntry, 2, RecRef);
  FilterRecord(ChangeLogEntry, 3, RecRef);

  IF RecRef.FINDFIRST THEN
```

```
     IF "Type of Change" = "Type of Change"::Modification THEN
                                                         BEGIN
       FieldRef := RecRef.FIELD("Field No.");

       CASE FORMAT(FieldRef.TYPE) OF
         'Code', 'Text': BEGIN
           FieldRef.VALUE := "Old Value";
         END;
         'Option', 'Integer', 'Decimal': BEGIN
           EVALUATE(TypeNumber, "Old Value");
           FieldRef.VALUE := TypeNumber;
         END;
         'Boolean': BEGIN
           IF "Old Value" = 'No' THEN
             FieldRef.SETRANGE(FALSE)
           ELSE
             FieldRef.SETRANGE(TRUE);
           END;
         END;
         RecRef.MODIFY;
       END;
     ELSE
       ERROR('No record found!');
   END;
END;
```

12. Add a function named `Rollback` that takes the following parameters:

Name	Type
EntryStart	Integer
EntryEnd	Integer

13. Add the following local variables to the function:

Name	Type	Subtype
ChangeLogEntry	Record	Change Log Entry

14. Add the following code to the function:

```
ChangeLogEntry.SETRANGE("Entry No.", EntryStart, EntryEnd);
ChangeLogEntry.ASCENDING := FALSE;
IF ChangeLogEntry.FINDFIRST THEN
  REPEAT
  ReverseEntry(ChangeLogEntry);
  UNTIL ChangeLogEntry.NEXT = 0;
```

15. Add the following code to the `OnRun` trigger:

```
Rollback(149, 199);
```

16. Save and close the codeunit.

How it works...

NAV has a built-in functionality to track changes to records called a **Change Log**. It must be turned on for tracking specific tables and fields. We can build on this functionality to create our own rollback routine. Each entry in the Change Log Entry table represents a change to a record. It stores the first three fields of the primary key, the field that was changed, the original value, and the new value. As we do not know what table or field was changed before we look at the record, we will rely heavily on **Record References** and **Field References**. This example is very basic and does not cover every possible field type or change that can be made, but it will get you started in developing your own. Let's look at each function to get a better understanding.

We'll start with the `FilterRecord` function. We tell this function which of the primary key fields to filter on. The first `CASE` statement pulls the primary key value from the Change Log Entry and stores it in a temp variable. If that field exists we then take appropriate actions based on what type of field it is. For example, in the Change Log, option values are stored as strings so we must match that string to the actual integer value of the `OptionString`.

That brings us to our next function, `MatchOptionToInteger`. This is a simple helper function. An **OptionString** is a comma-separated list. In this function, we parse the `OptionString` that removes all the text in it until we find a comma. The text we find represents a single option. We continue this process until we find the option we want, that is the one stored in the Change Log Entry.

Now that we have these helper functions, we need to use them to actually reverse an entry. Using the `ReverseEntry` function we tell the codeunit to filter for the record described by the primary key fields in the Change Log Entry. We do this three times to account for each of the primary key fields. After these filters are applied, we attempt to find the record and change its value. Again, because all of the values are stored as text we have to convert the data to the appropriate data type in order to change the value.

Our final function, `Rollback`, simply loops through all of the Change Log entries we tell it to and calls the `ReverseEntry` function on each of those records.

See also

- ▸ Repeating code using a loop
- ▸ Checking for conditions using an IF statement
- ▸ Creating a function
- ▸ Referencing dynamic fields and tables
- ▸ Creating transactions to alter data
- ▸ Retrieving a single record from the database
- ▸ Using advanced filtering
- ▸ Retrieving data using FIND

4
Designing Forms

In this chapter, we will cover:

- ▸ Obtaining input without a form
- ▸ Using the Form Generation Wizard
- ▸ Changing text appearance
- ▸ Preventing editable lookup forms
- ▸ Adding an editable field to a non-editable form
- ▸ Creating a matrix form
- ▸ Creating a wizard-style form
- ▸ Designing a form based on a temporary table
- ▸ Updating a subform from a parent form
- ▸ Updating a parent form from a subform

Introduction

Forms are a predominant visual element in Dynamics NAV. They allow the user to view, insert, modify, and delete data from the tables in the database. Forms also allow the user to initiate events that perform actions on that data.

There are 937 tables in the base NAV software and 1,820 forms that display information from those tables. Apart from learning how to create a form using the wizard, this chapter will not discuss the basic elements of form design. That information can be found in the C/SIDE Reference Guide and Development Coursework from Microsoft.

If you have not designed a form before, it is highly recommended that you go through the chapters based on forms first.

With NAV 2009, Microsoft released the **RoleTailored client**, or **RTC**. This was a huge change from the existing NAV product. In this release, Microsoft introduced the RTC as a second client or interface in addition to what is called the Classic client, or more traditional interface. While the future of NAV is definitely with the RTC, it is still important to understand what forms are and how they work, in order to support customers who might not upgrade to the latest version of the product.

Obtaining input without a form

Sometimes you don't want to use an entire form to get user input. Dialog boxes are not a substitute for forms, but they work just fine for quick input.

How to do it...

1. Create a new codeunit from **Object Designer**.

2. Add the following global variables:

Name	Type	Subtype	Length
Customer	Record	Customer	
CustomerNo	Code		20
Window	Dialog		

3. Add the following code to the OnRun trigger of the codeunit:

```
Window.OPEN('Customer No: #1##################');
Window.INPUT(1, CustomerNo);
Window.CLOSE;

IF Customer.GET(CustomerNo) THEN
  MESSAGE('Customer Name: %1', Customer.Name)
ELSE
  MESSAGE('No customer found!');
```

4. Save and close the codeunit.

How it works...

The first line of code opens an input dialog window that looks like one shown in the following screenshot:

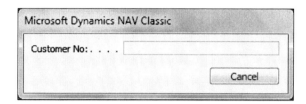

The next line lets the user input a value and stores it in the `CustomerNo` variable. The dialog window then closes and the result can be used later in code.

There's more...

As you can tell from the input window, dialogs are much weaker than forms when it comes to functionality. You can't do lookups, data validation, or anything other than basic text input. From a licensing aspect, forms are one of the cheapest objects to buy. They also don't match the look and feel for the rest of the system. For these reasons it is almost always better to use a form than an input dialog, but it is important to know what you can do using dialogs.

See also

▸   Displaying a Progress Bar

Using the Form Generation Wizard

You can always create a form manually, but using the **Form Generation Wizard** is a quick and painless way to create the skeleton.

How to do it...

1. With the form selected in **Object Designer** click the **New** button.

2. Choose the **Customer** table.
3. Select **Create a form using a wizard**.
4. Select **Tabular-Type Form**.
5. Click **OK**.

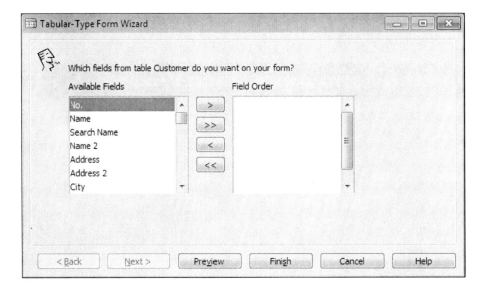

6. Use the arrow buttons between the two lists to add the **No.** and **Name** fields.

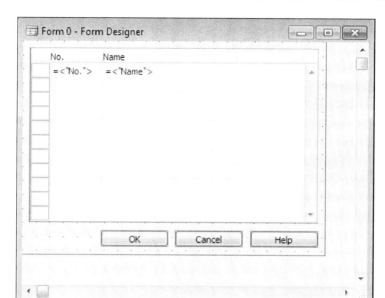

7. Click on **Finish**.

How it works...

The Form Generation Wizard allows you to tell the system what fields you want on the form and the format or order in which you want them to appear. NAV will then automatically place the fields on the form for you. There is no manual positioning of labels or textboxes; no creating tabs or list boxes. It is all done automatically.

There's more...

The wizard will only create a basic form for you. If you need to create special functions or do any specific data validation, you will have to code that manually. A wizard is only designed to get you started, not to do anything advanced.

See also

▸ Creating a matrix form
▸ Creating a wizard-style form

Changing text appearance

A great way to improve the user experience is to change the way text appears on the screen. This recipe will explore several options that are available to you.

Getting ready

Design the **Customer List** form and save it as a new object.

How to do it...

1. Design the copy of the **Customer List** form.

2. Create a function named GetColor that returns an integer.

3. Add the following code to the function:

```
IF "Location Code" = 'BLUE' THEN
   EXIT(16711680)
ELSE IF "Location Code" = 'GREEN' THEN
   EXIT(65280)
ELSE IF "Location Code" = 'RED' THEN
   EXIT(255)
ELSE IF "Location Code" = 'YELLOW' THEN
   EXIT(65535)
```

4. Create a function named GetBold that returns a boolean value.

5. Add the following code to the function:

```
EXIT("Credit Limit (LCY)" > 1000);
```

6. In the OnFormat trigger for the name column, add the following code:

```
CurrForm.Name.UPDATEFORECOLOR(GetColor);
CurrForm.Name.UPDATEFONTBOLD(GetBold);
```

7. Save and close the form.

How it works...

The trigger that controls the appearance of text is the OnFormat trigger. The first function we use is UPDATEFORECOLOR. This method is found on every text field in a form. It takes one parameter—the color we want the text to be. In our example, we pass a function as the parameter and that function returns the color we should use.

UPDATEFONTBOLD works in a similar way. It takes a boolean parameter that tells the form whether or not to emphasize the text.

The resulting form will look similar to the one shown in the following screenshot:

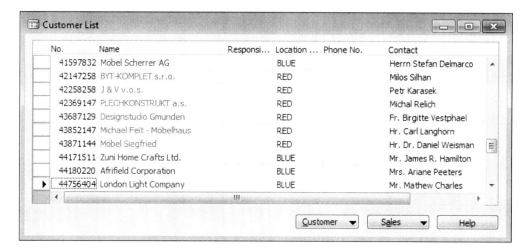

There's more...

The look and feel of a system is important for user satisfaction. Finding ways to make the information easier to understand, such as displaying the text in the same color as the warehouse location, can improve user understanding and decrease the time it takes to look up information.

That said, don't go overboard. Having a form with multiple colors that have no direct relation to the data can be confusing. You don't want to the user to have a "cheat sheet" of what everything means. If it takes longer than a couple of minutes to explain what certain characteristics mean and you can't remember them an hour later, then you probably have gone too far. It also makes your upgrade-time to the RoleTailored client longer because display colors only have limited support.

See also

▶ Converting a value to a formatted string

Preventing editable lookup forms

You may want users to only add records when running a form from a setup location. This example will show you how to prevent users from adding or modifying values when only trying to look up a record.

Getting ready

This example will use the Salesperson/Purchasers form (14).

How to do it...

1. Design the **Salesperson/Purchasers** form from **Object Designer**.

2. In the `OnOpen` trigger for the form, add the following code:

```
IF CurrForm.LOOKUPMODE THEN
   CurrForm.EDITABLE := FALSE;
```

3. Save and close the form.

How it works...

The code here is pretty self-explanatory. If the form is in lookup mode, it will not be editable.

There's more...

The **Lookup mode** is a special mode in which forms can run. Essentially, when in lookup mode, the **OK** and **Cancel** buttons are displayed; when not in lookup mode, they are hidden. When using these buttons you can retrieve the selected value from the form. It is often a good idea to make forms uneditable in lookup mode, although you will find many forms in base NAV where this is not the case. When the purpose of running a form is only to retrieve a value, it is a good idea to make sure that the form is not editable to make sure those values are not accidentally changed.

See also

▶ Checking for conditions using an `IF` Statement

▶ Adding an editable field to a non-editable form

Adding an editable field to a non-editable form

Have you ever needed to make a form uneditable rather than just one field? This recipe will show you a quick and easy way to do it.

Getting ready

Create a list form based on the **Customer** table that displays the number and name of the customer. The `Editable` property of the form should be set to **No**.

How to do it...

1. View the code for the **Name** column in the list form.

2. In the `OnActivate` trigger, add the following code:

   ```
   CurrForm.EDITABLE := TRUE;
   ```

3. In the `OnDeactivate` trigger add the following code:

   ```
   CurrForm.EDITABLE := FALSE;
   ```

4. Save and close the form.

How it works...

When you click on a textbox its `OnActivate` trigger is executed. In our form, we have told the system to override the default `Editable` property when we click on the textbox. We set it to true so that the field becomes editable. In fact, the entire form becomes editable. We must make the entire form editable because that overrides the editable property of the controls on the form.

But when we click-off or tab-off of the field the `OnDeactivate` trigger fires. We then reset the form back to uneditable. Whenever the field is activated you can edit it, otherwise you cannot edit anything.

 In the RoleTailored client there is no `OnActivate` or `OnDeactivate` trigger. You will have to do it the hard way, that is, by setting the `Editable` property on every field.

See also

▸   Preventing editable lookup forms

Creating a matrix form

A matrix shows information from multiple tables at the same time. This recipe will show you how to create a matrix that shows the amount a customer has spent on specific items.

How to do it...

1. Add a global function `CalculateData` that returns a text variable.

2. Add a global function `ColumnHeader` that returns a text variable.

3. Add a matrix box to the form.

4. Set the following properties on the matrix box control:

Property	Value
Name	MatrixBox
Editable	No
MatrixSourceTable	Item

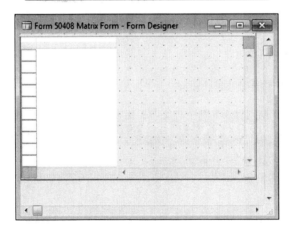

5. Set the following property on the form:

Property	Value
SourceExpr	Customer

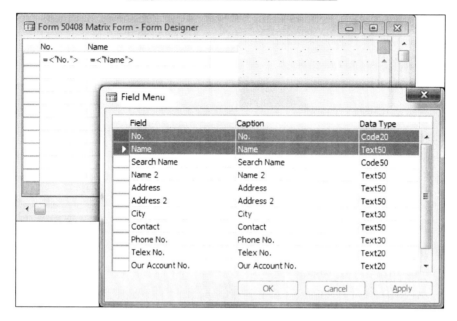

6. Add the **No.** and **Name** fields to the left-hand side of the matrix box using the **Field** menu.

7. Add a textbox to the right-hand side of the matrix box.

8. Set the following property on the textbox:

Property	Value
SourceExpr	CalculateData

9. Add a textbox as a column header above that textbox.

10. Set the following property on the textbox:

Property	Value
SourceExpr	ColumnHeader

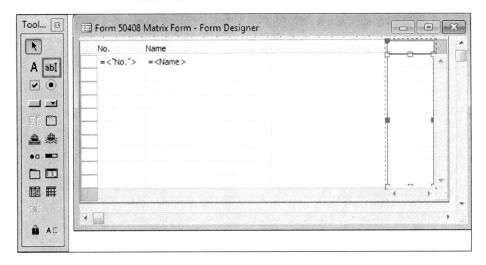

11. Add the following code to the `ColumnHeader` function

```
EXIT(CurrForm.MatrixBox.MatrixRec."No.");
```

12. Add the following local variables to the `CalculateData` function:

Name	Type	Subtype
ItemLedgerEntry	Record	Item Ledger Entry
TotalSales	Decimal	

13. Add the following code to the `CalculateData` function

```
ItemLedgerEntry.RESET;
ItemLedgerEntry.SETCURRENTKEY("Source Type", "Source No.",
                "Item No.", "Variant Code", "Posting Date");
ItemLedgerEntry.SETRANGE("Source Type", ItemLedgerEntry."Source
                                        Type"::Customer);
ItemLedgerEntry.SETRANGE("Source No.", "No.");
ItemLedgerEntry.SETRANGE("Item No.",
                        CurrForm.MatrixBox.MatrixRec."No.");
ItemLedgerEntry.SETRANGE("Entry Type", ItemLedgerEntry."Entry
                                        Type"::Sale);

IF ItemLedgerEntry.FINDSET THEN
```

```
REPEAT
    ItemLedgerEntry.CALCFIELDS("Sales Amount (Actual)");
    TotalSales := TotalSales + ItemLedgerEntry."Sales Amount
                                                       (Actual)";
  UNTIL ItemLedgerEntry.NEXT = 0;
EXIT(FORMAT(TotalSales));
```

14. After running the resulting form, you should see something similar to the following screenshot:

No.	Name	1964-W	1968-S	1968-W	1972-S	1972-W
10000	The Cannon Group PLC	4,500	541.78	0	0	0
20000	Selangorian Ltd.	0	0	0	0	0
30000	John Haddock Insurance Co.	0	0	0	0	0
40000	Deerfield Graphics Company	0	0	0	0	0
50000	Guildford Water Department	0	0	0	0	0
60000	Blanemark Hifi Shop	0	0	0	0	0
61000	Fairway Sound	0	0	0	0	0
62000	The Device Shop	0	0	0	0	0
01121212	Spotsmeyer's Furnishings	0	0	0	0	0
01445544	Progressive Home Furnishings	0	0	0	190.1	0
01454545	New Concepts Furniture	0	0	0	0	0
01905893	Candoxy Canada Inc.	0	0	0	0	0
01905899	Elkhorn Airport	0	0	0	0	0
01905902	London Candoxy Storage Campus	0	0	0	0	0
20309920	Metatorad Malaysia Sdn Bhd	0	0	0	0	0
20312912	Highlights Electronics Sdn Bhd	0	0	0	0	0
20339921	TraxTonic Sdn Bhd	0	0	0	0	0
21233572	Somadis	0	0	0	0	0

Caption: 10000 The Cannon Group PLC - Matrix Form

How it works...

A matrix form consists of two tables and some calculation based on those two tables. One set of records runs vertically along the left-hand side of the **matrix box** while the other set runs horizontally across the top. A grid is displayed on the rest of the form displaying a calculated value. We'll examine each of these pieces individually.

We begin by creating a normal form that is bound to the **Customer** table. For this special form we add a matrix box control. The left-hand side operates exactly the same as a standard list form. It will display all of the customers and there will be a scrollbar to look through the list. As we don't want the user to change anything on this form, we set the `Editable` property of the matrix box to **No**. We will also have to write code that refers to this control so we must give it a name.

Also, the matrix box itself operates on a table. In this case it is the **Item** table. As there is so much data stored in a table, we have to tell the control what we want to see. That's why we add a textbox as a column header to the top of the form. The source expression for that textbox is the `ColumnHeader` method. Let's take a look at the code there.

```
EXIT(CurrForm.MatrixBox.MatrixRec."No.");
```

`CurrForm` is the current form. `MatrixBox` is the value in the name property of our matrix box control. `MatrixRec` is the record in the matrix box that we are referring to (just like `rec` on a normal form). Finally, **No.** is the field from the `MatrixSourceTable` property(in this case the Item No). So our column headers will just be the Item Number from the **Item** table.

Lastly, we have to tell the form how to calculate the data we want to see. We add another textbox to the form and give it a source expression of `CalculateData`, which is a function on our form. This function could return anything, but in our case it returns the amount a customer has spent on a specific item. Let's take a look at the important code that combines the data from both tables.

```
ItemLedgerEntry.SETRANGE("Source No.", "No.");
ItemLedgerEntry.SETRANGE("Item No.",
            CurrForm.MatrixBox.MatrixRec."No.");
```

The **Item Ledger Entry** table already has fields that refer to the **Customer** table and to the **Item** table. The first filter uses the **No.** field from the source table (**Customer**). The second filter determines the current Item Number from the matrix box and uses it. Later in the function, a number is calculated and returned as a text variable.

See also

▶ Using the Form Generation Wizard

▶ Creating a function

Creating a wizard-style form

A wizard is a form that steps you through specific sections using **Next** and **Back** buttons. Here we will show you how to design a form which will do exactly that.

How to do it...

1. Add a frame to the form.

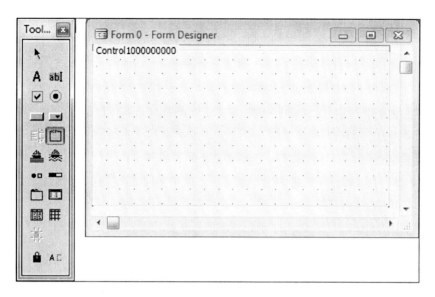

2. Set the following properties on the textbox:

Property	Value
ShowCaption	No
Name	Frame1

3. Add a label to the frame with the caption "Frame 1".

4. Set the following properties on the **Label**:

Property	Value
Caption	Frame 1

5. Copy the frame and paste two copies of it on the form.

6. Change the labels in the new frames to be **Frame 2** and **Frame 3**.

7. Change the Name properties of the frames to Frame2 and Frame3 respectively.

8. Your form should look like the one shown in the following screenshot:

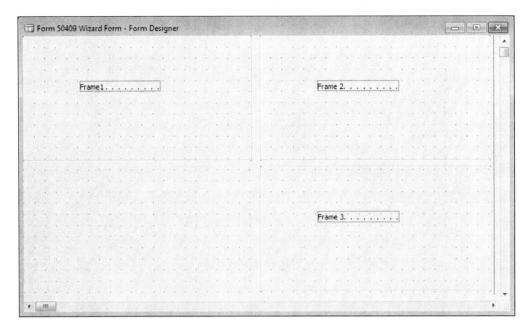

9. Add four buttons to the form beneath **Frame 1**. The name and caption properties on each should be **Back**, **Next**, **Finish**, and **Cancel** respectively.

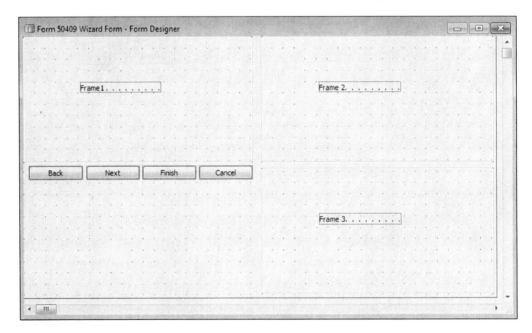

10. Add the following code to the `OnOpenForm` trigger:

```
CurrForm.Frame1.XPOS := 0;
CurrForm.Frame1.YPOS := 0;
CurrForm.Frame2.XPOS := 0;
CurrForm.Frame2.YPOS := 0;
CurrForm.Frame3.XPOS := 0;
CurrForm.Frame3.YPOS := 0;


CurrForm.HEIGHT := CurrForm.Cancel.YPOS +
                        CurrForm.Cancel.HEIGHT + 220;
CurrForm.WIDTH := CurrForm.Cancel.XPOS + CurrForm.Cancel.WIDTH
                                                        + 220;


WizardStep := 1;
ShowStep(TRUE);
```

11. Add a function named `ShowStep` that takes in a boolean value named `Show` as a parameter.

12. Add the following code to the function:

```
CASE WizardStep OF
  1: BEGIN
    CurrForm.Frame1.VISIBLE := Show;
    CurrForm.Frame2.VISIBLE := NOT Show;
    CurrForm.Frame3.VISIBLE := NOT Show;
    CurrForm.Back.ENABLED := NOT Show;
    CurrForm.Next.ENABLED := Show;
    CurrForm.Finish.ENABLED := NOT Show;
  END;

  2: BEGIN
    CurrForm.Frame1.VISIBLE := NOT Show;
    CurrForm.Frame2.VISIBLE := Show;
    CurrForm.Frame3.VISIBLE := NOT Show;
    CurrForm.Back.ENABLED := Show;
    CurrForm.Next.ENABLED := Show;
    CurrForm.Finish.ENABLED := NOT Show;
  END;

  3: BEGIN
    CurrForm.Frame1.VISIBLE := NOT Show;
    CurrForm.Frame2.VISIBLE := NOT Show;
```

```
    CurrForm.Frame3.VISIBLE := Show;
    CurrForm.Back.ENABLED := Show;
    CurrForm.Next.ENABLED := NOT Show;
    CurrForm.Finish.ENABLED := Show;
  END;
END;
```

13. Add the following code to the `OnPush` trigger of the **Back** button:

```
ShowStep(FALSE);
WizardStep -= 1;
ShowStep(TRUE);
```

14. Add the following code to the `OnPush` trigger of the **Next** button:

```
ShowStep(FALSE);
WizardStep -= 1;
ShowStep(TRUE);
```

15. Add the following code to the `OnPush` trigger of the **Finish** button:

```
CurrForm.CLOSE;
```

16. Add the following code to the `OnPush` trigger of the **Cancel** button:

```
CurrForm.CLOSE;
```

17. Save and close the form.

How it works...

The form contains three frames, only one of which is visible at any given time. In the design view, you can see that our form is quite wide and tall, but that would not look right when displaying a wizard form. That's why we place code in the `OnOpenForm` trigger.

The first set of lines places all of the frames on top of each other. The middle set changes the width and height of the form. Finally, the third sets the appropriate frames to be visible or not and enables the correct buttons.

Our custom method `ShowStep` decides what should be visible and what should not. It is just a large `CASE` statement based on the `WizardStep` variable. On the first frame for example, we can't move backwards to disable the **Back** button. We can't finish until we get to the last frame so that the **Finish** button is disabled until that point.

On the **Back** and **Next** buttons we decrement and increment the `WizardStep` variable so that the `ShowStep` method knows what to do. Other than the initial opening of the form we always call the function with `FALSE` as a parameter to "undo" what is currently displayed, change the `WizardStep` variable, and call the function with parameter `TRUE` to display new information.

See also

▶ Using the Form Generation Wizard

▶ Creating a function

Designing a form based on a temporary table

You may not always have the luxury of being able to save all of the information you need to the database. At other times you may want to calculate data on the fly and present it to the user in a form. Temporary tables come into play here and there is a special way to show their data on a form.

How to do it...

1. Follow the steps from the *Using the Form Generation Wizard* recipe in this chapter.

2. View the form properties by pressing *Shift + F4*.

3. Set the following properties on the form:

Property	Value
SourceTableTemporary	Yes

4. Add a global function named LoadData.

5. Add the following local parameters to the function:

Name	Type	Length
NoParam	Code	20
NameParam	Text	50

6. Add the following code to the function:

```
"No." := NoParam;
Name  := NameParam;
INSERT;
```

7. Add the following code to the OnOpenForm trigger:

```
AddCustomer('1', FIELDCAPTION(Name) + '1');
AddCustomer('2', FIELDCAPTION(Name) + '2');
AddCustomer('3', FIELDCAPTION(Name) + '3');
```

8. Save and close the form.

How it works...

By setting the SourceTableTemporary property to Yes we tell the form not to check the database for data when it loads. Just as with a normal record variable marked as temporary, there is no data to begin with. We have to tell the form what kind of data we want to see.

That's where the AddCustomer function comes in. When we open the form (OnOpenForm trigger) we load three customers into the temporary table. These customers will never be stored to the actual database. You can modify, delete, rename, or even add more customers, but these changes will be temporary.

See also

- ▶ Creating a function
- ▶ Creating transactions to alter data
- ▶ Using temporary tables to store data

Updating a subform from a parent form

Subforms only reload data when they know they need to. Unfortunately they are not very smart. This recipe will show you how to force a subform to refresh itself.

How to do it...

1. Create a new form from **Object Designer**.
2. Add the following global variables:

Name	Type
A	Integer
B	Integer

3. dd a global function named SetValues.
4. Add the following parameters to the function:

Name	Type
Aparam	Integer
Bparam	Integer

5. Add the following code to the function:

```
A := Aparam;
B := Bparam;
```

6. Add a global function called `UpdateSelf`.

7. Add the following code to the function:

```
CurrForm.UPDATE;
```

8. Set the following properties on the form:

Property	Value
Width	5720
Height	1430

9. Your form should look like the following screenshot:

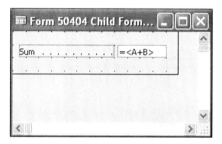

10. Save and close the form (for later use, remember the ID it is saved under).

11. Create a new form using the **Object Designer**.

12. Add the following global variables:

Name	Type
A	Integer
B	Integer

13. Add two textboxes with labels for each variable.

14. In the `OnAfterValidate` trigger for each textbox add the following code:

```
CurrForm.ChildForm.FORM.SetValues(A,B);
CurrForm.ChildForm.FORM.UpdateSelf;
```

15. Add a **Subform** control to the form.

16. View the properties for the **Subform** control.

17. Set the following properties on the form:

Property	Value
SubFormID	The ID of the form you just created
Name	ChildForm
Width	5720
Height	1430

18. Your form should look like the one shown in the following screenshot:

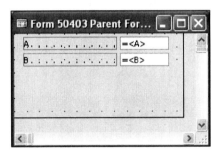

19. Save and close the form.

How it works...

To understand the concepts behind this recipe we use the following image:

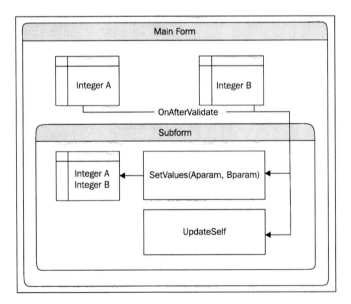

The main form knows only about things that are directly on itself; that is, two integer variables and a subform. The main form can request the subform to return some values and can also tell the subform to set values if it needs to, but it cannot do it directly.

The subform also only knows about things on its own form. Those are the two integer variables (completely different and separate than the two integer variables on the main form), the `SetValues` function, and the `UpdateSelf` function. While the main form can request information from the subform, the opposite does not hold true. The subform knows nothing about the main form.

That explains why we add code where we do. For the subform to display the sum of A and B, we have to tell it what the values of A and B are. Remember that just changing the values on the main form is not enough. That's why we have the `SetValues` function. We call this function every time the values are changed (`OnAfterValidate`) in the main form.

That again is not enough, though. Just because the values have changed in the subform doesn't mean the subform is smart enough to understand that it must display the new information. Ordinarily you would have to click on the subform (or select it; anything that makes it the active control on the page) for it to refresh. You can also do this with code, using the `CurrForm.UPDATE` command. There is a problem, though, when using it on a subform. Using the suggested code would generate the following error:

```
CurrForm.ChildForm.FORM.SetValues(A,B);
CurrForm.ChildForm.FORM.UPDATE;
```

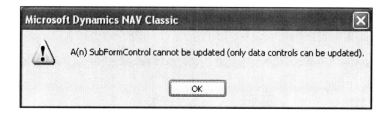

Hence, we have to create a wrapper function on the subform that can be called outside the subform. That's the `UpdateSelf` function.

See also

- Creating a function
- Updating a parent form from a subform

Updating a parent form from a subform

Subforms do not know about their parent form and there is no way to pass a reference of the parent form to a subform to "link" the two. Instead we have to go an unconventional route which is described in this recipe.

How to do it...

1. Create a new form using the **Object Designer**.

2. Add the following global variables:

Name	Type	Subtype
A	Integer	
B	Integer	
XMLDoc	Automation	'Microsoft XML, v6.0'.DOMDocument60

3. Add a global function named `SendMessage` with the following code:

    ```
    XMLDoc.loadXML('<root></root>');
    ```

4. Add a global function named `GetA` that returns an integer with the following code:

    ```
    EXIT(A);
    ```

5. Add a global function named `GetB` that returns an integer with the following code:

    ```
    EXIT(B);
    ```

6. Add a global function named `SetXMLDoc` that takes in the following parameter:

Name	Type	Subtype
XMLDocParam	Automation	'Microsoft XML, v6.0'.DOMDocument60

7. Add the following code to the function:

    ```
    XMLDoc := XMLDocParam;
    ```

8. Add two textboxes to the form.

9. Set the `SourceExpr` property on each of them:

Property	Value
SourceExpr	A (for textbox A)
SourceExpr	B (for textbox B)

10. Add the following code to the `OnAfterValidate` trigger for each textbox:

    ```
    SendMessage;
    ```

11. Your form should look similar to the one shown in the following screenshot:

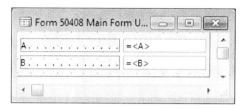

12. Save and close the form. Remember the ID for the next form.

13. Create a new form using the **Object Designer**.

14. Add the following global variables:

Name	Type	Subtype
XMLDoc	Automation	'Microsoft XML, v6.0'.DOMDocument60
A	Integer	
B	Integer	

15. Set the following property on the variable:

Property	Value
WithEvents	Yes

16. Add the following code to the `OnOpenForm` trigger:

    ```
    CREATE(XMLDoc);
    CurrForm.Subform.FORM.SetXMLDoc(XMLDoc);
    ```

17. Add the following code to the `OnCloseForm` trigger:

    ```
    CLEAR(XMLDoc);
    ```

18. Add the following code to the `XMLDoc::OnReadyStateChange` event:

    ```
    IF (XMLDoc.readyState = 4) THEN BEGIN
      A := CurrForm.Subform.FORM.GetA();
      B := CurrForm.Subform.FORM.GetB();
      CurrForm.UPDATE;
    END;
    ```

19. Add a textbox to the form.

20. Set the following properties on the textbox:

Property	Value
SourceExpr	A+B
Editable	No

21. Add a subform control to the form.

22. Set the following property on the textbox:

Property	Value
SubFormID	The id of the form you just created

23. Make sure the width and height of the subform control match the width and height of the actual subform.

24. Your form will look similar to the one shown in the following screenshot:

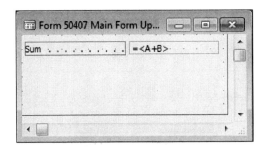

25. Save and close the form.

How it works...

Let's understand how these steps allow us to complete the task or solve the problem.

When we open the form we have to create an instance of our Automation variable. We then copy the XMLDoc to the subform to make sure that each form refers to the same automation.

By setting the WithEvents property on the XMLDoc in the parent form we get two "functions" added to our object. These cannot be called directly, but instead are called when certain things happen. In this case, we are concerned about the OnReadyStateChange event. First we check to see if the ReadyState is equal to 4, which stands for complete. When that happens we get the new values from the subform and call an UPDATE.

But how do we fire that event? After we validate the number that is input by the user, we call our custom `SendMessage` function. This calls the `LoadXML` function on our XMLDoc variable. Every time you load a new value (even if it is the same value as before) the state changes and the `OnReadyStateChange` event is executed.

See also

- ▸ Creating a function
- ▸ Updating a subform from a parent form

5
Report Design

In this chapter, we will cover:

- ▸ Using the Report Generation Wizard
- ▸ Adding custom filters to the request form
- ▸ Setting filters when a report is loaded
- ▸ Creating a report to process data
- ▸ Displaying a check mark on a report
- ▸ Dynamically showing sections on reports
- ▸ Grouping data to display totals
- ▸ Adding page totals to reports
- ▸ Display page X of Y
- ▸ Using virtual tables to loop through data
- ▸ Adding a watermark to a report

Introduction

Although reports are similar to forms, they serve a different purpose in NAV. Forms exist primarily for data entry while reports show a higher level view of what is going on in the database. Reports can be customer-facing documents such as order confirmations and invoices, or used for internal analysis like Aged Accounts Receivables and Aged Accounts Payable. They can also be used to process large amounts of data.

As a developer, it is your job to design the layout and business logic of these reports. Development of reports builds upon the same principles of development for other object types. Just as with every other object type, you can define variables and functions and add code to triggers. The layout design is just like building a form. You use the toolbox to add textboxes, labels, and other controls.

It is important to note that the report designer for the Classic client is significantly weaker than the one for the RoleTailored client. In this chapter, we'll show you how to build different types of reports as well as how to perform some advanced integration with PDF documents. Many of the advanced recipes in this chapter are done trivially with the report designer in Visual Studio for the RTC, but you will not always have the luxury of supporting clients that are only on the latest version of the software. We will note in many of the recipes how to perform them in the RoleTailored client, but for more on the subject you can read *Chapter 12, The RoleTailored Client*.

Using the Report Generation Wizard

When you need to create a quick report, the Report Generation Wizard can help. Instead of adding fields manually, you can make a useful report in a matter of minutes.

How to do it...

1. Create a new report using the **Object Designer**.

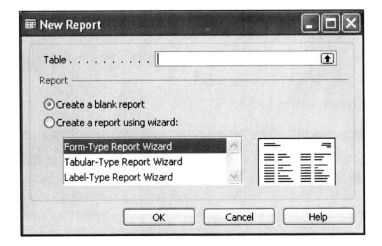

2. In the **Table** field, select the **Customer** table.
3. Select **Create a report using wizard**.

4. Click **OK**.

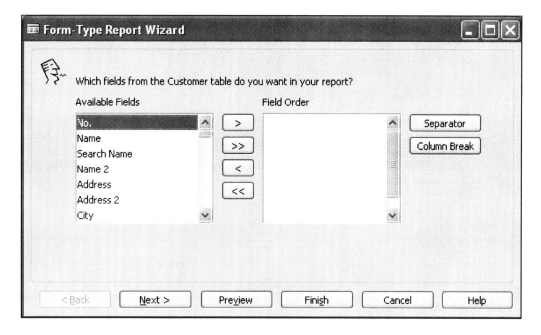

5. Select the **No.** and **Name** fields using the buttons in the middle of the screen.

6. Click **Next**.

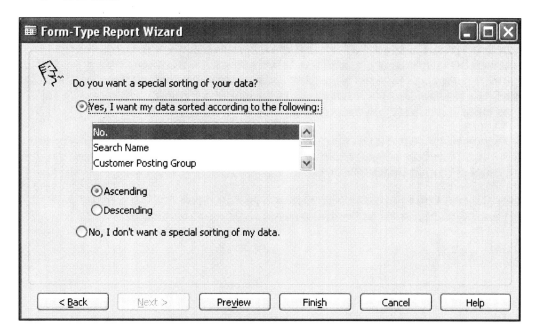

7. Select **No.** from the list of sort options.

8. Click **Finish**. You will be presented with a report that looks like the one shown in following screenshot:

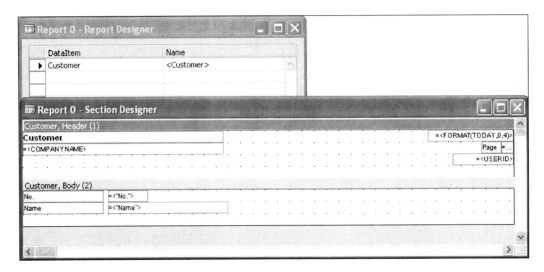

How it works...

The Report Generation Wizard starts in a way similar to the Form Generation Wizard. You must select the table that you want to base the report on and what type of report you want to create. In this example, we'll generate a form-type report.

On the next page, you select the fields that you want to see on the report. You are only creating a basic report so you may choose to add only the **No.** and **Name** fields. If you want to add more fields after the wizard is complete you can easily do so. The section designer works exactly like the form designer. You can use the **Toolbox** to add labels and textboxes or the **Field Menu** to add fields from the data item.

The third and final page lets you select how you want to order the data. You can choose any of the keys defined on the table to sort data. If you want to change this later you can view the properties of the data item and change the `DataItemTableView` property.

When you click **Finish** you will be presented with the final report. You can use the *Ctrl+R* shortcut key and then click on **Preview** to see what the report will look like.

There's more...

Although the wizard is limited in functionality, it is a very useful tool. You can quickly and easily create reports that conform to NAV standards and contains a lot of useful information such as the company name, page numbers, and user ID of the person running it.

See also

▸ Using the Form Generation Wizard

▸ Exporting data using the Excel buffer

▸ Building the report layout

Adding custom filters to the request form

Sometimes you want the user to be able to filter on something that is not a field in a table. This recipe will show you how to add a filter to the request form for such a purpose.

How to do it...

1. Create a report by following the *Using the Report Generation Wizard* recipe.
2. Add the following global variable:

Name	Type	Length
CustomerNoFilter	Code	250

3. Click on **View | Request Form** (*Alt + V, Q*).
4. Add a textbox with a label for the **Request Form**.
5. Set the following property on the textbox control:

Property	Value
SourceExpr	CustomerNoFilter

6. Set the following property on the label control:

Property	Value
Caption	Customer No. Filter

7. Your request form should look like the following screenshot:

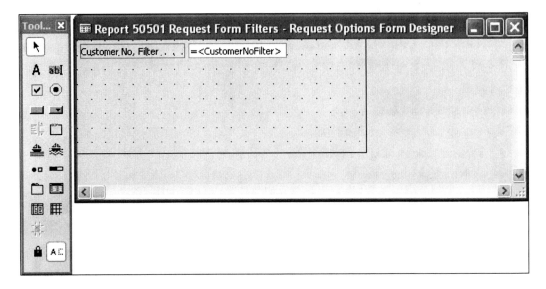

8. Add the following code to the `OnPreDataItem` trigger for the customer data item:

```
IF CustomerNoFilter <> '' THEN
    SETFILTER("No.", '%1', CustomerNoFilter);
```

9. Save and close the report.

How it works...

The **Request Form** is just a normal form. You design it in the same way you would for any other form.

Our example is basic. We could just as easily add the **No.** field to the filters on the data item. Instead we store the filter in a global text variable and then use that text variable to properly set the filter before loading the data by adding the code to the `OnPreDataItem` trigger. The trick is to set the filter only if the user has filled something in. If the filter was left blank, and we filtered for blank, we would get an empty recordset.

Ordinarily when you run a report assuming you have added fields to the `ReqFilterFields` property and nothing has been added to the request form, you would see a window similar to the following screenshot:

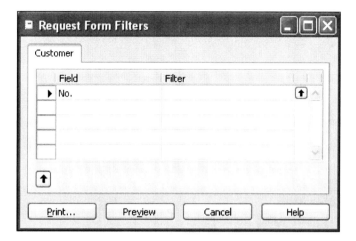

When you run this report you'll notice a new tab called **Options**. This is the tab that holds the request form, but it only appears when you have added something to it.

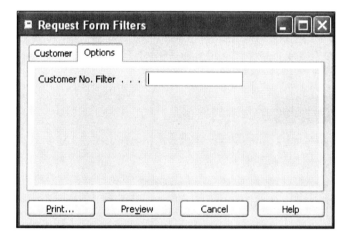

There's more...

Textboxes on the request form have the same triggers and properties as textboxes on normal forms. This means that you don't have to rely on the user to remember the customer number. We can add the lookup functionality as shown:

Add the following local variables to the OnLookup trigger for the textbox:

Name	Type	Subtype
Customer	Record	Customer
CustomerLookupForm	Form	Customer List

Add the following code to the `OnLookup` trigger:

```
CustomerLookupForm.LOOKUPMODE := TRUE;
IF CustomerLookupForm.RUNMODAL = ACTION::LookupOK THEN BEGIN
   CustomerNoFilter := CustomerLookupForm.GetSelectionFilter;
END;
```

This code enables the **lookup arrow** on the textbox. When you use it, it runs the **Customer List** form in lookup mode and retrieves the records that you selected. That value is assigned to the `CustomerNoFilter` variable which is what the textbox displays.

See also

- ► Using advanced filtering
- ► Setting filters when a report is loaded
- ► Dynamically showing sections a report

Setting filters when a report is loaded

You will often want to run a report on a specific record. This recipe will show you how to set the record that the report will use to execute.

How to do it...

1. Create a new report by following the *Using the Report Generation Wizard* recipe.
2. Save and close the report.
3. Create a new codeunit from **Object Manager**.
4. Add the following global variable:

Name	Type	Subtype
Customer	Record	Customer

5. Add the following code to the `OnRun` trigger:

```
Customer.FINDFIRST;

Customer.SETRANGE("No.", Customer."No.");
REPORT.RUN(REPORT::"Report on Record", TRUE, FALSE, Customer);
```

6. Save and close the codeunit.

How it works...

The FINDFIRST in this example is used here just so we have some data to work with. It is not necessary for you to implement this example. We use this data to apply a filter for the first customer number in the table.

Next comes the important part. NAV has a built-in variable named REPORT that has several methods associated with it. One of these is the RUN() method which takes four parameters. The first parameter is the ID of the report to run. It is best to reference the report using the same syntax as an Option variable, REPORT::"Name of Report".

The second and third parameters are Booleans. The second tells the system whether or not to display the request form. We definitely want to display it because we want to see how it looks when we run it on a specific record. The third parameter tells it whether or not to use the system printer.

Our final parameter is a record variable that matches the first data item of the report. This parameter holds all of the filters that have been previously applied.

When you run the codeunit, the report request form will be shown and the **No.** filter will be filled in.

There's more...

The most common place in NAV to see this being used is when printing reports from specific documents such as an invoice. You can take a look at the flow of data between the actual forms and the document-print codeunit to get a better understanding.

See also

- ▸ Using advanced filtering
- ▸ Adding custom filters to the request form

Creating a report to process data

Reports are very useful for performing an operation on multiple records. Here we will see how to build a report to process changes to data.

How to do it...

1. Create a new blank report from **Object Designer**.

2. Set the following property on the report:

Property	Value
ProcessingOnly	Yes

3. Add a data item for the **Customer** table.

4. In the OnAfterGetRecord trigger for the customer data item add the following code:

```
"Last Date Modified" := TODAY;
MODIFY;
```

5. Save and close the report.

How it works...

A **Data Item** is a record variable. However, instead of us writing our own code to loop through each record, this functionality is built into a report. That makes a report a great place to perform a mass processing of records. For this type of report we don't want any pages to be displayed. This slows down the processing speed dramatically. To do this we set the ProcessingOnly property of the report to **Yes**.

The OnAfterGetRecord trigger is fired after each record is retrieved from the database. This is where we need to place our code. Here we are just changing the **Last Modified Date** field, but you could do any sort of change you want.

When you run the report you will see different buttons on the button of the request form. Instead of the normal print and preview buttons there is an **OK** button in its place.

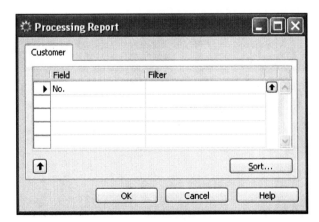

There's more...

When a normal report is running you can see the **Generating Page X** on the bottom right corner of the preview pane. This lets the user know the system is still doing something and has not stopped. **Processing Only** reports don't have sections, and hence they don't tell the user what is going on. That means it is your responsibility to keep the user informed. The best way to do this is by displaying a Progress Bar. You can assign the variables and open the dialog in the `OnPreDataItem` trigger. The `OnAfterGetRecord` trigger is used to update the progress bar while the `OnPostDataItem` trigger can be used to close the dialog.

See also

- ▸ Displaying a Progress Bar
- ▸ Creating transactions to alter data

Displaying a check mark on a report

Small visual changes to reports can make them easier to use. This recipe will show you how to represent a Boolean value with a check mark.

How to do it...

1. Create a new report by following the _Using the Report Generation Wizard_ recipe and add one additional column for the **Tax Liable** field.
2. View the **Sections** for the report.
3. Click on the header and press _F3_ to add a new header section below the current one.
4. Move the column headers to this new header section.
5. Add the following global variable:

Name	Type
TaxLiableCheckMark	Char

6. Add the following code to the `OnAfterGetRecord` trigger for the customer data item:

```
IF "Tax Liable" THEN
  TaxLiableCheckMark := 129
ELSE
  TaxLiableCheckMark := 0;
```

7. Add a textbox to the body section of the customer data item.

8. Set the following properties on the textbox control:

Property	Value
SourceExpr	TaxLiableCheckMark
FontName	WingDings

9. Your sections should look like the following screenshot when you are finished:

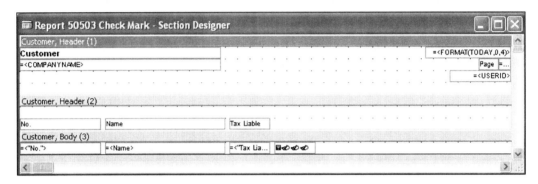

10. Save and close the report.

How it works...

The default font for every textbox is Helvetica. This font does not have a check-mark symbol. Luckily, we can change the font style that the textbox uses. It has a property called `FontName` and here we want to change it to Wingdings. If you are unfamiliar with the Wingdings font you can run the **CharMap** utility from Windows to see all of the available symbols. Notice how the text becomes illegible when you change the font.

The check-mark symbol is number 129 in the Wingdings set of characters. As a `char` variable is an integer, we can assign this value to our `TaxLiableCheckMark` variable, but only when tax liable is true; otherwise we set it to **0**.

The resulting report will look like the following screenshot:

Customer			
CRONUS USA, Inc.			May 13, 2010
			Page 1
			MATTTRAX

No.	Name	Tax Liable	
10000	The Cannon Group PLC	Yes	✓
20000	Selangorian Ltd.	Yes	✓
30000	John Haddock Insurance	Yes	✓
40000	Deerfield Graphics Comp	Yes	✓
50000	Guildford Water Departm	No	
60000	Blanemark Hifi Shop	No	
61000	Fairway Sound	No	

See also

▶ Changing text appearance

Dynamically showing Sections on reports

NAV does not limit you to one section of each type. You can have as many of each section type as you want, but you usually do not want to show every section on every report. This recipe will show you how to choose which sections to display.

How to do it...

1. Create a new report by following the *Using the Report Generation Wizard* recipe.

2. View the **Sections** for the report.

3. Add two headers below the current header and a body below the existing body section. The report should have five sections in total.

4. Move the column labels for the existing fields to the **Header (2)** section.

5. Add the following fields to the **Body (5)** section using the field menu: **No.**, **Name**, **Address**, **City**, **Country/Region Code**, **Post Code**.

6. Move the column labels to the **Header (3)** section.

7. Your sections should be as shown in the following screenshot:

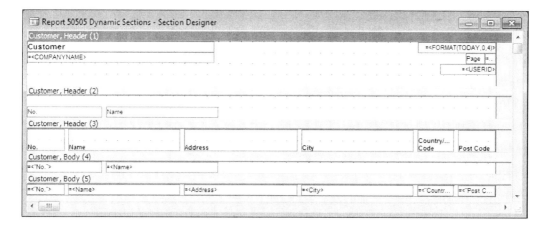

8. Add the following global variable:

Name	Type
ShowDetail	Boolean

9. Add a checkbox and a label to the report request form.

10. Set the following property on the **Check box** control:

Property	Value
SourceExpr	ShowDetail

11. Set the following property on the **Label** control:

Property	Value
Caption	Show Detail

12. Add the following code to the OnPreSection trigger for the **Header (2)** section:

```
CurrReport.SHOWOUTPUT(NOT ShowDetail);
```

13. Add the following code to the OnPreSection trigger for the **Header (3)** section:

```
CurrReport.SHOWOUTPUT(ShowDetail);
```

14. Add the following code to the OnPreSection trigger for the **Body (4)** section:

```
CurrReport.SHOWOUTPUT(NOT ShowDetail);
```

15. Add the following code to the OnPreSection trigger for the **Body (5)** section:

```
CurrReport.SHOWOUTPUT(ShowDetail);
```

16. Save and close the report.

17. The resulting reports will look similar to the following screenshots:

```
Customer                                              May 13, 2010
CRONUS USA, Inc.                                         Page    1
                                                        MATTTRAX


No.              Name
10000            The Cannon Group PLC
20000            Selangorian Ltd.
30000            John Haddock Insurance
40000            Deerfield Graphics Comp
50000            Guildford Water Departm
60000            Blanemark Hifi Shop
61000            Fairway Sound
```

```
Customer                                              May 13, 2010
CRONUS USA, Inc.                                         Page    1
                                                        MATTTRAX


No.    Name                   Address           City      ZIP Code
10000  The Cannon Group PLC   192 Market Square  Atlanta   31772
20000  Selangorian Ltd.       153 Thomas Drive   Chicago   61236
30000  John Haddock Insurance C 10 High Tower Green Miami   37125
40000  Deerfield Graphics Compan 10 Deerfield Road Atlanta 31772
50000  Guildford Water Departmen 25 Water Way    Atlanta   31772
60000  Blanemark Hifi Shop    28 Baker Street    London    GB-W1 3AL
61000  Fairway Sound          159 Fairway        Atlanta   31772
```

How it works...

Here we create one header and body for each type of report, standard and detailed. Unlike with a form, we can't control the visibility of specific textboxes from the code. We can, however, control the visibility of an entire section using the `CurrReport.SHOWOUTPUT` command. This function takes in a single Boolean variable, which when FALSE tells the system to hide the section. It is always placed in the `OnPreDataItem` trigger for a section.

There's more...

This is just a basic example of how to dynamically show sections on reports. If you want to see a more advanced report take a look at **Aged Accounts Receivable (10040)**.

Section triggers should only be used to show or hide sections, and not to perform calculations. In the RoleTailored client, these section triggers are not executed so any calculations placed in these triggers will not function properly. Calculations should almost always be performed inside their own function and are usually called from the `OnAfterGetRecord` trigger.

See also

▸ Adding custom filters to the request form

Grouping data to display totals

The easiest way to display totals in a report is to group records under specific criteria. This recipe will show you how to specify what fields to total and what criteria to use.

How to do it...

1. Create a new report using the Report Generation Wizard on table 21, **Cust. Ledger Entry**.

2. On the second wizard window, add the **Customer No.**, **Posting Date**, and **Amount** fields.

3. On the third wizard window, set the sorting order to **Customer No.**, **Posting Date**, **Currency Code**.

4. Click **Finish**.

5. View the sections for the report.

6. Add a second **Header** section.

7. Move the column labels to the **Header** section.

8. Add a **GroupFooter** section.

9. Move the textboxes from the **Body** section to the **GroupFooter** section.

10. Delete the **Body**.

11. Your sections should be as shown in the following screenshot:

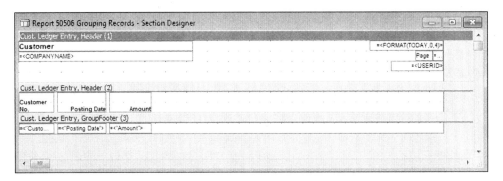

12. Add the following code to the **GroupFooter** section:

```
CurrReport.SHOWOUTPUT(CurrReport.TOTALSCAUSEDBY =
                          FIELDNO("Posting Date"));
```

13. View the properties of the **Cust. Ledger Entry** data item.

14. Set the following properties on the data item:

Property	Value
TotalFields	Amount
GroupTotalFields	Customer No., Posting Date

15. The properties window should look like the following screenshot:

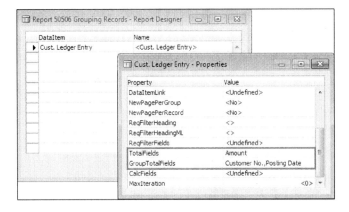

16. Save and close the report.

How it works...

In order to group records together we have to tell the system which fields we want to group on. This is where the `GroupTotalFields` property comes into picture. Here we are going to group records by their **Customer No.** and **Posting Date** fields, which means that for every combination of **Customer No.** and **Posting Date** we will have one line on the report.

When we group records it is usually because we want to total the values of some field on those records. Here we want to sum the **Amount** field so we add it to the `TotalFields` property.

An important fact to remember is that the fields we are grouping on must be contained in the key being used by the data item. The field you want to sum must be contained in the `SumIndexFields` for that key.

With grouping, we don't use the standard **Body** section. Instead we use a `GroupFooter`. This trigger is displayed every time we reach the end of grouping records. Remember, though, that we are grouping by **Customer No.** *and* **Posting Date**. That means every time the **Customer No.** *or* **Posting Date** changes, the `GroupFooter` is displayed. This can cause duplication of lines. We only want to display the section when the last field in our `GroupTotalFields` changes. We use the `TOTALSCAUSEDBY` function, which returns an integer, to determine which field has changed.

There's more...

You can manually create the totals in your code by using the `CREATETOTALS` function. This function has an advantage over the `TotalFields` property in which one can create totals on variables as well as fields.

See also

- ▸ Adding a key to a table
- ▸ Creating a `SumIndex` field
- ▸ Adding page totals to reports

Adding page totals to reports

Listings can often span multiple pages making it easy to lose track of the totals. NAV allows you to easily add a textbox to the bottom or top of a page to show these subtotals to the user.

How to do it...

1. Create a new report using the **Report Generation Wizard** on table 21, **Cust. Ledger Entry**.

2. On the second wizard window, add the **Customer No., Posting Date**, and **Amount** fields.

3. On the third wizard window, set the **Sorting Order** to **Customer No., Posting Date, Currency Code**.

4. Click **Finish**.

5. View the sections for the report.

6. Add a second **Header** section.

7. Move the column labels to the **Header** section.

8. Add a **TransHeader** section.

9. Add a **TransFooter** section.

10. Add a textbox to both sections.

11. Set the following property on each textbox control:

Property	Value
SourceExpr	Amount

12. Add a textbox to the **TransHeader** section.

13. Set the following property on the textbox control:

Property	Value
SourceExpr	'Transferred from previous page'

14. Add a textbox to the **TransFooter** section.

15. Set the following property on the textbox control:

Property	Value
SourceExpr	'Transferred to next page'

15. View the properties of the **Cust. Ledger Entry** data item.

16. Set the following property on the data item:

Property	Value
TotalFields	Amount

17. Save and close the report.
18. A portion of the resulting report is shown in the following screenshot:

46897889	01/23/11	7,841.00
47563218	01/25/11	115,966.31
49525252	01/07/11	3,852.74
49525252	01/08/11	3,082.20
49525252	01/10/11	5,393.84
Transferred To Next Page		1,434,592.96

How it works...

In addition to the GroupHeader and GroupFooter sections, NAV Reports have sections called **TransHeader** and **TransFooter**. These sections are displayed every time the page number changes. The TransFooter is displayed on the bottom of the page right before the change and the TransHeader is displayed on the top of the next page.

In this report, we add the **Amount** field to these sections with a label so that the subtotals are not mistakenly added into the main total.

There's more...

▶ Adding a key to a table
▶ Creating a SumIndex field
▶ Grouping data to display totals

Display page X of Y

What sounds like a simple task is actually quite complicated in NAV. This recipe will show you how to print the total number of pages on every page of a report.

Getting ready

You must have **PDFCreator** installed on your machine. This recipe was tested with version 0.9.8 and 0.9.9, and is not guaranteed to work with future or previous releases of PDFCreator.

You must also have Visual Studio 2005 or later installed on your machine in order to write the C# code for this recipe.

How to do it...

1. Create a new class library project named NAVUtilities in Visual Studio.

2. Add a new file called PDFPageCounter with the following code:

```csharp
using System.IO;
using System.Text.RegularExpressions;
using System.Runtime.InteropServices;

namespace NAVUtilities
{
  [ClassInterface(ClassInterfaceType.AutoDual)]
  [ProgId("PDFPageCounter")]
  [ComVisible(true)]
  public class PDFPageCounter
  {
    public int GetNoOfPagesPDF(string FileName)
    {
      int result = 0;
      FileStream fs = new FileStream(FileName, FileMode.Open,
                                       FileAccess.Read);
      StreamReader r = new StreamReader(fs);
      string pdfText = r.ReadToEnd();

      System.Text.RegularExpressions.Regex regx = new
                        Regex(@"/Type\s*/Page[^s]");
      System.Text.RegularExpressions.MatchCollection matches =
                            regx.Matches(pdfText);
      result = matches.Count;

      r.Close();
      fs.Close();

      return result;
    }
  }
}
```

3. View the **Properties** of the project.

4. On the **Application** tab set the **Assembly Name** to Packt-PDFWatermark.

5. On the **Build** tab set the **Register for COM interop** property to **True** (checked).

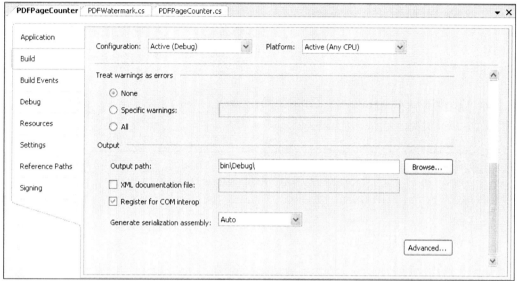

6. Save and compile your objects.

7. Create a new report by following the *Using the Report Generation Wizard* recipe.

8. Add the following global variable:

Name	Type
NoOfPages	Integer

9. Add a global function named `SetNoOfPages`.

10. The function should take the following parameter:

Name	Type
NoOfPagesIn	Integer

11. Add the following code to the function:

```
NoOfPages := NoOfPagesIn;
```

12. Delete the **Page No.** label and textbox from the **Header** section.

13. Replace them with a single textbox.

14. Set the following property on the textbox control:

Property	Value
SourceExpr	`'Page ' + FORMAT(CurrReport.PAGENO) + ' of ' + FORMAT(NoOfPages)`

15. Save and close the report.

16. Create a new codeunit from **Object Designer**.

17. Add the following global variables:

Name	Type	Subtype	Length
PrintToPDF	Codeunit	(See Printing Reports to PDF recipe)	
FileName	Text		1024
FileDir	Text		1024
FullFileName	Text		1024
NoOfPages	Integer		

18. Add a global function named `GetNumberOfPages`.

19. The function should take the following parameter:

Name	Type	Length
FileNameIn	Text	1024

20 It should return an integer named `NoOfPagesOut`.

21. Add the following local variable:

Name	Type	Subtype
PDFUtil	Automation	'Packt-PDFPageCounter'.PDFPageCounter

22. Add the following code to the function:

```
IF ISCLEAR(PDFUtil) THEN
  CREATE(PDFUtil);

IF EXISTS(FileNameIn) THEN
  NoOfPagesOut := PDFUtil.GetNoOfPagesPDF(FileNameIn);

CLEAR(PDFUtil);

EXIT(NoOfPagesOut);
```

23. Add a global function named `PrintReportToPDF`.

24. Add the following code to the function:

```
IF EXISTS(FullFileName) THEN
  ERASE(FullFileName);
PrintToPDF.SetupPDFCreator(FileDir, FileName);
RunReport;
PrintToPDF.ClearPDFCreator;
```

25. Add a global function named `RunReport`.

26. Add the following global variable:

Name	Type	Subtype
ReportToRun	Report	Page X of Y

27. Add the following code to the function:

```
CLEAR(ReportToRun);
ReportToRun.USEREQUESTFORM := FALSE;
ReportToRun.SetNumberOfPages(NoOfPages);
ReportToRun.RUNMODAL;

IF NOT PrintToPDF.WaitUntilFileExists(FullFileName) THEN
  ERROR(Text001, FullFileName);
```

28. Add a global function named `SetupFile`.

29. The function should take in the following parameters:

Name	Type	Length
FileDir	Text	1024
FileNameIn	Text	1024

30. Add the following code to the function:

```
FileDir := FileDirIn;
FileName := FileNameIn;
FullFileName := COPYSTR(FileDirIn + '\' + FileName, 1,
                        MAXSTRLEN(FullFileName));
```

31. Add the following code to the `OnRun` trigger:

```
SetupFile(ENVIRON('Temp'), 'TempPDF.pdf');

PrintReportToPDF;
NoOfPages := GetNumberOfPages(FullFileName);
PrintReportToPDF;

HYPERLINK(FullFileName);
```

32. Save and close the codeunit.

How it works...

The problem with knowing how many pages will there be in a printed report is that it's something you won't know until the report has finished printing! There's no way around this so, unfortunately, we will have to process our report twice. That means double the execution time. This is not recommended for large or process-intensive reports.

There is a lot going on in this recipe, but don't worry. We will take it step-by-step. In order to use the code from this recipe, you will need to import the print to PDF codeunit explained in *Chapter 10, Integration*. We will not see how that code works in this recipe. Just know that it takes the report you are running and saves it to a temporary PDF file.

To start, we need to create an Automation control to count the number of pages in our PDF document. NAV doesn't have built-in support for analyzing PDF files so we have to build this part of our solution in another programming language. In this case we are going to use C# which we can compile and use inside NAV.

Let's take a look at the libraries we will be using. `System.IO` is used for reading and writing to files. The `System.Text.RegularExpressions` library is used to find patterns of characters in strings or text variables. The last library, `System.RunTime.InteropServices` is used to register the program on the computer so that it can be seen and used by other applications like NAV.

Now we need to examine the attributes of our class. The first attribute is called `ClassInterface`. By setting the value to `ClassInterfaceType.AutoDual` we tell the program to automatically register itself on the system, if we choose to register it at all (which we will). The second attribute is called `ProgId` and is the name that our program will be referenced by. The last is called `COMVisible`, which tells the system that this class can be registered on the computer.

 For more information on libraries and attributes you can go to `msdn.microsoft.com`.

Alright, now we get to the meat of the program. It is a function called `GetNoOfPages` that takes in a file name and returns an integer named `result`. The first two lines about streams are fairly standard for opening a file. The text of the file is stored in the `PDFText` variable by doing a `ReadToEnd` on the stream.

This part will be confusing if you have never encountered a Regular Expression before. Basically, we are looking for a pattern like this:

```
/Type + "some optional, unknown amount of whitespace" + /Page (but
not /Pages)
```

If you open a PDF file in Notepad and search for bits and pieces of this text you'll find that it appears as metadata on every page in the file.

Finally we have to close our streams. If we fail to do this the PDF file will be locked and we won't be able to use it.

That's the coding part for the automation. But there are some properties that need to be set, specifically the **Register COM for interop**. Remember those attributes that we set so that *if we ever registered this program, it would work?* Well now we have to register it. Check the box, compile it, and you are ready to go.

For the report, we need to create a function to tell it how many pages will print in all. We pass it an integer variable and it stores it in a global integer variable called NoOfPages. We also have to change the page number in the header to display the total number of pages.

Lastly, we need to create a codeunit to manage the printing of this report. This codeunit will consist of four functions. The first is a helper function called SetupFile. This function just sets some global text variables that point to the path or folder of the PDF file, the name of the PDF file, and the combined path plus name of the file.

We also need a wrapper function for our Automation class. This function will be called GetNumberOfPages. It creates a new instance of the Automation class, checks to make sure that the file exists, and counts the number of pages using the GetNoOfPagesPDF function from the C# code. This value is then returned from the function.

Our third function is used to actually run our report. This function takes in the number of pages we found by using the GetNumberOfPages function. It passes that value to the report and runs it.

The last function is called PrintReportToPDF. The details of how this works can be found in *Chapter 10*, *Integration*, in the *Printing reports to PDF* recipe. To give you a quick overview, we delete any files that have the same name, set up PDFCreator, print the report, and then clear any changes that were made.

So how does all of that work together? Let's step through it. In the OnRun trigger, we set up our file to go to the local Temp directory on the computer. We then print our report to that PDF file. At this point we don't know how many pages will be printed, so the upper right-hand corner of the report would look like "**Page 1 of 0**". Next, we determine how many pages are in the PDF file. We then call the same function to print the report to PDF, but this time we pass the real number of pages instead of zero. Finally, we use the HYPERLINK command to open the file and display it to the user.

There's more...

This is a huge pain to do in the Classic client. Not only is there a lot of code, but it also requires you to run the report twice. That means double the execution time just to get the total number of pages on the report. On large, calculation-heavy reports' benefits just do not outweigh the lost productivity time.

Fortunately for RoleTailored client users this is incredibly easy to do. In the design layout in Visual Studio you can add a new textbox and set the expression on it like this:

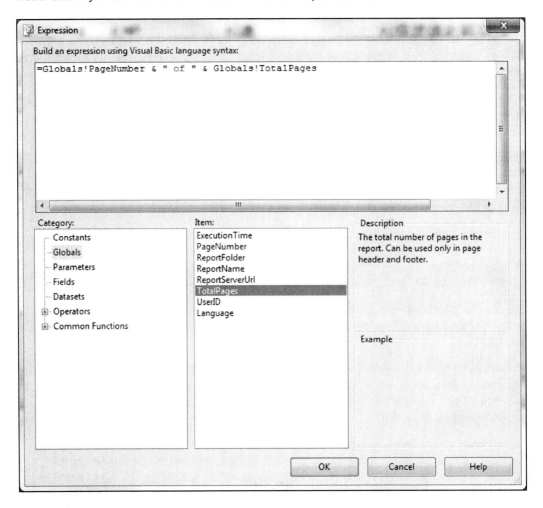

See also

▸ Creating a function

▸ Adding a watermark to a report

Using virtual tables to loop through data

Just as you can repeat code using a loop, you can also repeat data items in a report using a virtual table. This recipe will show you how to use the most common virtual table, Integer.

How to do it...

1. Create a new report by following the *Using the Report Generation Wizard* recipe.

2. Add the following global variable:

Name	Type
NoOfCopies	Integer

3. Add a label and textbox control to the request form.

4. Set the following property on the textbox control:

Property	Value
SourceExpr	NoOfCopies

5. Set the following property on the label control:

Property	Value
Caption	No. of Copies

6. Insert an **Integer** data item above the **Customer** data item.

7. Change the **Name** field for the **Integer** data item to **CopyLoop**.

8. Indent the **Customer** data item by using the right arrow button on the bottom of the form.

9. Delete the **CopyLoop Body** section from the **Section Designer**.

10. Add the following code to the OnPreDataItem trigger for **CopyLoop**:

    ```
    SETRANGE(Number, 0, NoOfCopies);
    ```

11. Save and close the report.

How it works...

Think of the **Customer** data item, including all of the code and sections, as a function called DisplayCustomerData. If you were to write code for it, it would look similar to this:

```
IF Customer.FINDSET THEN
  REPEAT
    DisplayCustomerData;
  UNTIL Customer.NEXT = 0;
```

If you want to repeat this code multiple times you would have to add another loop to it, like the following:

```
FOR i := 0 TO NoOfCopies DO BEGIN
  IF Customer.FINDSET THEN
    REPEAT
      DisplayCustomerData;
    UNTIL Customer.NEXT = 0;
END;
```

Our report is already handling the `REPEAT..UNTIL` part of the code. There is no reason for it to not handle the `FOR` loop as well. The main purpose of a `FOR` loop is to iterate through a set of numbers. For that we can use the virtual table called **Integer**. The **Integer** table has a single field called Number that we can filter on.

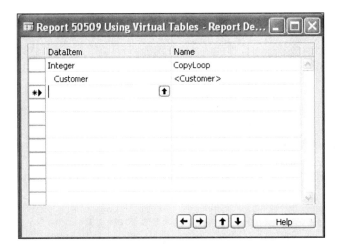

Just as the code indented beneath the `FOR` loop will be executed a number of times, the data items indented under other data items will also be executed a number of times depending on the filters that are set.

There's more...

There are plenty of virtual tables in NAV. You won't find these tables in **Object Designer** and you might not even know they were there. The following report has been included, which lists all of the virtual tables and their fields.

List of virtual tables in NAV

Object Type	Object ID	Object Name
Table	2000000001	Object
Table	2000000007	Date
Table	2000000009	Session
Table	2000000010	Database File
Table	2000000020	Drive
Table	2000000022	File
Table	2000000024	Monitor
Table	2000000026	Integer
Table	2000000028	Table Information
Table	2000000029	System Object
Table	2000000037	Performance
Table	2000000038	AllObj
Table	2000000039	Printer
Table	2000000040	License Information
Table	2000000041	Field
Table	2000000042	OLE Control
Table	2000000043	License Permission
Table	2000000044	Permission Range
Table	2000000045	Windows Language
Table	2000000046	Automation Server
Table	2000000049	Code Coverage
Table	2000000050	Windows Object
Table	2000000051	Service Connection Point
Table	2000000052	Windows Group Member
Table	2000000055	SID - Account ID
Table	2000000056	User SID
Table	2000000058	AllObjWithCaption
Table	2000000059	Breakpoint
Table	2000000063	Key
Table	2000000070	Error List

See also

▶ Repeating code using a loop

Adding a watermark to a page

Watermarks can be used in a variety of ways to make reports stand out. This recipe will show you how to add a "draft" watermark to the background of a report.

Getting ready

You must have PDFCreator installed on your machine. This recipe was tested with version 0.9.8 and 0.9.9 and is not guaranteed to work with future or previous releases of PDFCreator. PDFCreator requires the .NET Framework 1.1 to install the dll files used with this example.

You must also have Visual Studio 2005 or later installed on your machine in order to write the C# code for this recipe.

You should understand the *Printing reports to PDF* recipe from *Chapter 10, Integration*. This recipe builds on that one and the details will not be explained here. The codeunit for printing to PDF from the Integration chapter is included in this chapter as well.

How to do it...

1. Open a new text file.
2. Add the following code:

```
Option Explicit

Dim Arguments
Dim pdfforge
Dim tools
Dim fso
Dim FilePath
Dim ImagePath
Dim WatermarkImage
Dim OriginalFile
Dim StampedFile

Set Arguments = WScript.Arguments

Set fso = CreateObject("Scripting.FileSystemObject")

Set pdfforge = Wscript.CreateObject("pdfforge.pdf.pdf")
```

```
Set tools = Wscript.CreateObject("pdfforge.tools")

OriginalFile = Arguments(0)
FilePath = fso.GetParentFolderName (Arguments(0))
if FilePath = "" then
  if FilePath = "" then FilePath = fso.GetParentFolderName
                                    (Wscript.ScriptFullname)
  if Right(FilePath,1) <> "\" then FilePath = FilePath & "\"
  OriginalFile = FilePath & OriginalFile
End if

WatermarkImage = Arguments(1)
ImagePath = fso.GetParentFolderName (Arguments(1))
if ImagePath = "" then
  ImagePath = fso.GetParentFolderName (Wscript.ScriptFullname)
  if Right(ImagePath,1) <> "\" then ImagePath = ImagePath & "\"
  WatermarkImage = ImagePath & WatermarkImage
End if

StampedFile = Left(OriginalFile, Len(OriginalFile) - 4) & " -
                Watermark" + Right(OriginalFile, 4)

pdfforge.StampPDFFileWithImage OriginalFile, StampedFile,
                    WatermarkImage, 1, 0, true, 1, 9

set Arguments = Nothing

WScript.Echo StampedFile
```

3. Save the file as `AddWatermark.vbs`.

4. Create a new class library project named `NAVUtilities` in Visual Studio.

5. Add a new file called `PDFPageCounter` with the following code:

```
using System.Runtime.InteropServices;
using System.Diagnostics;

namespace NAVUtilities
{
  [ClassInterface(ClassInterfaceType.AutoDual)]
  [ProgId("PDFWatermark")]
  [ComVisible(true)]
  public class PDFWatermark
  {
    private string Script;
    private string PDFFile;
```

```csharp
      private string WatermarkImageFile;
      private string WatermarkedPDFFile;

      public void SetScript(string newScript)
      {
        Script = newScript;
      }

      public void SetPDFFile(string newPDFFile)
      {
        PDFFile = newPDFFile;
      }

      public void SetWatermarkImage(string
                                    newWatermarkImageFile)
      {
        WatermarkImageFile = newWatermarkImageFile;
      }

      public string GetWatermarkedPDFFile()
      {
        return WatermarkedPDFFile;
      }

      public void CreateWatermark()
      {
        Process p = new Process();
        p.StartInfo.FileName = @"cscript";

        p.StartInfo.Arguments = Script + " " + PDFFile + " "
                                + WatermarkImageFile;
        p.StartInfo.UseShellExecute = false;
        p.StartInfo.RedirectStandardOutput = true;
        p.Start();

        p.StandardOutput.ReadLine();
        p.StandardOutput.ReadLine();
        p.StandardOutput.ReadLine();
        WatermarkedPDFFile = p.StandardOutput.ReadLine();
      }
    }
  }
```

6. View the **Properties** of the project.

7. On the **Application** tab set the **Assembly Name** to Packt-PDFWatermark.

8. On the **Build** tab check the **Register for COM interop** checkbox.

9. Save and compile the objects.

10. Create a new report by following the *Using the Report Generation Wizard* recipe.

11. Save and close the report (remember the ID for later use).

12. Create a new codeunit from **Object Designer**.

13. Add the following global variables:

Name	Type	Subtype	Length
Customer	Record	Customer	
PrintToPDF	Codeunit	(See Printing Reports to PDF Recipe)	
FileName	Text		1024
FileDir	Text		1024
FullFileName	Text		1024
WatermarkedFile	Text		1024
ReportToRun	Report	Watermark Report	
PDFWatermark	Automation	'Packt-PDFWatermark'. PDFWatermark	

14. Add a global function named `SetupFile`.

15. The function should take in the following parameters:

Name	Type	Length
FileDirIn	Text	1024
FileNameIn	Text	1024

16. Add the following code to the function:

```
FileDir := FileDirIn;
FileName := FileNameIn;
FullFileName := COPYSTR(FileDirIn + '\' + FileName, 1,
               MAXSTRLEN(FullFileName));
```

17. Add the following code to the OnRun trigger (change the path to the vbs and watermark images based on your system):

```
IF ISCLEAR(PDFWatermark) THEN
  CREATE(PDFWatermark);

SetupFile(ENVIRON('Temp'), 'TempPDF.pdf');
PrintToPDF.SetupPDFCreator(FileDir, FileName);
ReportToRun.USEREQUESTFORM := FALSE;
ReportToRun.RUNMODAL;
```

```
PrintToPDF.WaitUntilFileExists(FileDir + '\' + FileName);
PrintToPDF.ClearPDFCreator;

PDFWatermark.SetScript('"C:\Packt\AddWatermark.vbs"');

PDFWatermark.SetWatermarkImage(
                    '"C:\Packt\DraftWatermark.png"');

PDFWatermark.SetPDFFile(FileDir + '\' + FileName);

SLEEP(1000); //Need to make sure the file isn't locked
PDFWatermark.CreateWatermark;

WatermarkedFile := PDFWatermark.GetWatermarkedPDFFile;

IF WatermarkedFile = '' THEN
  ERROR(Text001);
HYPERLINK(WatermarkedFile);

CLEAR(PDFWatermark);
```

18. Save and close the codeunit.

19. An example report is shown in the following screenshot:

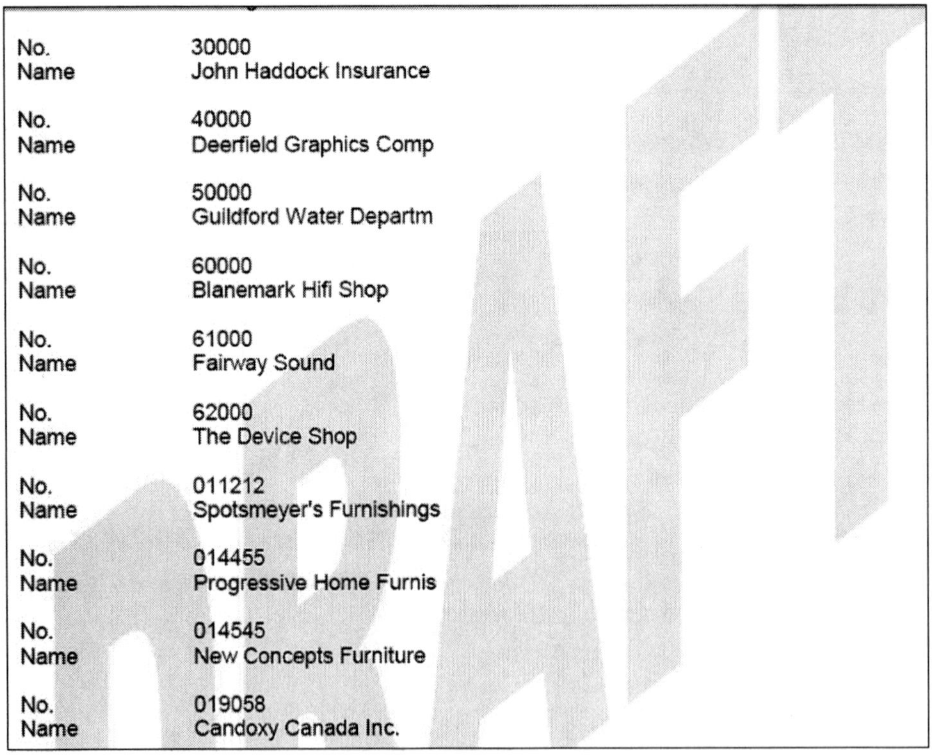

No.	30000
Name	John Haddock Insurance
No.	40000
Name	Deerfield Graphics Comp
No.	50000
Name	Guildford Water Departm
No.	60000
Name	Blanemark Hifi Shop
No.	61000
Name	Fairway Sound
No.	62000
Name	The Device Shop
No.	011212
Name	Spotsmeyer's Furnishings
No.	014455
Name	Progressive Home Furnis
No.	014545
Name	New Concepts Furniture
No.	019058
Name	Candoxy Canada Inc.

How it works...

As you can see, much of the code in this recipe is complicated. It involves development in three different languages, VBScript, C#, and C/AL. We will tackle each one separately in order to understand how they all work together.

Take a look at the VBScript file first. Remember, this is not a VBScript book. We will only explain how the file works in general terms. This file works similar to a batch file and takes in two arguments. The first is the PDF File to which we want to add a watermark and the second is the watermark image.

To start we set up all of our variables using the `Dim` keyword. We then instantiate our more complex variables using the `Set` function. The important variable here is `pdfforge`. This is installed with PDFCreator (as long as you have the .NET Framework 1.1).

The next two sections of code deal with each of the arguments passed to the script. The code here makes sure that there is a complete path and filename stored in the variables and sets them up if it is not.

Next we have to set up a new filename (the old filename + " – Watermark") and use the `pdfforge` variable to stamp the file. The key parameters to use with the `StampPDFFileWithImage` function are the first two integers. These represent the page range to watermark. A zero as the second parameter means "watermark everything".

Finally we perform some cleanup on our variables and echo the watermarked file to the command window.

Now let's examine the C# code. Let's take a look at the libraries we will be using. `System.IO` is used for reading and writing to files. `System.Diagnostics` provides classes that allow you to interact with system processes (such as launching a VBScript file).

Now we need to examine the attributes of our class. The first attribute is called `ClassInterface`. By setting the value to `ClassInterfaceType.AutoDual`, we tell the program to automatically register itself on the system. The second attribute is called `ProgId` and is the name that our program will be referenced by. The last is called `COMVisible` and tells the system that this class can be registered on the computer.

Our class is composed of three setter functions: one getter function, and one function to call the VBScript. We will focus on the latter.

First we create a new **Process** instance and tell it that we will be running a script file. We then set the arguments to the script which are the script name, PDF file, and image file that we set using our setter methods. As we need to use the output of our script file (remember that it is going to tell us the location of the watermarked file) we have to set the `UseShellExecute` property to `False` and the `RedirectStandardOutput` property to `True`. We then start the process.

The redirected output returns four lines of text. We don't care about the first three lines so we just read them and let them fall off somewhere in the memory. The fourth and last line, though, is the path to our watermarked PDF document. We store that in a variable that can be retrieved with our getter method.

Now we can look at the final piece of code in NAV. The codeunit contains one function called `SetupFile`. This function just sets some global text variables that point to the path or folder of the PDF file, the name of the PDF file, and the combined path plus the name of the file.

The `OnRun` trigger is where the bulk of the code is placed. First we instantiate our `PDFWatermark` Automation variable. We then create pointers to our temporary PDF file in the `Temp` folder and set up PDFCreator.

In this case we do not want to use the request form so we set the `USEREQUESTFORM` property to `False` before running the report. As this report will be output to a PDF file we have to wait until that file is created before clearing our PDFCreator setup.

Now we can begin to use our C# code. We set the script, PDF File, and watermark image using the setter methods in the C# class. Before adding the watermark to the file we issue a `SLEEP(1000)` command. This pauses the system for one second in order to make sure the locks on the PDF file are removed. If there are locks on the file the `CreateWatermark` function would fail because that would make it impossible to access and modify the file.

Finally, we retrieve the watermarked file name and if it is not empty (meaning an error occurred) we open it for the user to see.

There's more...

There are many other things you can do using `pdfforge` and PDFCreator. The VBScript code files can be found in the PDFCreator `install` directory under the `Plugins` folder. In that folder, you'll find scripts to merge and split files, copy files, and even convert images to PDF.

See also

- ▸ Creating a function
- ▸ Display page X of Y
- ▸ Displaying a graph on a report

6
Diagnosing Code Problems

In this chapter, we will cover:

- ▸ Using the debugger
- ▸ Setting breakpoints
- ▸ Using Code Coverage
- ▸ Handling runtime errors
- ▸ Using Client Monitor to diagnose problems
- ▸ Finding errors when using NAS
- ▸ Implementing `Try` / `Catch` / `Finally`

Introduction

No one writes perfect code on their first attempt. When running hundreds or even thousands of lines of code at a time, it can be extremely difficult to determine exactly where an error occurred and what caused it. That's why we have tools like the Debugger, Code Coverage, and Client Monitor in Microsoft Dynamics NAV.

For the most part the recipes in this chapter will not deal with writing your own code or writing better code. Instead we will focus more on how you can determine what is happening with code you have already written.

Using the debugger

This recipe will show you how to use the debugger to examine the code that is currently executing. We will demonstrate how to go through the code line-by-line and watch how values and objects change.

How to do it...

1. Create a new codeunit from **Object Designer**.

2. Add the following global variable:

Name	Type	Subtype
Customer	Record	Customer

3. Add the following global text constant:

Name	ConstValue
Text001	Matt Traxinger

4. Add a global function called `ChangeCustomerName`.

5. The function should take in the following parameter:

Name	Type	Length
NewName	Text	50

6. Add the following code to the function:

```
Customer.Name := NewName;
```

7. Add the following code to the `OnRun` trigger:

```
Customer.FINDFIRST;
ChangeCustomerName(Text001);
Customer.VALIDATE("Post Code");
```

8. Save and close the codeunit.

9. From the **Tools** menu in the NAV client select **Debugger | Active** (*Shift + Ctrl + F11*).

10. From the **Tools** menu in the NAV client select **Debugger | Breakpoint on Triggers** (*Shift + Ctrl + F12*).

11. Run the codeunit.

How it works...

When you run the codeunit, the **Microsoft Dynamics NAV Debugger** window will appear just like the one shown in the following screenshot:

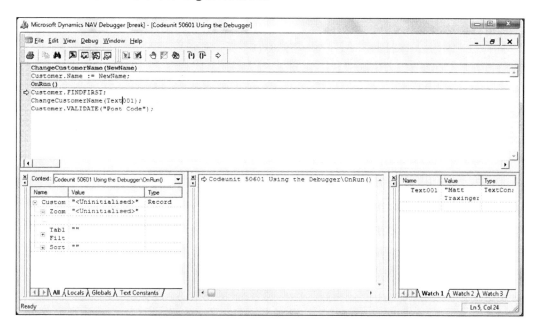

Before we get into the details of this window, we need to understand what caused it to appear. Setting the debugger to **Active** from the **Tools | Debugger** menu means that the debugger window will open every time the system encounters an error. In this case, though, we know our code doesn't produce any errors. We want to look at it anyway so we turn on the **Breakpoint on Triggers** option as well.

There are five components to the debugger window. The first is the menu and toolbar at the very top. They function just like any other toolbars you've seen. You can mouse over each button to get a tool tip of what it does.

The second component sits right below and contains the actual code from the current object. Here you can see a small yellow arrow pointing to the first line of our codeunit in the OnRun trigger. This is the line that is about to execute. Note that it has NOT executed yet. We'll explore each of the other three components as we move through our code.

Use the *F8* key or click the **Step Into** button on the toolbar. The window will now look like the one shown in following screenshot:

The yellow arrow has moved to the second line of code and the first line has executed. Notice the red text in the bottom left-hand corner. This is the **Variables** window (bottom left window). It lists all the variables and their values from the current object. At first, our customer variable was uninitialized because we had not executed the Customer.FINDFIRST line. That line retrieved a record from the database causing the value of the variable to change. This text will only remain red until you take another step into the program.

The next line of code that will execute is:

```
ChangeCustomerName(Text001);
```

What is this Text001 variable? If you're unsure of the value of a text constant, or you don't want to scroll through a possibly long list of variables in the **Context** window, you can add a shortcut to the **Watch List** (bottom right window). Right-click on **Text001** and go to **Add Watch**. The variable will be added to the **Watch List** along with its current value. Go ahead and hit *F8* to step into the next line.

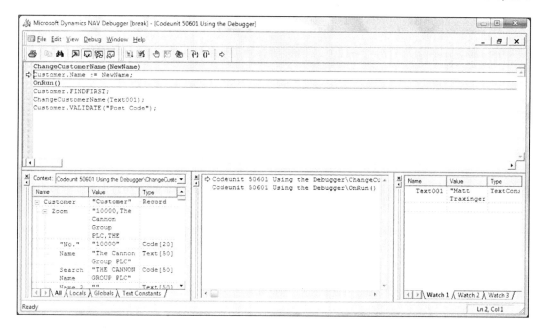

The yellow arrow jumps to the function that we just called. That brings us to our last window, the **Call Stack** (bottom middle window). It is important to know how you got to the code you are currently viewing. By looking at the **Call Stack** you can see that we were in the OnRun trigger of the codeunit and then jumped to the ChangeCustomerName function. You can click on each level of the stack to see the code for that object.

You may not always want to go through your code line-by-line, though. Try hitting the *F5* key or the **Go** command from the **Debug** menu. This will cause you to jump to the next function which is called instead of the next line. You will find yourself in a complete new object, the **Customer** table. Notice how the **Context** menu completely changes because the old variables are no longer in scope. They do not belong to the current object being examined.

There's more...

One common annoyance is trying to stop the debugger. You will find yourself in the middle of debugging your code and have that "Aha! I know what's wrong!" moment. You will click on the "X" to close the window only to have the debugger pop right back up at you.

From the **Debug** menu click on **Stop Debugging** (*Shift* + *F5*). This will stop the debugger until you turn it on again and, more importantly, allow you to continue with your development. **Stop Debugging** also performs a rollback of the changes that have happened to the database since you started the debugger.

See also

▸ Setting breakpoints

Setting breakpoints

Stepping through code line-by-line or function-by-function can take forever. Luckily there is an easy way to tell the debugger to stop right where we want it to.

How to do it...

1. Create and save the same codeunit discussed in the *Using the debugger* recipe in this chapter.
2. Design the codeunit.
3. Go to the following line of code in the OnRun trigger:

   ```
   ChangeCustomerName(Text001);
   ```
4. Press *F9* twice.
5. Go to the following line of code in the OnRun trigger:

   ```
   VALIDATE("Post Code");
   ```
6. Press *F9* once.

7. Your window should look like the following screenshot:

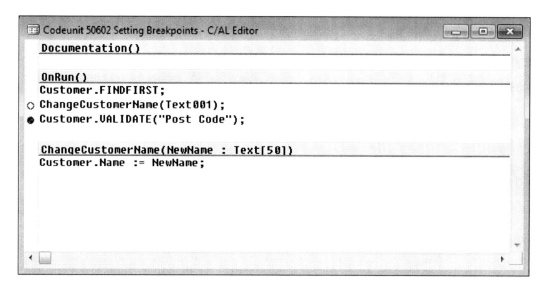

8. Save and close the codeunit.

9. From the **Tools** menu in the NAV client select **Debugger** | **Active** (*Shift + Ctrl + F11*).

10. Run the codeunit.

How it works...

When running the debugger on this codeunit, it should stop on `Customer.VALIDATE("Post Code")` line of code. This is because we have set a breakpoint here, which was the filled-in red circle at the left of that line. The debugger stops right where we tell it to, that is right before that line of code executes.

You will notice another mark. It is a red circle that is not filled. This is used to mark old breakpoints that you are not currently using. This is useful when you are trying to debug large amounts of code and want to temporarily remove a breakpoint or remember where you had one.

There's more...

The debugger is not perfect by any means. Some might even say it has a mind of its own sometimes. It doesn't always stop *exactly* where you want it to. It is common practice to set a breakpoint on a few successive lines of code in order to ensure that you stop in the general area.

See also

▸ Using the debugger

Using Code Coverage

In some scenarios, it may be useful to see a high-level overview of which objects are used when running a process and what code is executed in those objects. This recipe will show you how to use the **Code Coverage** tool for exactly that purpose.

How to do it...

1. From the NAV client menu, click on **Tools | Debugger | Code Coverage**. This will open the **Code Coverage** window.

2. Click the **Start** button.

3. Navigate to the **Customer Card** in the menu suite by clicking on **Sales and Marketing | Order Processing | Customers**.

4. Press *F3* to insert a new record followed by *Tab* or *Enter* to save that record to the database.

5. Close the **Customer Card**.

6. Click the **Stop** button on the **Code Coverage** window.

7. You should now see a form similar to the one shown in the following screenshot:

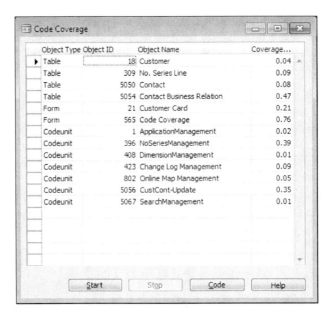

How it works...

The **Code Coverage** tool logs every line of code that is executed during a process. In this window, you can see every object that was used during the insertion process as well as the percentage of code (coverage ratio) that was executed in each object.

To view the details of the exact code that was executed in an object, select it in the list and click the **Code** button. The **Code Overview** window will open.

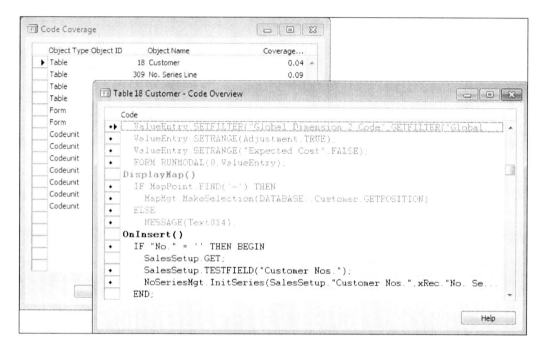

Unfortunately, this window is not as straightforward as it might first appear. The lines of code that *have* been executed are shown in black. The lines of code that are not executed are shown in red.

The lines that are marked with the small diamond to the left of the line are executable lines of code. These lines are the only lines for which you can be sure that the information displayed is correct.

There's more...

One great use of Code Coverage is to determine all of the possible places where a value may have changed. For example, the **Description** field on a Sales Line.

You can use Code Coverage to log all of the code that is executed and then view it in the **Code Overview** window. This window actually shows all the code that has been logged, but applies a filter for the selected object. This filter can be removed like any other in order to view every line of code.

From there you can set a filter like "*Description*" or "*Description :=*" to find every line of code where the **Description** field is used or assigned a value. Using the **Zoom** feature (*Ctrl + F8*), you can select a line and quickly view which object it is in.

Running Code Coverage from code

You can also turn on Code Coverage from within your own code.

```
CodeCoverage.DELETEALL;

CODECOVERAGELOG := TRUE;

CODECOVERAGELOG := FALSE;
FORM.RUN(FORM::"Code Coverage");
```

You will first need to define a record variable named `CodeCoverage` of subtype Code Coverage and delete all records from it.

You can then turn Code Coverage on/off using the `CODECOVERAGELOG` function. To see what was logged, run the Code Coverage form (565).

Handling runtime errors

Runtime errors happen when you are actually executing code. Most of these errors present error messages that users cannot easily understand. This recipe will show you how to handle these errors as well as some of the most common ones.

How to do it...

1. Create a new codeunit from **Object Designer**.
2. Add the following global variables:

Name	Type	Subtype
Customer	Record	Customer
Selection	Integer	

3. Add the following code to the OnRun trigger:
```
Selection := STRMENU('Show Error,Handle Error', 1);
IF Selection = 1 THEN
```

```
      Customer.GET
ELSE
  IF NOT Customer.GET THEN
    ERROR(' Unable to find a customer with a blank number.
           \Are you sure you have selected a customer?');
```

4. Save and close the codeunit.

How it works...

This codeunit allows you to select between having NAV handle an error for you or handling it with custom code. If you choose to let NAV handle the error for you, you will be presented with this error message:

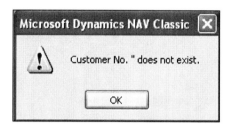

This message can be confusing for new users. Its interpretation can be different depending on the user. The following is not a stretch:

Customer No.. Double quote does not exist.

For those who have been using NAV for a while, this message is obvious. Those users know that two single quotes represents something blank and that this message is saying that a customer record with a blank number does not exist.

Now look at the message that is displayed when we handle the error:

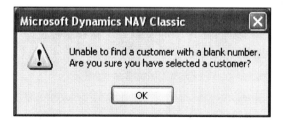

This error message was "trapped" by surrounding the function call with a conditional. The GET function, and many others, returns a Boolean value. If this value is not used by the developer and it is false, an error is thrown. We still want to throw an error, but we want one that makes sense to everyone. Here we tell the user what went wrong and a possible solution.

See also

▸ Creating transactions to alter data

Using Client Monitor to diagnose problems

Client Monitor is a tool that collects statistics about client/server communication. It will let you find out where your code is slow and show you every line of code that executes from start to finish. This recipe will show you how to use it.

How to do it...

1. Create a new codeunit from **Object Designer**.

2. Add the following global variable:

Name	Type	Subtype
Customer	Record	Customer

3. Add the following code to the OnRun trigger:

```
Customer.FINDFIRST;
SLEEP(5000);
Customer.FINDLAST;
```

4. Save and close the codeunit.

5. From the **Tools** menu in the NAV client click on **Client Monitor**.

6. Click the **Start** button in the window that then appears.

7. Run the codeunit you created.

8. Click the **Stop** Button on the **Client Monitor** window.

9. You should now see a form similar to the following screenshot:

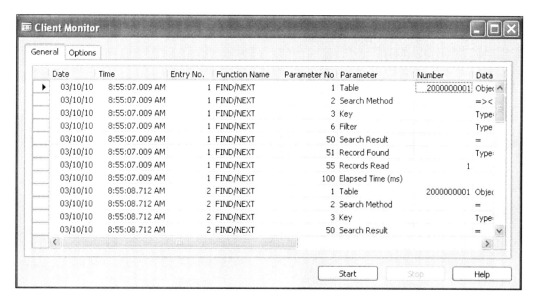

How it works...

It can be difficult to parse through all of the data that programs like this collect. We will not begin to cover everything that the Client Monitor reports on, but instead will examine our very short codeunit.

Let's look at the output from the Client Monitor to see if we can match it up to what our codeunit did.

 Please note that some output that deal with selecting the Object from **Object Designer** have been removed from the following result set shown.

Date	Time	Entry No.	Function Name	Parameter No	Parameter	Number	Data
3/10/2010	8:55:08.712 AM	4	FIND/NEXT	1	Table	18	Customer
3/10/2010	8:55:08.712 AM	4	FIND/NEXT	2	Search Method		-
3/10/2010	8:55:08.712 AM	4	FIND/NEXT	3	Key		No.
3/10/2010	8:55:08.712 AM	4	FIND/NEXT	14	Source Object		Codeunit 50605 Client Monitor

Date	Time	Entry No.	Function Name	Parameter No	Parameter	Number	Data
3/10/2010	8:55:08.712 AM	4	FIND/ NEXT	15	Source Trigger/ Function		OnRun()
3/10/2010	8:55:08.712 AM	4	FIND/ NEXT	16	Source Line No.	2	
3/10/2010	8:55:08.712 AM	4	FIND/ NEXT	17	Source Text		Customer. FINDFIRST;
3/10/2010	8:55:08.712 AM	4	FIND/ NEXT	50	Search Result		-
3/10/2010	8:55:08.712 AM	4	FIND/ NEXT	51	Record Found		No.='10000'
3/10/2010	8:55:08.712 AM	4	FIND/ NEXT	55	Records Read	2	
3/10/2010	8:55:08.712 AM	4	FIND/ NEXT	60	Reads	2	
3/10/2010	8:55:08.712 AM	4	FIND/ NEXT	100	Elapsed Time (ms)		
3/10/2010	8:55:13.712 AM	5	FIND/ NEXT	1	Table	18	Customer
3/10/2010	8:55:13.712 AM	5	FIND/ NEXT	2	Search Method		+
3/10/2010	8:55:13.712 AM	5	FIND/ NEXT	3	Key		No.
3/10/2010	8:55:13.712 AM	5	FIND/ NEXT	14	Source Object		Codeunit 50605 Client Monitor
3/10/2010	8:55:13.712 AM	5	FIND/ NEXT	15	Source Trigger/ Function		OnRun()
3/10/2010	8:55:13.712 AM	5	FIND/ NEXT	16	Source Line No.	4	
3/10/2010	8:55:13.712 AM	5	FIND/ NEXT	17	Source Text		Customer. FINDLAST;
3/10/2010	8:55:13.712 AM	5	FIND/ NEXT	50	Search Result		+
3/10/2010	8:55:13.712 AM	5	FIND/ NEXT	51	Record Found		No.='IC1030'
3/10/2010	8:55:13.712 AM	5	FIND/ NEXT	55	Records Read	2	

Date	Time	Entry No.	Function Name	Parameter No	Parameter	Number	Data
3/10/2010	8:55:13.712 AM	5	FIND/NEXT	60	Reads	1	
3/10/2010	8:55:13.712 AM	5	FIND/NEXT	100	Elapsed Time (ms)		

Each action corresponds to an **Entry No.** in the table. Each entry number has multiple parameters. We will begin with entry number **4**.

Parameters **1** and **3** tell us that we are dealing with the **Customer** table and have it sorted on the Parameter No. key, which in this case is the primary key. That means we probably did not use the SETCURRENTKEY command. Parameter 2, Search Method, has a value of "-". From older versions of NAV we know that this is a FIND('-'), or what is now a FINDFIRST (the actual code is shown in Parameter No. 17, but it is nice to be able to understand the output).

Parameter numbers 14 and 15 tell us that this code is being called from the OnRun trigger of our Client Monitor codeunit. Parameter 16 gives more specifics about the exact line number of the code. Note that this is based on the *entire* object, not the line number of the trigger or function. Trigger definitions (gray bars is Code View) also count as lines. This is important to know because we could have multiple Customer.FINDFIRST commands and we will need to know which one we are dealing with.

The remaining parameters show us the record that was returned and the number of database reads (or writes if this was an INSERT/MODIFY/RENAME command).

Note that this code executed at 8:55:08 AM. Entry No. 5 did not execute until 8:55:13 AM. This tells us that we have some sort of network problem. In reality, this is an artificial problem created by the SLEEP(5000) command. We introduced a five second delay to show what the output would look like if there were actual network issues.

See also

▸ Using SQL Profiler

Finding errors when using NAS

The **Navision Application Server**, or **NAS**, does everything a normal NAV client can do, except that it doesn't show anything on the screen. This can present challenges to figuring out what has gone wrong when running your code using NAS. This recipe will show you how to debug this type of code.

Getting ready

You must already have the NAV Application Server installed on the machine on which you are working.

How to do it...

1. Copy your developer license into the install directory for the application server. On a typical install this is `C:\Program Files (x86)\Microsoft Dynamics NAV\60\Application Server`. The license file should be named `fin.flf`.

2. Open a command prompt.

3. Run the following command:

```
"Path to Application Server\nassql" debug, appservername="NAS",
servername="Your Server Name", database="Your Database
Name",company="Your Company Name", startupparameter="NEP-",
objectcache=32000, nettype=tcp
```

How it works...

The **NAS Snap-in Console** does not allow you to start an NAS service in debug mode, so we have to start it manually from the command line. This command is designed to error-out quickly by passing a start up parameter of `NEP-` instead of `NEP-1`.

When the command is run, the normal NAV debugger window will open with Codeunit 1 loaded. From here you can use the normal debugger commands to step through the code.

There's more...

You can also create your own codeunit that calls the `NASHandler` function in Codeunit 1, `ApplicationManagement` to get similar results.

See also

▶ Using the debugger
▶ Setting breakpoints

Implementing Try / Catch / Finally

The `Try` / `Catch` / `Finally` syntax has been around in languages like C# .NET for a very long time. Unfortunately, it has never made it into C/AL. This recipe will show you how to implement this type of control structure so that you can display error messages and still have your code continue to execute.

How to do it...

1. In Visual Studio create a new **Class Library Project**.

2. Add a file named `ITryCatchFinally.cs` with the following code:

```
using System.Runtime.InteropServices;

namespace TryCatchFinally
{
    [ComVisible(false)]
    public delegate void OnTry();

    [ComVisible(false)]
    public delegate void OnCatch(string errMessage);

    [ComVisible(false)]
    public delegate void OnFinally();

    [InterfaceType(ComInterfaceType.InterfaceIsIDispatch)]
    [ComVisible(true)]
    public interface ITryCatchFinally
    {
        event OnTry NAVTry;
        event OnCatch NAVCatch;
        event OnFinally NAVFinally;

        void Execute();
    }
}
```

3. Add a file named `ITryCatchFinallyEvents.cs` with the following code:

```
using System.Runtime.InteropServices;

namespace TryCatchFinally
{
    [InterfaceType(ComInterfaceType.InterfaceIsIDispatch)]
    [ComVisible(true)]
```

```
      public interface ITryCatchFinallyEvents
      {
        [DispId(0x60020001)]
        void NAVTry();

        [DispId(0x60020002)]
        void NAVCatch(string errMessage);

        [DispId(0x60020003)]
        void NAVFinally();
      }
    }
```

4. Add a file named `TryCatchFinally.cs` with the following code:

```
using System;
using System.Runtime.InteropServices;

namespace TryCatchFinally
{
  [ComSourceInterfaces(typeof(ITryCatchFinallyEvents))]
  [ProgId("TryCatchFinally")]
  [ComVisible(true)]
  [ClassInterface(ClassInterfaceType.None)]
  public class TryCatchFinally : ITryCatchFinally
  {
    public event OnTry NAVTry;
    public event OnCatch NAVCatch;
    public event OnFinally NAVFinally;

    public TryCatchFinally()
    {
    }

    public void Execute()
    {
      OnTry();
    }

    private void OnTry()
    {
      try
      {
        NAVTry();
      }
      catch (Exception e)
```

```
    {
      try { OnCatch(e); } catch { }
    }
    finally
    {
      try { OnFinally(); } catch { }
    }
  }

  private void OnCatch(Exception exception)
  {
    if (exception != null)
    {
      NAVCatch(exception.Message);
    }
  }

  private void OnFinally()
  {
    NAVFinally();
  }
    }
}
```

5. View the **Properties** of the project.

6. On the **Build** tab check the **Register for COM interop** checkbox.

7. Save and compile the objects.

8. Create a new codeunit from **Object Designer**.

9. Add a global Automation variable named `TCF` of subtype `'TryCatchFinally'.TryCatchFinally`

10. Add the following global variable:

Name	Type	Subtype
TCF	Automation	'TryCatchFinally'.TryCatchFinally

11. Set the following property on the variable:

Property	Value
WithEvents	Yes

12. Add the following code to the `OnRun` trigger:

```
CREATE(TCF);
TCF.Execute();
```

13. Add the following code to the `TCF::NAVTry` event:

```
ERROR('NAV has encountered an error.');
MESSAGE('This message should never be displayed.');
```

14. Add the following code to the `TCF::NAVCatch` event:

```
MESSAGE('The following error was caught:\%1', errMessage);
```

15. Add the following code to the `TCF::NAVFinally` event:

```
MESSAGE('NAV will now perform some cleanup.');
```

16. Save and close the codeunit.

How it works...

We will not go into the details about how the C# .NET code works. For that you should refer related articles on `msdn.microsoft.com/`.

The `ITryCatchFinally.cs` file is a basic interface. Any class that implements this interface will need to define three events (`NAVTry`, `NAVCatch`, and `NAVFinally`) and a method called `Execute`.

We also need to implement an interface that will expose the events in our NAV object. This is the `ITryCatchFinallyEvents.cs` file. We again define our three events, but give each of them a special attribute called `DispId`. This ID allows the code that will be written in the NAV events to be linked back to these functions.

The last file is a class named `TryCatchFinally`. Our `Execute` method, which will be called from NAV, is simply a wrapper for our `OnTry` method. `OnTry` executes the code we have added in the `NAVTry` method in our NAV object. If an error is found, it is caught and execution moves to the `OnCatch` event. Lastly, no matter what happens, the `OnFinally` event is called.

When we add the Automation control to our NAV object and set the `WithEvents` property to `Yes`, our three events appear. In our `NAVTry` event we intentionally throw an error. A message action has been placed under that error to show that execution of the event does in fact stop when the error is encountered. In the other events, `OnCatch` and `OnFinally`, we add messages to show that although we have encountered an error, NAV code will continue to execute.

There's more...

The downside to this solution is that you must declare an Automation variable for every try / catch / finally block you want to execute. This can cause your code to become difficult to read and follow.

You can also mimic this behavior using the `IF CODEUNIT.RUN THEN` syntax. This is easier, but you have to buy a codeunit (admittedly, a cheap thing to buy) for every line of code you need to do this on.

Most errors can be caught using simple conditionals and this form of error trapping should be used only when absolutely necessary.

See also

- Checking for conditions using an `IF` Statement
- Using a `CASE` statement to test multiple conditions

7

Roles and Security

In this chapter, we will cover:

- ▶ Adding roles through the User Setup table
- ▶ Creating and assigning a security role
- ▶ Using `FILTERGROUP` to restrict data
- ▶ Checking for user-assigned roles
- ▶ Checking Active Directory groups
- ▶ Using security filters
- ▶ Field-level security
- ▶ Assigning menu suites based on company
- ▶ Ending an idle session
- ▶ Automatically adding users to NAV
- ▶ Hiding values in Zoom

Introduction

ERP systems like Dynamics NAV need a built-in security model to make sure that appropriate people have access to appropriate information. NAV supports two forms of user authentication: Database and Windows. Each login is assigned roles, which in turn have permissions, which the system checks every time data is accessed or an object is run.

NAV security is somewhat limited and difficult to maintain. However, as system-security data is stored in tables of the NAV database, we can write custom code to handle permissions in any way we like. We can even make calls to the Active Directory to examine user groups and other Windows properties. As you will see in this chapter, the boundaries of NAV security are limitless, but there will be a large amount of work involved for certain tasks.

Adding roles through the User Setup table

A common way to give permissions to users is by adding a field to the User Setup table. Although not the best practice, this recipe will show you how this common type of permission works.

How to do it...

1. Design the **User Setup** table (91) from **Object Designer**.

2. Add a Boolean field named **Sample Permission** with ID as **50000**.

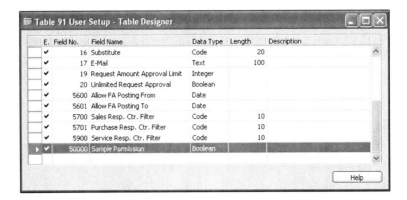

3. Save and close the table.

4. Design the **User Setup** form (119).

5. Use the **Field Menu** to add a column for the **Sample Permission** field.

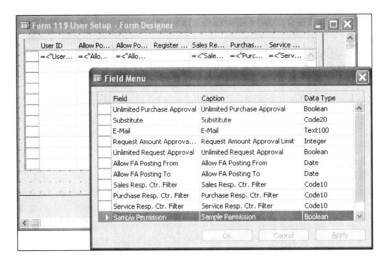

6. Save and close the form.

7. Create a new codeunit from **Object Designer**.

8. Add the following global variable:

Name	Type	Subtype
UserSetup	Record	User Setup

9. Add the following code to the OnRun trigger:

```
IF NOT UserSetup.GET(USERID) THEN
  ERROR('You do not have permission to perform this action.');

IF UserSetup."Sample Permission" THEN
  MESSAGE('Permission granted.')
ELSE
  ERROR('You do not have permission to perform this action.');
```

10. Save and close the codeunit.

How it works...

We start by adding a field that will give or deny permission for a specific action. That field is then added to the form so that the permission can be assigned.

In our codeunit we first make sure that a user setup record exists for our ID. If it does not, we throw an error stating that we do not have the correct permissions. If a record is found we check the value of the **Sample Permission** field using a standard conditional statement and take an appropriate action.

There's more...

This method of assigning permissions is not the best practice. NAV already has a working security system, so if you need to modify the database, you might as well build that modification on top of the existing functionality. Although this method works just fine, it can get confusing when there are multiple places to check for user permissions.

See also

- Creating and assigning a security role
- Checking for user-assigned roles

Creating and assigning a security role

NAV has its own built-in methods for controlling access to certain parts of the system. This recipe will show you how to create roles to limit that access.

How to do it...

1. From the NAV client click **Tools | Security | Roles**.

2. Use the *F3* key to enter a new role called **SAMPLE** with a **Description** of "PACKT – Sample Role".

3. With your cursor on the **SAMPLE** line, click on the **Role** button, then **Permissions**.

4. Add a permission for **Object Type** = TableData, **Object Type** = 18.

5. Close the **Permissions** window.

6. Close the **Role** window.

7. From the NAV client click on **Tools | Security | Windows Logins** (or **Database Logins** depending on the system).

8. Select a user from the list and click on **Roles**.

9. Add the sample role to the user.

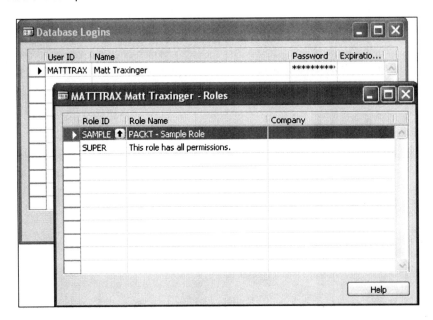

10. Close the **Roles** window.

11. Close the **Logins** window.

How it works...

The security system in NAV is maintained using roles and permissions. A **role** is made up of permissions to access specific objects in the database such as tables, forms, reports, and even system objects such as items in the NAV client menu. These roles are then assigned to database users, Windows users, or Windows groups.

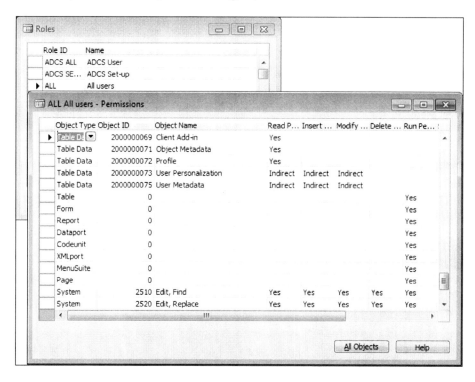

Everything related to security in NAV can be found under the **Tools | Security** menu in the NAV client. Roles are inserted into the system using the same shortcuts as in every other record, the *F3* key. These roles have a short name called the **Role ID** and a longer **Description** field.

Our role contains a permission that will allow the user full access to customer records. For Table Data object types, there are four permission levels that can be combined in any order. They include the ability to read, insert, modify, and delete records from this table. The fifth permission level is run or execute and is used for the other object types. The options for each of these permission levels are blank (No), **Yes**, and **Indirect.**

In order to test this you will need to assign the role to a user who does not already have permission to the **Customer** table. Once that role is assigned, the user will need to close the NAV client and reopen it in order to gain their new permissions.

For more information about roles and security, search for **Security** in Microsoft Dynamics NAV Help from the NAV client **Help** menu.

There's more...

If you are using SQL Server you may need to take an additional step in order to make sure the permissions in the NAV system are the same as those in SQL. This depends on the security model you are using. You can check this by going to **File | Database | Alter** in the NAV client. Click on the **Advanced** tab and check the security model.

If you are using **Standard** security then no further action is required. However, if you are using **Enhanced** security then you need to selet **Tools | Security | Synchronize All Logins**. This will make sure everything between the NAV Client and SQL Server matches.

Leveraging the User Rights tool

Microsoft provides a great product with the NAV software called the User Rights tool. This code examines records produced by the Client Monitor tool and automatically creates a role with the permissions you need. You can find it on the NAV product CD.

See also

- ▸ Adding roles through the User Setup table
- ▸ Checking for user-assigned roles

Using FILTERGROUP to restrict data

Filter groups are used to apply filters that cannot be removed by the user. This recipe will show you how to write code to utilize them and what to watch out for.

How to do it...

1. Create a new codeunit from **Object Designer**.

2. Add the following global variables:

Name	Type	Subtype
CurrFilterGroup	Integer	
Customer	Record	Customer

3. Add the following code to the `OnRun` trigger of the codeunit:

```
CurrFilterGroup := Customer.FILTERGROUP;

Customer.FILTERGROUP(255);
Customer.SETRANGE("No.", '50000');
Customer.FILTERGROUP(CurrFilterGroup);

Customer.FINDFIRST;
MESSAGE('Filters: %1\First Customer: %2', Customer.GETFILTERS,
                                          Customer.Name);
```

4. Save and close the codeunit.

How it works...

A FILTERGROUP is used to set filters on a `Record` variable that cannot be removed by the user. This function takes in a single integer as a parameter between the numbers 0 and 255. Although you can use numbers one to six, they are reserved by the system and manually assigning filters to those groups can override default functionality. For example, NAV uses FILTERGROUP number four to apply the link between header and line values on forms such as **Sales Order** and **Purchase Order**.

In our short code segment, we first need to determine the FILTERGROUP that is currently assigned to the user so that we can set it back when we are finished. Like other functions in NAV, when the optional parameter is not used the function returns the current value. Next we set the FILTERGROUP to 255, assign a filter, and then reset the FILTERGROUP. Finally, we find the first record in the table and display a message with the filters applied and the record that was found.

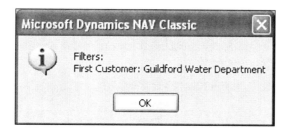

As you can see from the expected output, we cannot see that we have applied any filters to the record. However, if we look at the **Customer List** from the standard form, we can see that **Guildford Water Department** is not the first customer in the list.

See also

▶ Using advanced filtering

Checking for user-assigned roles

The NAV system checks permissions every time you look at data or run an object, but what if you need to check permissions manually? This recipe will show you how to examine a user ID to check for a specific role.

How to do it...

1. Create a new codeunit from **Object Designer**.

2. Add a global function called `VerifySecurity` that returns a Boolean value named `HasPermission`.

3. This function should take in three parameters:

Name	Type	Length
RoleID	Code	20
CompanyRequired	Boolean	
SuperAllowed	Boolean	

4. Add the following code to the function:

```
HasPermission := CheckUserId(RoleID, CompanyRequired,
                                      SuperAllowed);
```

5. Add a global function called `CheckUserID` that returns a Boolean value.

6. This function should take in the same three parameters as the `VerifySecurity` function.

7. Add the following local variable to the function:

Name	Type	Subtype
Session	Record	Session

8. Add the following code to the function:

```
Session.SETRANGE("My Session", TRUE);
IF NOT Session.FINDFIRST THEN
  EXIT(FALSE);
```

```
IF Session."Login Type" = Session."Login Type"::Database THEN
BEGIN
    EXIT(CheckDatabaseLogin(USERID, RoleID, CompanyRequired,
                                            SuperAllowed))
END ELSE BEGIN
    EXIT(CheckWindowsLogin(USERID, RoleID, CompanyRequired,
                                            SuperAllowed));
END;
```

9. Add a global function named `CheckDatabaseLogin` that returns a Boolean value named `HasPermission`.

10. The function should take in the following parameters:

Name	Type	Length
UserIDIn	Code	20
RoleID	Code	20
CompanyRequired	Boolean	
SuperAllowed	Boolean	

11. Add the following local variable:

Name	Type	Subtype
DatabaseUserRoles	Record	Member Of

12. Add the following code to the function:

```
DatabaseUserRoles.SETRANGE("User ID", UserIDIn);
IF NOT SuperAllowed THEN
    DatabaseUserRoles.SETRANGE("Role ID", RoleID)
ELSE
    DatabaseUserRoles.SETFILTER("Role ID", '%1|%2', RoleID,
                                            'SUPER');
IF CompanyRequired THEN BEGIN
    DatabaseUserRoles.SETFILTER(Company, '%1|%2', COMPANYNAME, '');
END;
IF DatabaseUserRoles.FINDFIRST THEN
    HasPermission := TRUE;
```

13. Add a global function named `CheckWindowsLogin` that returns a Boolean value named `HasPermission`.

14. The function should take in the same parameters as the `CheckDatabaseLogin` function.

15. Add the following local variable to the function:

Name	Type	Subtype
WindowsUserRoles	Record	Windows Access Control

16. Add the following code to the function:

```
IF NOT SuperAllowed THEN
  WindowsUserRoles.SETRANGE("Role ID", RoleID)
ELSE
  WindowsUserRoles.SETFILTER("Role ID",'%1|%2', RoleID, 'SUPER');
IF CompanyRequired THEN
  WindowsUserRoles.SETFILTER("Company Name",'%1|%2',
                                  COMPANYNAME, '');
IF WindowsUserRoles.FINDSET THEN
  REPEAT
    WindowsUserRoles.CALCFIELDS("Login ID") ;
    IF UPPERCASE(ShortUserID(WindowsUserRoles."Login ID")) =
                          UPPERCASE(UserIDIn) THEN
      HasPermission := TRUE;
  UNTIL (WindowsUserRoles.NEXT = 0) OR (HasPermission);
```

17. Add a global function named `ShortUserID` that returns a code variable of length 20.

18. The function should take in the following parameter:

Name	Type	Length
UserIDIn	Code	132

19. Add the following code to the function:

```
IF STRPOS(UserIdIn,'\') IN [0,STRLEN(UserIdIn)] THEN
  EXIT(COPYSTR(UserIdIn,1,MAXSTRLEN(UserIdIn)));
EXIT(COPYSTR(UserIdIn,STRPOS(UserIdIn,'\') +
                          1,MAXSTRLEN(UserIdIn)));
```

20. Add the following code to the `OnRun` trigger:

```
IF VerifySecurity('S&R-CUSTOMER', FALSE, FALSE) THEN
  MESSAGE('Security Check Passed')
ELSE
  MESSAGE('Security Check Failed');
```

21. Save and close the codeunit.

How it works...

NAV security can be quite complex, but this codeunit breaks out the process of checking it. Our `OnRun` trigger calls the `VerifySecurity` function so we will start there.

This function takes in three parameters which are used throughout the codeunit. The first is the Role ID. This identifies the role that we want to check for in the system. Usually you will want to store this value in a setup table so that it can be changed by the customer, but here we have hard coded it into the business logic. The second parameter tells the function whether or not the user must have permission specifically for the company they are in (TRUE) or if they can have it for any company in the database (FALSE). The last is whether or not the user is allowed to have SUPER access which overrides any lower-level permission. This function will call the `CheckUserID` function and pass the same parameters to it.

In the `CheckUserID` function we take a look at the **Session** table, a virtual table in NAV. This table contains all of the users currently logged into NAV. There is a field in this table called **My Session** which identifies the session of the user running the code. The other important field in this table is the **Login Type**. This field tells us whether the user is connected through a database login or a Windows login. Security-related data is stored in different tables for each type so we have to know in which order to do a correct check.

Security-related data for database users is stored in the **Member Of** table. In order to check the security we apply three filters. The first is for the user we are looking for. The next two depend on the values of our parameters. If we want it to be the company name then we must set a filter for the current company name; if not, we will leave the filter blank. The last filter is applied if SUPER is an allowed role. If it is then we filter for _either_ the Role ID or SUPER. If not, we only filter for the Role ID. If a record is found, the function returns TRUE.

Checking Windows logins is a little different. In Windows, the logins actually map to a SID, or security identifier. The security identifier is stored in the Windows Access Control table. Based on this SID and the actual username is a FlowField. Here we will set the same filters as the database-login check, other than the User ID. This will give us a recordset containing everyone who has the correct role. We will then loop through that set, calculating the value of the FlowField, and comparing it to the ID we are looking for.

In order to properly perform this comparison we have to implement one final function. The **User Name** field contains the user's full name; that is the domain and/or user ID. The `USERID` function in NAV only returns the ID of the current user. The `ShortUserId` function removes the domain part of the name, if it exists, and returns a value in-line with what NAV is expecting.

When you run the codeunit you will see a message depending on the security validation:

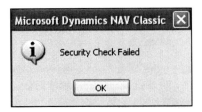

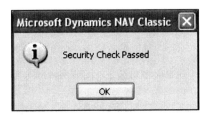

See also

▶ Checking conditions using an IF statement

▶ Adding roles through the User Setup table

▶ Creating and assigning a security role

▶ Checking Active Directory groups

▶ Automatically adding users to NAV

Checking Active Directory groups

A common practice is to assign security through Active Directory groups. NAV supports this out-of-the-box, but does not give a way to manually check those groups from code. For that you will need to implement a .NET class.

Getting ready

The codeunit from the *Checking for user-assigned roles* recipe should be created.

How to do it...

1. Create the following class in Visual Studio. You will need to add a reference to `System.DirectoryServices`.

```csharp
using System;
using System.Collections;
using System.DirectoryServices;
using System.DirectoryServices.ActiveDirectory;
using System.Runtime.InteropServices;
using System.Security.Principal;

namespace NAV_ActiveDirectory
{
  [ProgId("NAV_ActiveDirectory")]
  [ComVisible(true)]
  [ClassInterface(ClassInterfaceType.AutoDual)]
  public class NAV_ActiveDirectory
  {
    private ArrayList properties;
    private string userdn;
    private int propertiesIndex;

    public NAV_ActiveDirectory()
    {
      properties = new ArrayList();
      propertiesIndex = 0;
    }

    public void SetConnectionString(string userid, string userdn)
    {
      this.userdn = userdn;
      this.userdn = userdn.Replace("%1", userid);
    }

    public bool MorePropertiesExist()
    {
      return (propertiesIndex < properties.Count);
    }

    public string GetNextProperty()
    {
      string dnstring = properties[propertiesIndex].ToString();
      dnstring = dnstring.Substring(dnstring.IndexOf("CN=") + 3,
                                    dnstring.IndexOf(",") - 3);
```

```
        propertiesIndex++;
        return dnstring;
      }


      public void LoadADGroups(bool recursive)
      {
        LoadProperty("memberof");
      }

      private void LoadProperty(string property)
      {
        DirectoryEntry ent = new DirectoryEntry(userdn);
        PropertyValueCollection ValueCollection =
                            ent.Properties[property];
        IEnumerator en = ValueCollection.GetEnumerator();

        while (en.MoveNext())
        {
          if (en.Current != null)
          {
            if (!properties.Contains(en.Current.ToString()))
            {
              properties.Add(en.Current.ToString());
            }
          }
        }
        ent.Close();
        ent.Dispose();
      }
    }
  }
```

2. Add a function to your codeunit called `CheckADGroups`.

3. This function should take three parameters:

Name	Type	Length
RoleID	Code	20
CompanyRequired	Boolean	
SuperAllowed	Boolean	

4. Add the following global variable to the codeunit:

Name	Type	Subtype
ADGroups	Automation	'NAV_ActiveDirectory'.NAV_ActiveDirectory

```
CREATE(ADGroups);
ADGroups.SetConnectionString( USERID,
  'LDAP://DomainName/CN=%1,OU=your_organizational_unit,
                              DC=your_domain');
ADGroups.LoadADGroups(TRUE);
WHILE (ADGroups.MorePropertiesExist()) AND (NOT HasPermission) DO
BEGIN
  GroupName := ADGroups.GetNextProperty();
  HasPermission := CheckWindowsLogin(GroupName, RoleID,
                              CompanyRequired, SuperAllowed);
END;
CLEAR(ADGroups);
```

5. Add the following code to the `VerifySecurity` function:

```
IF NOT HasPermission THEN
  HasPermission := CheckADGroups(RoleID, CompanyRequired,
                              SuperAllowed);
```

6. When you run the codeunit you will see a message depending on the security validation:

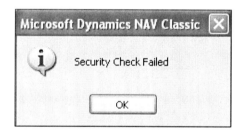

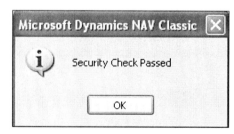

How it works...

Our Visual Studio class creates an **LDAP (Lightweight Directory Access Protocol)** to a domain controller on your network using a string like this:

```
LDAP://DomainName/CN=%1,OU=your_organizational_unit,DC=your_domain
```

You can find the domain name using **Active Directory Users and Computers**.

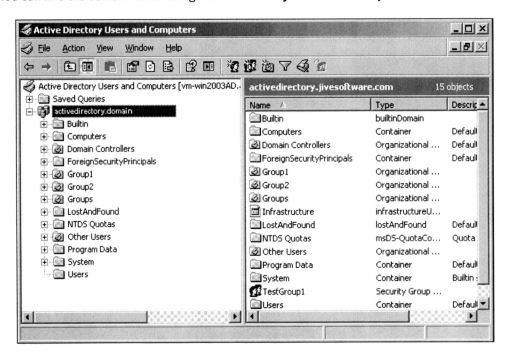

The objects within the domain are grouped into **Organizational Units**, or **OU**s. Examples in the preceding image include **Computers** and **Users**. If the object you are looking for resides deep down in the hierarchy you must pass each OU to the LDAP query and you have to do it in a specific way. For example, if a **User** object was found in Users\Company1\Service Accounts, you would pass an LDAP string like this:

```
LDAP://DomainName/CN=%1,OU=Service Accounts,OU=Company1,
  OU=Users,DC=your_domain
```

That is, you have to pass them in order, from the bottom up, to the query.

You should be able to find your domain very easily. It is displayed every time you log into your system. You can also find it in **Control Panel** under **System and Maintenance**.

Once the LDAP connection has been established, the program then loads all of the values found in the `MemberOf` property for the user into an `ArrayList` object. As NAV cannot handle these types of objects, code is included to loop through the values and return them one-by-one. As these AD groups are listed in the Windows Login table, just like a normal user, we can use our `CheckWindowsLogin` function to see what permissions have been assigned to it.

See also

- ▸ Checking conditions using an `IF` statement
- ▸ Adding roles through the User Setup table
- ▸ Creating and assigning a security role
- ▸ Checking for user-assigned roles
- ▸ Automatically adding users to NAV

Using security filters

The SQL Server option for Microsoft Dynamics NAV allows you to specify record-level security using the **Security Filters** field on **Permissions**. Here we will discuss how to set up these filters and some pitfalls to watch out for when using them.

Getting ready

You must be using a SQL database in order to use this recipe.

How to do it...

1. If you have not done so, create the SAMPLE role as described in the *Creating and assigning a security role* recipe.

2. View the permissions for this role.

3. Using the assist button, set the **Security Filter** field to filter based on a Service Zone Code equal to the letter 'M'.

4. Close the **Security** windows.

5. Create a new codeunit from **Object Designer**.

6. Add the following global variable:

Name	Type	Subtype
Customer	Record	Customer

7. Add the following code to the `OnRun` trigger:

```
Customer.SETPERMISSIONFILTER;
FORM.RUNMODAL(0, Customer);
```

8. Save and close the codeunit.

9. The resulting form will only list a single customer:

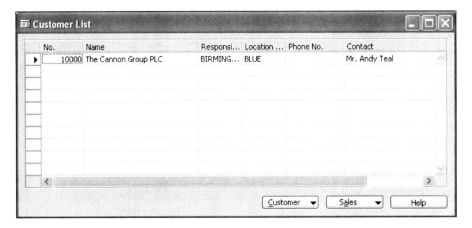

How it works...

With SQL Server, you can limit the records the user can see in a table using the **Security Filter** option. This attribute is assigned in a way similar to the read / insert / modify / delete attributes in the **Permissions** window for a **Role**.

If the user opens a form these filters will automatically be applied. This is not the case, though, when the form is opened through code. In these cases you must call the `SETPERMISSIONFILTER` function on the `Record` variable that is passed to the form.

There's more...

When used correctly, security filters can be of great use when setting up permissions. They can also cause a lot of headaches.

For example, let's imagine a manager who needs to view the **General Ledger** entries to make sure his department is not going over budget. He should be able to view entries only in the accounts that relate directly to his department. This seems like a great use for security filters. But what about all of those other General Ledger Entries that are created when he posts documents? Tax and VAT are great examples. That security filter will not allow him to post to those accounts and he will receive errors during posting.

Be careful when and how you use this type of security. If you apply a security filter to a Customer permission, don't just open the Custom List form to test it out. As with all forms of security you will want to test your code extensively to make sure that you do not introduce any problems into the system.

See also

▸   Using advanced filtering

Field-level security

Field-level security does not exist out-of-the-box in NAV and is not easy to implement. In fact, real field-level security is impossible to implement. This recipe will show you an example of how to quickly create a work around for this type of security model in your system.

Getting ready

Part of the code in this recipe relies on code from the codeunit created in the *Checking for user-assigned roles* recipe in this chapter.

How to do it...

1.   Create a new table in **Object Manager** named **Field Level Security**.

2.   Add the following fields:

Name	Type	Length
Table No.	Integer	
Field No.	Integer	
Security Type	Option	
Applies To	Text	119
Editable	Boolean	
Visible	Boolean	
Show Text	Boolean	

3. Set the following properties for these fields:

Field Name	Property	Value
Table No.	`TableRelation`	`Object.ID WHERE (Type=CONST(Table))`
Field No.	`TableRelation`	`Field.No. WHERE (TableNo=FIELD(Table No.))`
Security Type	`OptionString`	`Database User, Windows User`

Applies To	`Text`	`IF (Security Type=CONST(Database User)) User`
		
		`ELSE IF (Security Type=CONST(Windows User)) "Windows Login"`

4. Set the primary key for the table to **Table No., Field No., Security Type, Applies To**.

5. Save and close the table.

6. Using the **Form Generation Wizard**, create a form that displays all of the fields from this table.

7. Add the following local variables to the `OnFormat` trigger of the **Applies To** field:

Name	Type	Subtype
WindowsLogin	Record	Windows Login
SecurityCheck	Codeunit	Security Check (or the name you gave your codeunit in the "Checking for user-assigned roles" recipe)

8. In the `OnFormat` trigger for the **Applies To** field add the following code:

```
IF "Security Type" = "Security Type"::"Windows User" THEN BEGIN
   WindowsLogin.GET("Applies To");
   WindowsLogin.CALCFIELDS(ID);
   Text := SecurityCheck.ShortUserID(WindowsLogin.ID);
END;
```

9. Save and close the form.

10. A sample form with data might look like this:

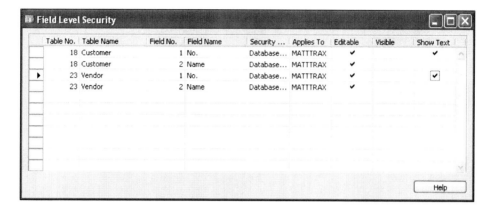

11. Create a new codeunit from **Object Designer**.

12. Create a global function named `CheckSecurity`.

13. This function should take in the following parameters:

Name	Type	Length
UserIDIn	Code	119
TableID	Integer	
FieldID	Integer	
CurrentStatus	Boolean	
PropertyToCheck	Option	

14. Set the following property for these fields:

Field Name	Property	Value
PropertyToCheck	OptionString	Editable,Visible,ShowText

15. The function should return a Boolean value.

16. Define the following local variables in the function:

Name	Type	Subtype
FieldLevelSecurity	Record	Field Level Security
Session	Record	Session

17. Add the following code to the `CheckSecurity` function:

```
Session.SETRANGE("My Session", TRUE);
IF NOT Session.FINDFIRST THEN
  EXIT(FALSE);

FieldLevelSecurity.SETRANGE("Table No.", TableID);
FieldLevelSecurity.SETRANGE("Field No.", FieldID);
CASE Session."Login Type" OF
  Session."Login Type"::Database: BEGIN
    FieldLevelSecurity.SETRANGE("Security Type",
        FieldLevelSecurity."Security Type"::"Database User");
    FieldLevelSecurity.SETRANGE("Applies To", USERID);
  END;
  Session."Login Type"::Windows: BEGIN
    FieldLevelSecurity.SETRANGE("Security Type",
        FieldLevelSecurity."Security Type"::"Windows User");
    FieldLevelSecurity.SETRANGE("Applies To",
                          GetSIDFromLogin(USERID));
  END;
END;

IF FieldLevelSecurity.FINDFIRST THEN
  CASE PropertyToCheck OF
    PropertyToCheck::Editable:
      EXIT(FieldLevelSecurity.Editable AND CurrentStatus);
    PropertyToCheck::Visible:
      EXIT(FieldLevelSecurity.Visible AND CurrentStatus);
    PropertyToCheck::Show:
      EXIT(FieldLevelSecurity."Show Text" AND CurrentStatus);
  END;

EXIT(CurrentStatus);
```

18. Add a function named `GetSIDFromLogin` that takes in the following parameter:

Name	Type	Length
Login	Text	119

19. It should return a **Text** value of length **132**.

20. Add the following local variables to the function:

Name	Type	Subtype
WindowsLogin	Record	Windows Login
SecurityCheck	Codeunit	Security Check (or the name you gave your codeunit in the "Checking for user-assigned roles" recipe)

21. Add the following code to the function:

```
IF WindowsLogin.FINDSET THEN
  REPEAT
    WindowsLogin.CALCFIELDS(ID);
    IF UPPERCASE(USERID) =
        UPPERCASE(SecurityCheck.ShortUserID(WindowsLogin.ID)) THEN
      EXIT(WindowsLogin.SID);
  UNTIL WindowsLogin.NEXT = 0;

EXIT('');
```

22. Create a form as described in the *Using the Form Generation Wizard* recipe. You should have a form displaying the **No.** and **Name** fields from the **Customer** table.

23. Add the following global variable:

Name	Type	Subtype
FieldLevelSecurity	Codeunit	Field Level Security

24. Add the following code to the `OnOpenForm` trigger:

```
CurrForm."No.".EDITABLE := FieldLevelSecurity.CheckSecurity(
    USERID, DATABASE::Customer, Rec.FIELDNO("No."),
    CurrForm."No.".EDITABLE, 0);
CurrForm."No.".VISIBLE := FieldLevelSecurity.CheckSecurity(
    USERID, DATABASE::Customer, Rec.FIELDNO("No."),
    CurrForm."No.".VISIBLE, 1);
```

25. Add the following code to the `OnFormat` trigger for the **No.** field:

```
IF NOT FieldLevelSecurity.CheckSecurity(
    USERID, DATABASE::Customer, Rec.FIELDNO("No."), TRUE, 2) THEN
  Text := '***';
```

26. Save and close the form.

27. The resulting form might look something like the one shown in the following screenshot, depending on the security assigned:

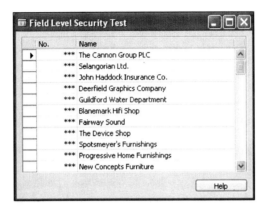

How it works...

NAV does not have a place to store security settings on a field level so we need to create our own table and form to hold this information. This table will hold the user, table, and field number that security needs to be tracked for. Similar to the read/insert/modify/delete permissions, we will track the `Editable/Visible/ShowText` properties.

We also need a codeunit to check the permissions when the fields are accessed. This function will take in the table and field to check, the ID of the user, the current status of the property, and the property to check. We check the **Session** table to determine how we have logged into the database and then set appropriate filters on the **Field Level Security** table based on our parameters. If a record is found, we return the value in the table *and* the current status. This is so that we do not change the default value of the form to allow more access. For example, if a field is not editable on a form we do not want to allow our code to make the field editable. It would be fine if it was the other way around. If no value is found, we return the current value of the property.

Finally we need a test form. When the form opens we need to set the properties of the fields based on the **Field Level Security** table. We will be setting security for the **No.** field in the customer table so we add the appropriate code to the `OnOpenForm` trigger.

As this is a list form we also need to take into account the fact that hiding a column wont really hide a column. The user can still right-click on the column heading and show the field. We need to add code to the `OnFormat` trigger for the field to change the display value if the user is not allowed to see it.

 Note that the value can still be viewed using the **Zoom** feature. To change that refer to the *Hiding values in Zoom* recipe in this chapter.

There's more...

The concept of Field-level security is neither difficult to understand nor something you will need to write code for. The problem is that in order to do it properly we have to add code to _every_ form in the database. For this to work on a large scale, you would need to build your own parser to analyze NAV objects in their text form. The code would then be added to the correct areas and the objects imported into the system.

Adding so much of code to forms before they open can also cause some slowness. The **Customer Card**, for example, has 68 fields on it. That is, 136 checks (68 for Editable, 68 for Visible) that need to be made before the form can appear on the screen. Of course many of these fields will never have security set up for them, but you would need to determine that before making modifications. You would also need to keep a documentation of the fields whose security you wont be checking, as those fields could still be added to the permissions table, but never utilized.

See also

- ▸ Checking conditions using an IF statement
- ▸ Creating a table
- ▸ Using the Form Generation Wizard
- ▸ Changing text appearance
- ▸ Checking for user-assigned roles

Assigning menu suites based on company

Unfortunately, NAV only supports assigning one menu suite to a user. This recipe will show you how to set a user's menu suite at runtime based on the current company.

How to do it...

1. Design the **User Menu Level** table (2000000061).

2. Save the table as **User Menu Level by Company** with a new object ID.

3. Add the following field to the table:

Name	Type	Length
Company	Text	30

4. Set the following properties for the field:

Field Name	Property Name	Value
Company	TableRelation	Company
Company	NotBlank	Yes

5. Add the **Company** field as the first field under **Primary Key**.

6. Save and close the table.

7. Create a new codeunit from **Object Designer**.

8. Add a global function named LoadMenusuite.

9. Add the following local variables to the function:

Name	Type	Subtype
UserMenuLevelComp	Record	User Menu Level by Company
UserMenuLevel	Record	User Menu Level
Session	Record	Session

10. Add the following code to the function:

```
Session.SETRANGE("My Session", TRUE);
IF NOT Session.FINDFIRST THEN
  EXIT;

UserMenuLevelComp.SETRANGE(Company, COMPANYNAME);
UserMenuLevelComp.SETRANGE(ID, USERID);
IF Session."Login Type" = Session."Login Type"::Database THEN
  UserMenuLevelComp.SETRANGE("ID Type", UserMenuLevelComp."ID
                                        Type"::Database)
ELSE IF Session."Login Type" = Session."Login Type"::Windows THEN
  UserMenuLevelComp.SETRANGE("ID Type", UserMenuLevelComp."ID
                                        Type"::Windows);

IF UserMenuLevelComp.FINDFIRST THEN BEGIN
  UserMenuLevel.GET(UserMenuLevelComp.ID, UserMenuLevelComp."ID
                    Type", UserMenuLevelComp.Level);
  UserMenuLevel.DELETE;
END;

UserMenuLevelComp.CALCFIELDS(Object);
UserMenuLevel.TRANSFERFIELDS(UserMenuLevelComp);
UserMenuLevel.INSERT;
```

11. Add a global function named LoadMenusuite.

12. Add the following local variables to the function:

Name	Type	Subtype
UserMenuLevelComp	Record	User Menu Level by Company
UserMenuLevel	Record	User Menu Level
Session	Record	Session

13. Add the following code to the function:

```
Session.SETRANGE("My Session", TRUE);
IF NOT Session.FINDFIRST THEN
  EXIT;

UserMenuLevel.SETRANGE(ID, USERID);
IF Session."Login Type" = Session."Login Type"::Database THEN
  UserMenuLevel.SETRANGE("ID Type", UserMenuLevel."ID
                         Type"::Database)
ELSE IF Session."Login Type" = Session."Login Type"::Windows
                                                      THEN
  UserMenuLevel.SETRANGE("ID Type", UserMenuLevel.
                                "ID Type"::Windows);

IF UserMenuLevel.FINDFIRST THEN BEGIN
  IF UserMenuLevelComp.GET(COMPANYNAME, UserMenuLevel.ID,
        UserMenuLevel."ID Type", UserMenuLevel.Level) THEN BEGIN
    UserMenuLevel.CALCFIELDS(Object);
    UserMenuLevelComp.Object := UserMenuLevel.Object;
    UserMenuLevelComp.MODIFY;
  END ELSE BEGIN
    UserMenuLevel.CALCFIELDS(Object);
    UserMenuLevelComp.TRANSFERFIELDS(UserMenuLevel);
    UserMenuLevelComp.Company := COMPANYNAME;
    UserMenuLevelComp.INSERT;
  END;
END;
```

14. Save and close the codeunit.

15. Design **Codeunit 1, Application Management**.

Name	Type	Subtype
MenusuiteMgt	Codeunit	Menusuite Management (our custom codeunit)

16. Add the end of the `LoginStart` function add the following code:

    ```
    MenusuiteMgt.LoadMenusuite;
    ```

17. Add the end of the `LoginEnd` function add the following code:

    ```
    MenusuiteMgt.SaveMenusuite;
    ```

18. Save and close the codeunit.

How it works...

MenuSuites allow the user to navigate to different parts of the NAV system. Users can customize their menus by hiding links or adding shortcuts. These changes are stored as a **BLOB** field in the **User Menu Level** table. The problem is that each user is only allowed one entry in this table. This is also a system table used by the NAV executables so we want to avoid modifying it if possible. We may not be able to change *how* the system loads a menu suite, but we can definitely change *what* it loads.

First we need to create a wrapper for the **User Menu Level** table. We will call this table **User Menu Level by Company**. It is a duplicate of the **User Menu Level** table, but it also has a **Company** field which is part of the primary key. This will allow each user to have one entry per company.

Next we should create a codeunit to manage our new table. We will need a way to load a menu suite into the real **User Menu Level** table as well as a way to save the menusuite into the **User Menu Level by Company** table.

In order to load the correct record containing the menu suite, you need to determine the current session type (Database or Windows login) and set appropriate filters like the user ID and company. We then delete the record from the **User Menu Level** system table. In order to properly copy the **BLOB** field, we must do a `CALCFIELDS` on it before we use the `TRANSFERFIELDS` function. The copy is then saved to the system table, which changes what it loads.

Our `Save` function works the opposite way. We first find the menu suite in the system table. If a copy already exists we replace the **BLOB** field, but if there is no copy we insert a new record. Once this is done the load function will pick up on it.

Lastly, we need to tell NAV to use these functions. This involves modifying **Codeunit 1**, **Application Management**. This should be done with extreme caution. You do not want to introduce any errors into this codeunit as it could potentially cause you to be unable to log into the database. When someone changes companies or opens the database, the `LoginStart` or `LoginEnd` methods are called. It is in these methods that we tell NAV to load or save the menu suite.

See also

▶ Creating a table

Ending an idle session

Idle users utilize sessions in the system and also leave the application available to people who should not be using it. This recipe will show you how to create a small program to end these sessions.

How to do it...

1. Create a new codeunit from **Object Designer**.

2. Add the following global variable:

Name	Type	Subtype
Session	Record	Session

3. Add the following code to the OnRun trigger:

```
Session.SETFILTER("Idle Time", '>%1', 1800000);
Session.DELETEALL;
```

4. Save and close the codeunit.

How it works...

The session table contains a field called **Idle Time**. This field is a Duration data type which is similar to an integer. The value in the field represents the number of milliseconds that have elapsed since the user was active. In our example, we use the number 1,800,000 which is equal to 30 minutes. If we find any sessions that have been idle for longer than that, we delete them from the **Session** table which kills their connection to the database.

There's more...

This code is obviously more beneficial if it runs periodically throughout the day. You can schedule this code to run through several methods including the OnTimer property of forms, a custom NAS process, or through SQL Server. There is an example of the latter in *Chapter 11, SQL Server and Performance Tuning*.

Automatically adding users to NAV

Adding users to groups in Active Directory and Windows Groups is not enough to give access to NAV. Here we will show a way to automatically add a user to NAV Windows Logins when they are added to a specific group.

Getting ready

You will need to create the .NET project described in the *Checking Active Directory groups* section of the *Checking for user-assigned roles* recipe in this chapter.

How to do it...

1. Add the following functions to your .NET class:

```
public string RetrieveSID(string user, string domain)
{
  string connectionPrefix = "LDAP://" + domain;
  byte[] userSID;
  DirectorySearcher ADSearcher = new DirectorySearcher(new
                    DirectoryEntry(connectionPrefix));

  ADSearcher.Filter = @"(&(objectClass=user)(cn=" + user + "))";
  SearchResult result = ADSearcher.FindOne();

  if (result == null)
  {
    throw new NullReferenceException
      ("Could not find " + user + " in the " + domain + "
                                        domain");
  }

  DirectoryEntry ADUser = result.GetDirectoryEntry();
  ADUser = new DirectoryEntry(connectionPrefix + "/" +
        ADUser.Properties["distinguishedName"].Value);

  userSID = (byte[])ADUser.Properties["objectSid"][0];

  ADUser.Close();
  ADUser.Dispose();
  ADSearcher.Dispose();

  return (new SecurityIdentifier(userSID, 0).Value);
}
public void LoadADGroupMembers()
{
  LoadProperty("member");
}
```

2. Save and compile your class.

3. Create a new codeunit from **Object Designer**.

4. Add the following global variables to the codeunit:

Name	Type	Subtype	Length
ADGroupMembers	Automation	'NAV_ActiveDirectory'.NAV_ActiveDirectory	
IDtoSID	Automation	'NAV_ActiveDirectory'.NAV_ActiveDirectory	
WindowsLogin	Record	Windows Login	
GroupMember	Text		119
GroupMemberSID	Text		119

5. Add the following code to the `OnRun` trigger:

```
CREATE(ADGroupMembers);
CREATE(IDtoSID);
ADGroupMembers.SetConnectionString('NAV_ACCESS_GROUP',
  'LDAP://your_domain/CN=%1,OU=your_groups,DC=your_domain');
ADGroupMembers.LoadADGroupMembers();
WHILE (ADGroupMembers.MorePropertiesExist()) DO BEGIN
  GroupMember := ADGroupMembers.GetNextProperty();
  GroupMemberSID := IDtoSID.RetrieveSID(GroupMember,
                                        'corp.local');

  IF GroupMemberSID <> '' THEN BEGIN
    WindowsLogin.VALIDATE(SID, GroupMemberSID);
    IF WindowsLogin.INSERT THEN;
  END;
END;
```

6. Save and close the codeunit.

How it works...

For reference here is the `LoadProperty` function from a previous recipe.

```
private void LoadProperty(string property)
{
  DirectoryEntry ent = new DirectoryEntry(userdn);
  PropertyValueCollection ValueCollection = ent.Properties[property];
  IEnumerator en = ValueCollection.GetEnumerator();

  while (en.MoveNext())
  {
```

```
    if (en.Current != null)
    {
      if (!properties.Contains(en.Current.ToString()))
      {
        properties.Add(en.Current.ToString());
      }
    }
  }
  ent.Close();
  ent.Dispose();
}
```

In order to know which users to load into NAV, we need a way to determine which users are assigned to a specific group. For that we need to create an LDAP connection to the group in question. With this type of connection a property called "member" is exposed. We can load the members of the group into a ListArray so that we can iterate through them in NAV.

As we move through the list using the `MorePropertiesExist` and `GetNextProperty` function, we need to retrieve the SID for the group member. Remember, Windows Security in NAV is based completely off of the SID. As the group member could be stored anywhere in the Active Directory, we cannot create a hard coded LDAP string to get this information. Instead, we have to search the entire domain for them.

In order to search Active Directory we need to create a `DirectorySearcher` object. This is not unlike a `Record` variable in NAV. We apply filters for the user we are looking for and execute the `FindOne()` method. The `distinguishedName` property in Active Directory tells us exactly where to look to find the user. Essentially, the property is an LDAP string that points to the user. Using this connection we can get the user record and retrieve the `ObjectSid` for them. This SID is not in the correct format, however, and we need to convert it to a standard Security Identifier before returning the value.

From here, NAV can use the returned value to validate the SID and insert the record into the **Windows Login** table. Assuming NAV permissions are done through Active Directory groups and users are correctly assigned, there is no more setup to perform. The only exception would be if you are using SQL Server and the Enhanced Security Model which would require you to do a synchronization of the users.

There's more...

You can easily expand this recipe to remove users from the **Windows Login** table if they are removed from the Active Directory group or their accounts are disabled. The entirety of Active Directory is available for changes from NAV using .NET. You should be careful with your code, though. It can be very easy to accidentally delete something you did not mean to. If you do not catch the change before it replicates across all of the domain controllers or do not have a recent backup you are in serious trouble.

See also

- ▸ Adding roles through the User Setup table
- ▸ Creating and assigning a security role

Hiding values in Zoom

Users with the Zoom ability can see the values of fields that are hidden on forms. This recipe will show you how to hide these fields from the Zoom window.

How to do it...

1. Create a new table from **Object Designer**.

2. Add the following fields to the table:

Name	Type	Length
Field No.	Integer	
Field	Text	250
Value	Text	250
Table	Text	50
Table No.	Integer	

3. Save and close the table.
4. Create a new list form using the Form Generation Wizard.
5. Add the **Field** and **Value** fields from the table.
6. Set the following properties on the form:

Property Name	Value
Caption	Zoom
SourceTableTemporary	Yes
Editable	No
InsertAllowed	No
ModifyAllowed	No
DeleteAllowed	No
SourceTablePlacement	First

7. Add a global function named `LoadValues`.

8. The function should take in two parameters:

Name	Type
TableNo	Integer
RecRef	RecordRef

9. The `RecRef` parameter should be passed by reference.

10. Add the following local variables to the function:

Name	Type	Subtype
Field	Record	Field
FieldRef	FieldRef	

11. Add the following code to the `LoadValues` function:

```
Field.SETRANGE(TableNo, TableNo);
Field.SETRANGE(Enabled, TRUE);
IF Field.FINDSET THEN
  REPEAT
    FieldRef := RecRef.FIELD(Field."No.");

    Rec."Field No." := Field."No.";
    Rec.Field := Field.FieldName;
    Rec.Value := FORMAT(FieldRef.VALUE);
    Rec.Table := Field.TableName;
    Rec."Table No." := TableNo;
    Rec.INSERT;
  UNTIL Field.NEXT = 0;
```

12. Add the following local variable to the `OnFormat` trigger for the **Value** field:

Name	Type	Subtype
FieldLevelSecurity	Codeunit	Field Level Security (from previous recipe)

13. Add the following code to the `OnFormat` trigger of the **Value** field:

```
IF NOT FieldLevelSecurity.CheckSecurity(
  USERID, "Table No.", "Field No.", TRUE, 2) THEN
    Text := '***';
```

14. Save and close the form.

15. Create the test form as described in the *Field level security* recipe in this chapter.

16. Add a **Menu** button to the form with the `Caption` property set to **Custom Zoom**.

17. Add a menu item named **Custom Zoom** with a shortcut key of *Ctrl+F8*.

18. Add the following local variables to the OnPush trigger of the menu item:

Name	Type	Subtype
RecRef	RecRef	
CustomZoomForm	Form	Custom Zoom

19. Add the following code to the OnPush trigger for the menu item:

```
RecRef.GETTABLE(Rec);
CustomZoomForm.LoadValues(DATABASE::Customer, RecRef);
CustomZoomForm.RUNMODAL;
```

20. Save and close the form.

The folowing is an example of our **Custom Zoom** form run from our test form.

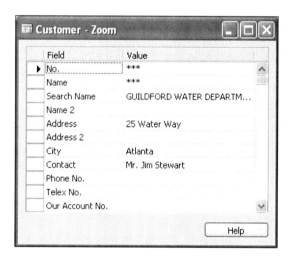

How it works...

There's no way to override what NAV chooses to display in the **Zoom** window. With some work, though, we can display another window in its place. First we need a table to store our Zoom data. We need to know the field number and the name, table number and name, and the **Value** of the field.

We also need a form to display our data. We want this form to look and function exactly like the **Zoom** form in base NAV. The form should only be used to display data (Editable = No, insertion, modification, and deletion are not allowed). Also, the form should focus on the first record when it loads (SourceTablePlacement = Yes). Finally we do not need this data to actually be stored in the database (SourceTableTemporary = Yes).

This form needs to know what data to display. As there is never any data in the table, we must tell it how to load this data. In order to do this we loop through all of the enabled fields for the table specified. We then create a field reference to that field based on the record reference, we pass to the `LoadData` function. From there we create a **Custom Zoom** record and insert into the temporary table on which our form works.

At this point, we have only duplicated the **Zoom** functionality. We now want to integrate that functionality with the **Field Level Security** table we developed in a previous recipe. That involves changing the display value using the `OnFormat` trigger.

Now we have to override the base Zoom functionality on the form. Adding a menu button with the same shortcut as Zoom will take care of that. We add our own code to the `OnPush` trigger of that **Custom Zoom** menu item that loads the values for the selected record and displays the form.

There's more...

Like other recipes in this chapter, this recipe is useful only under specific circumstances such as displaying social security numbers or credit card numbers. In order to implement it properly it would need to be added to every form in the system and the Zoom permission would need to be taken away from all users. If it is left assigned to a user they can still get to the base NAV feature by using the menu in the NAV Client.

The **Custom Zoom** menu button would also be resized so that it is nearly invisible on the screen. Better yet, it could be hidden behind another control on the form. This allows for a seamless integration of the code and the user will not see any change to the forms they have been using, but it is not so great for new developers trying to figure out what is going on with the form.

See also

- ▶ Referencing dynamic tables and fields
- ▶ Creating a table
- ▶ Using the Form Generation Wizard
- ▶ Changing text appearance
- ▶ Designing a form based on a temporary table
- ▶ Field-level security

8
Leveraging Microsoft Office

In this chapter, we will cover:

- ► Using the style sheet tool
- ► Sending data to Microsoft Word
- ► Sending an e-mail from NAV through Outlook
- ► Exporting data using the Excel buffer
- ► Creating a data connection from Excel to NAV
- ► Creating an InfoPath form with NAV data
- ► Instant messaging using Office Communicator
- ► Creating charts with Visio

Introduction

Microsoft Office is a related suite of applications. Just as the Dynamics platform encompasses multiple products, so does the Office product line. The three most popular programs are Word, Excel, and Outlook which serve as a word processor, spreadsheet application, and e-mail manager respectively. NAV does not offer the same functionality that these applications provide and integrating with them can open many new possibilities for the users of the software.

Office also comes with other, lesser known, programs that are used by many companies. We will also examine three of such products. The first is **InfoPath** which is used to generate XML-based forms for users to enter and view data. We will learn about **Office Communicator**, an enterprise instant messaging and meeting utility. Finally, we will take a look at Visio which is used for diagrams and flowcharts. With all of these products working together as one, you will easily be able to see how to get your data to the people who need it.

Using the style sheet tool

NAV has built-in functionality to send data to outside applications like Word and Excel. They allow you to view data on a style sheet which can make it look much better than just a black-and-white report. This recipe will show you how to create these style sheets using a tool within NAV.

Getting ready

Download and install the Style Sheet Tool version 2.0 (links can be found in the *There's More* section). Run the Style Sheet setup and form and if you are using the RTC, fill out the **RoleTailored Client** tab.

How to do it...

1. Run the **Style Sheet Card** form from **Object Designer**.

2. Create a new record and fill in these fields with the following values:

Field	Value
Code	CUSTLIST
Description	Customer List Style Sheet
Form No.	22
Page No.	22

3. Add a line with the following values:

Field	Value
Table No.	18
Base Record	Yes
Multiple Lines	Yes

4. Click on the **Style Sheet** button, then **Select Fields**.

5. Add lines with the following values:

Field No.	Field Name	Include Caption	Currency
1	No.	Yes	No
2	Name	Yes	No
58	Balance	Yes	Yes

6. Close the **Select Fields** window. You should now have a form that looks like the following screenshot:

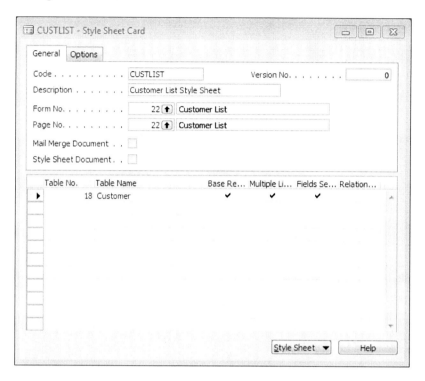

7. Click on **Style Sheet | Create Mail Merge**.

8. In the Microsoft Word window that opens, click on the **Mailings** menu.

9. Click **Insert Merge Field**.

10. Add a `MULTILINE_BEGIN_<Item>` and a `MULTILINE_END_<Item>` to the document.

11. In between, add a table with the following captions and field values. The resulting document should look like this:

«MULTILINE_BEGIN_Customer»		
«CAPTION_Customer_No»	«CAPTION_Customer_Name»	«CAPTION_Customer_Balance»
«Customer_No»	«Customer_Name»	«Customer_Balance»
«MULTILINE_END_Customer»		

12. Close the document and click on **Yes** to each of the messages that are presented.

13. The document will be converted to a style sheet and saved in the database.

How it works...

1. Note that this recipe is not compatible with the RoleTailored client. The Classic client calls the code found in **Codeunit 403, Application Launch Management**, but the RTC does not. You can still export to Word and Excel, but not with a custom style sheet.

2. With the **Customer List** form open, click on the **Send Options** button from the NAV toolbar.

3. You will be presented with a send options window.

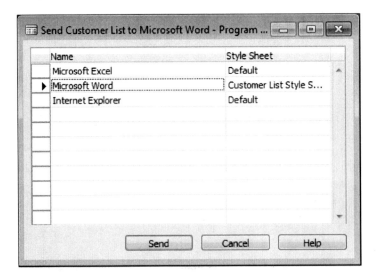

4. Notice that the style sheet has automatically changed from default to the one we just created. You could still switch back to the default if you so desired.

5. Click the **Send** button and the **Customer List** will be loaded into a Word Document.

There's more...

The style sheet tool can be used to generate a lot more complex documents than the one is this example. For a complete walkthrough of what can be done you can download the Style Sheet Tool User Guide, along with the tool itself, from one of the following addresses:

Customers:

```
https://mbs.microsoft.com/customersource/downloads/servicepacks/
navstylesheettool.htm?printpage=false&stext=nav%20style%20sheet%20
tool
```

Partners:

```
https://mbs.microsoft.com/partnersource/deployment/resources/
supplements/navstylesheettool.htm?printpage=false&stext=nav%20
style%20sheet%20tool
```

See also

▶ Sending data to Microsoft Word

Sending data to Microsoft Word

Creating attractive Word documents from NAV is a challenging task. This recipe will not show you how to create a document that looks exactly like your report from NAV, but it will introduce you to the basics of sending data to the application.

Getting ready

Microsoft Word must be installed on the client system.

How to do it...

1. Create a new codeunit from **Object Designer**.

2. Add the following global variables:

Name	Type	Subtype	Length
WordApp	Automation	'Microsoft Word 12.0 Object Library'.Application	
WordDoc	Automation	'Microsoft Word 12.0 Object Library'.Document	
WordAppSelection	Automation	'Microsoft Word 12.0 Object Library'.Selection	
WordFont	Automation	'Microsoft Word 12.0 Object Library'.Font	
CompanyInformation	Record	Company Information	
ExportedPicture	Text		250
NewLine	Char		

3. Save an uncompiled version of the codeunit and close it.

4. Export the codeunit to a text file.

5. Open the file and remove all of the events that were added by the Automation variables.

6. Save and close the text file.

7. Import the text file into NAV and compile the object.

8. Add the following code to the OnRun trigger:

```
NewLine := 13;
ExportedPicture := ENVIRON('TEMP') +
                   '\CompanyInformationPicture.bmp';

CompanyInformation.GET;
CompanyInformation.CALCFIELDS(Picture);
CompanyInformation.Picture.EXPORT(ExportedPicture);

CREATE(WordApp);

WordDoc := WordApp.Documents.Add;
WordDoc.Activate;

WordAppSelection := WordApp.Selection;
```

```
WordDoc.Shapes.AddPicture(ExportedPicture);

WordFont := WordAppSelection.Font;
WordFont.Size(40);
WordFont.Name('Arial');
WordAppSelection.TypeText('Big Text' + FORMAT(NewLine));

WordFont.Size(20);
WordFont.Name('Courier New');
WordAppSelection.TypeText('Medium Text' + FORMAT(NewLine));

WordFont.Size(10);
WordFont.Name('Times New Roman');
WordAppSelection.TypeText('Small Text' + FORMAT(NewLine));

WordApp.Visible := TRUE;
```

9. Save and close the codeunit.

How it works...

This recipe requires an odd step in which you have to manipulate the object from a text file and not within **Object Designer**. When you add Automation variables to your object, regardless of whether or not you set the `WithEvents` property, the events are added to the code. The `WithEvents` property just lets you see them when you are coding.

Unfortunately, NAV has a limit on just how long these event names can be and many of them are similarly named. When they are added to NAV, the application truncates the end of the event name which can result in duplicate events being defined. This throws an error when you compile the object. If you want to use these events in your NAV code you will have to write your own .NET wrapper class with names that are not as long.

Now we can move to the actual code. To start, we export the logo from **Company Information**. Ideally, we would place this on a shared drive, or use an image that is not stored in NAV, because the `ENVIRON` command is no longer supported in the RTC.

Next we create an instance of the Microsoft Word application. We then create a new blank document and activate it. Using the `Shape.AddPicture` method from the Word Document object we can insert the logo that we exported from **Company Information**.

We can also manipulate text just as we would if we were using the application manually. By changing the font size and name, the `TypeText` method will alter the way it displays the text on the screen. If you were trying to duplicate a NAV report you could set the font name to Helvetica and the font size to seven, for example.

There's more...

For detailed reading on the Microsoft Word Object Model you can visit the following MSDN site:

```
http://msdn.microsoft.com/en-us/library/kw65a0we%28VS.80%29.aspx
```

See also

▶ Using the style sheet tool

Sending an e-mail from NAV through Outlook

Dynamics NAV has code that will integrate with your Outlook client to send an e-mail. This recipe will show you how to leverage that code.

Getting ready

You must have Outlook, or some other e-mail client, installed on the machine.

How to do it...

1. Create a new codeunit from **Object Designer**.

2. Add the following global variables:

Name	Type	Subtype
SMTPMailSetup	Record	SMTP Mail Setup
SMTPMail	Record	SMTP Mail
Mail	Record	Mail
Selection	Integer	

3. Add the following code to the OnRun trigger of your codeunit:

    ```
    Selection := STRMENU('SMTP,Standard');

    IF Selection = 1 THEN BEGIN
      IF SMTPMailSetup.GET THEN BEGIN
        SMTPMail.CreateMessage('Matt Traxinger',
            'YourE-mail@microsoft.com', 'Someone@somewhere.com',
            'E-mail Subject', 'E-mail Body', FALSE);
        SMTPMail.Send;
      END;
    ```

```
END ELSE BEGIN
  Mail.NewMessage('Navision.Programmer@gmail.com',
      '','E-mail Subject','E-mail Body','',TRUE);
END;
```

4. Save and close the codeunit.

How it works...

When you run the codeunit you will be presented with the option to send the e-mail through **SMTP (Simple Mail Transfer Protocol)** or Outlook.

SMTP is the preferred way of sending e-mail with NAV. The code behind this functionality, and more specifically the `CreateMessage` function, is located in **Codeunit 400**, **SMTP Mail**. This function uses the `'Microsoft Navision Mail'.SmtpMessage` Automation to create a message for us based on the input parameters. These parameters are `Sender Name`, `Sender E-mail Address`, `Recipient E-mail Addresses`, `Subject`, `Body`, and `HTML Formatted`. We must manually call the `Send` function in the Codeunit if we want to actually send the message.

As a backup, you can use the `NewMessage` from **Codeunit 397**, **Mail**. This function also takes in six parameters, but they are not the same as the SMTP `CreateMessage` function. These inputs are `Recipient E-mail`, `CC E-mail`, `Subject`, `Body`, `Attachment Filename`, and `Open Dialog`. This function will automatically try to send the e-mail for you if you set the `Open Dialog` parameter to **FALSE**.

There's more...

For more details on the Microsoft Outlook object model you can visit the following MSDN site:

```
http://msdn.microsoft.com/en-us/library/ms268893%28VS.80%29.aspx
```

Sending an HTML formatted e-mail

Many CRM applications or other programs send e-mails out automatically. Anything that is customer-facing should look professional. That is not to say that simple text e-mails are bad, just that HTML formatted e-mails are more dynamic and more likely to get the customer's attention.

Here is some sample code which can be used to send an HTML formatted e-mail:

```
IF SMTPMailSetup.GET THEN BEGIN
  SMTPMail.CreateMessage('Matt Traxinger',
          YourE-mail@YourCompany.com', 'Someone@Somewhere.com',
          'E-mail Subject', '', TRUE);
  SMTPMail.AppendBody('<b><h2>Thank You!</h2></b><br><br>');
  SMTPMail.AppendBody('Your message has been received,<br><br>');
  SMTPMail.AppendBody('Administrator');
  SMTPMail.Send;
END;
```

By passing a value of TRUE as the last parameter to the CreateMessage function, we tell the system to format the e-mail for HTML. We can then use the AppendBody function to add lines to our message. These could be read from an external file, stored in NAV, or hard coded as we have done here.

Exporting data using the Excel buffer

NAV contains a wrapper object that allows you to export data to Microsoft Excel. This recipe will show you how to use it in its most common form—exporting a report to Excel.

Getting ready

Microsoft Excel must be installed on the client machine.

How to do it...

1. Create a new report based on the **Customer** table using the **Report Generation Wizard**.

2. Add the **No.**, **Name**, and **Balance** fields.

3. Add the following global variables:

Name	Type	Subtype
ExcelBuf	Record	Excel Buffer
PrintToExcel	Boolean	

4. The ExcelBuf variable should be **Temporary**.

5. Add a function named MakeExcelInfo.

6. Add the following code the function:

```
ExcelBuf.SetUseInfoSheed;
ExcelBuf.AddInfoColumn(FORMAT('Company Name'),
                              FALSE,'',TRUE,FALSE,FALSE,'');
ExcelBuf.AddInfoColumn(COMPANYNAME,FALSE,'',FALSE,FALSE,
                                                FALSE,'');
ExcelBuf.NewRow;
ExcelBuf.AddInfoColumn(FORMAT('Report Name'),
                              FALSE,'',TRUE,FALSE,FALSE,'');
ExcelBuf.AddInfoColumn(FORMAT('Print Report to Excel'),
                              FALSE,'',FALSE,FALSE,FALSE,'');
ExcelBuf.NewRow;
ExcelBuf.AddInfoColumn(FORMAT('Report No.'),
                              FALSE,'',TRUE,FALSE,FALSE,'');
ExcelBuf.AddInfoColumn(REPORT::"Print Report to Excel",
                              FALSE,'',FALSE,FALSE,FALSE,'');
ExcelBuf.NewRow;
ExcelBuf.AddInfoColumn(FORMAT('User Id'),
                                FALSE,'',TRUE,FALSE,FALSE,'');
ExcelBuf.AddInfoColumn(USERID,FALSE,'',FALSE,FALSE,FALSE,'');
ExcelBuf.NewRow;
ExcelBuf.AddInfoColumn(FORMAT('Date / Time'),
                                FALSE,'',TRUE,FALSE,FALSE,'');
ExcelBuf.AddInfoColumn(TODAY,FALSE,'',FALSE,FALSE,FALSE,'');
ExcelBuf.AddInfoColumn(TIME,FALSE,'',FALSE,FALSE,FALSE,'');
ExcelBuf.NewRow;
ExcelBuf.AddInfoColumn(FORMAT('Filters'),FALSE,'',
                                  TRUE,FALSE,FALSE,'');
ExcelBuf.AddInfoColumn(Customer.GETFILTERS,FALSE,'',
                                  FALSE,FALSE,FALSE,'');
ExcelBuf.ClearNewRow;
MakeExcelDataHeader;
```

7. Add a function called `MakeExcelDataHeader`.

8. Add the following code to the function:

```
ExcelBuf.NewRow;
ExcelBuf.AddColumn(Customer.FIELDCAPTION("No."),FALSE,'',
                                  TRUE,FALSE,TRUE,'@');
ExcelBuf.AddColumn(Customer.FIELDCAPTION(Name),FALSE,'',
                                  TRUE,FALSE,TRUE,'');
ExcelBuf.AddColumn(Customer.FIELDCAPTION(Balance),FALSE,
                                  '',TRUE,FALSE,TRUE,'');
```

9. Add a function called `MakeExcelDataBody`.

10. Add the following code to the function:

```
ExcelBuf.NewRow;
ExcelBuf.AddColumn(Customer."No.",FALSE,'',FALSE,
                                    FALSE,FALSE,'');
ExcelBuf.AddColumn(Customer.Name,FALSE,'',FALSE,
                                    FALSE,FALSE,'');
ExcelBuf.AddColumn(Customer.Balance,FALSE,'',FALSE,
                                    FALSE,FALSE,'#,##0');
```

11. Add a function called `CreateExcelBook`.

12. Add the following code to the function:

```
ExcelBuf.CreateBook;
ExcelBuf.CreateSheet('Data','',COMPANYNAME,USERID);
ExcelBuf.GiveUserControl;
ERROR('');
```

13. Add the following code to the `OnPreDataItem` trigger for the customer data item:

```
IF PrintToExcel THEN
  MakeExcelInfo;
```

14. Add the following code to the `OnAfterGetRecord` trigger for the customer data item:

```
IF PrintToExcel THEN
  MakeExcelDataBody;
```

15. Add the following code to the `OnPostReport` trigger:

```
IF PrintToExcel THEN
  CreateExcelbook;
```

16. Add a checkbox control and label to the **Request** form of the report.

17. Set the following properties on the control:

Property	Value
SourceExpr	PrintToExcel
Caption	"Print to Excel"

18. Save and close the report.

How it works...

Printing a report to Excel requires two variables. The first is a record variable that refers to the Excel Buffer table. This table contains several functions that we will use throughout our report to communicate with the Excel program. The second is Boolean, named `PrintToExcel`. There may be instances when we just want to see the report in its normal display so we need a flag to tell the report what to do.

We will use four functions in this report and go through each of them one-by-one. The first function is named `MakeExcelInfo` and contains a series of calls to the `AddInfoColumn` and `NewRow` functions in the Excel Buffer table. This function replicates what you see in the **Header** section of most reports, that is the name of the report, the date and time when it was created, whom was it created by, and any filters that may have been used.

The `AddInfoColumn` parameters deal with formatting of the text that will be entered in the cell. In order, the parameters are: `Value`, `IsFormula`, `CommentText`, `IsBold`, `IsItalics`, `IsUnderline`, and `NumFormat`.

At the end of our function, we make a call to `MakeExcelDataHeader`, which adds our column headings to the first row of a new sheet in the Excel Workbook.

There is a similar function, `MakeExcelDataBody`, which adds our actual data to the sheet.

Finally, we have a function called `CreateExcelBook`, which loads the data from the Excel Buffer and displays the Excel worksheet.

Now that we have these functions, we need to use them in our report. When thinking about what each one does and how the report flows from start to finish, it becomes obvious when we should use them. The header information about the report is displayed in a **Header** section for the **Customer** record, so we can use the `MakeExcelInfo` function in the `OnPreDataItem` trigger. We retrieve data from the database in the `OnAfterGetRecord` trigger, so here is where we should add the data to the Excel file. Lastly, we don't want to view the Excel file until the report is completely generated, so we place the call to the `CreateExcelBook` function in the `OnPostReport` trigger.

When you run the report and print to Excel, you should see a document like the one shown in the following screenshot:

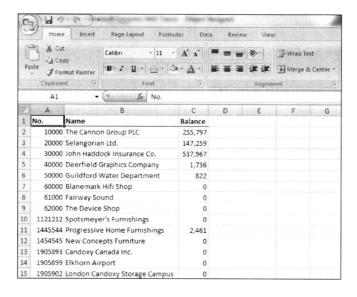

There's more...

Although the Excel Buffer will provide for most of your needs, you can also write your own Excel Automations.

 For more information on the Microsoft Excel Object Model visit the following MSDN site:

`http://msdn.microsoft.com/en-us/library/`
`wss56bz7%28VS.80%29.aspx`

See also

▶ Using temporary tables to store data

▶ Using the report generation wizard

▶ Creating a data connection from Excel to NAV

Creating a data connection from Excel to NAV

Instead of copying and pasting data from NAV into Excel, you can easily create an external connection to the NAV database.

Getting ready

Microsoft Excel must be installed on the client machine.

How to do it...

1. In Microsoft Excel select the **Data** tab.

2. From the **Get External Data** section of the menu select **From Other Sources** | **From SQL Server**.

3. In the data connection wizard, enter the name of the SQL Server and your **Log on credentials**.

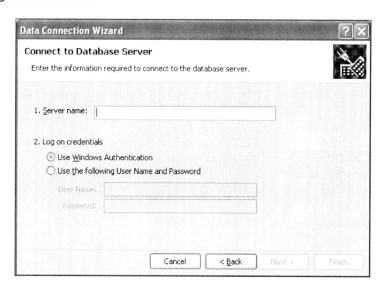

4. Click **Next**.

5. In the next window select the database and table you wish to view in Excel.

6. Click **Finish**.

7. It may take a moment for the data to load into the workbook.

How it works...

Microsoft Excel maintains an active connection to the database when you setup an external data connection. When you save and close a file with a connection in it the data is automatically reloaded the next time you open the document. This eliminates the need to log in to NAV to copy and paste data. For users that only need this basic level of access to the data a company can save thousands of dollars by licensing users for this type of connection to the database, known as DCO or Dynamics Client for Office.

There's more...

The following MSDN article provides more information about managing your connections in Microsoft Excel:

`http://msdn.microsoft.com/en-us/library/bb545041%28office.11%29.aspx`

See also

> ▸ Exporting data using the Excel Buffer

Creating an InfoPath form with NAV data

Microsoft InfoPath allows you to create forms to view and enter data outside of the NAV application. There is no programming involved, other than having an existing NAV Page exposed as a web service.

Getting ready

Microsoft InfoPath must be installed on the client machine.

How to do it...

1. Create a web service as described in the *Creating a web service recipe* in *Chapter 10, Integration*.
2. From the **Getting Started** window in InfoPath, select **Design a Form Template**.
3. Select **Web Service** as the source that the form should be based on.

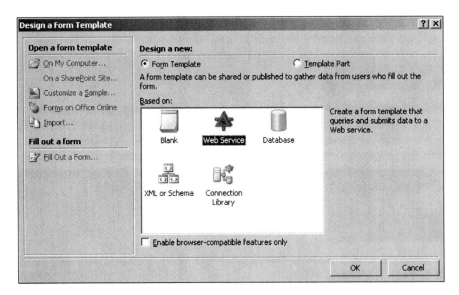

4. Click **OK**.
5. Select **Receive Data**.

6. From the **Dynamics NAV Web Server** go to the following address and find the web service: `http://localhost:7047/DynamicsNAV/WS/services`

7. In this case we will be using `http://localhost:7047/DynamicsNAV/WS/Page/CustomerExample`, but this could be different on your system.

8. Enter this address in the **Data Connection Wizard** window.

9. Click **Next**.

10. Select **Read Multiple**.

11. Click **Next** and finally **Finish**.

12. You should now have a **Design Template** that looks like the following screenshot:

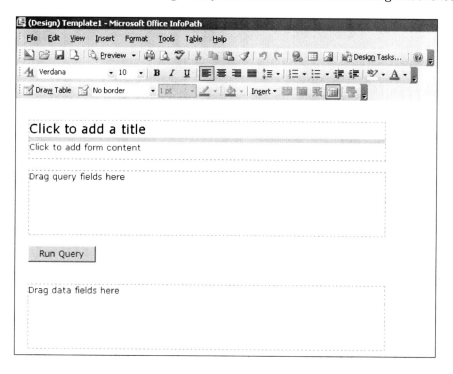

13. Change the title to **Customer List**.

14. From the **queryFields** node in the data source tree view on the right-hand side of the screen, drag the **Field** node into the **Drag query fields here** box on the form.

15. Select **Drop Down List Box**.

16. Drag the **Criteria** and **Set Size** nodes to the same area on the form.

17. Click on the box labeled **Drag data fields here**.

18. From the menu, select **Insert | Repeating Table**.

19. Drill down in the **Data Fields** node and select `CustomerExample`.

20. Click **Next**.

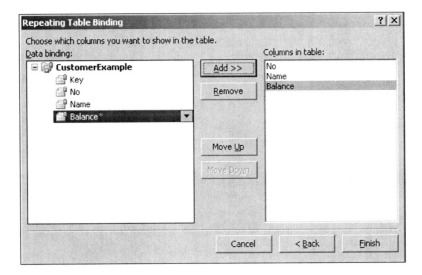

21. Add the **No.**, **Name**, and **Balance** fields.

22. Click **Finish**.

23. Your completed InfoPath form should look like the following screenshot:

How it works...

To view the form click **Preview** in the InfoPath toolbar. Just like NAV, you can select your filter fields, but you must select **Run Query** in order to retrieve the data. The data will be presented in a list format at the bottom of the page.

There's more...

The most common use of InfoPath forms is to add them to a Forms Library in SharePoint. Although this example is used only for viewing data, you can also create forms to enter and modify data in NAV. The licensing costs for these type of users are significantly less than those for users of the Classic and RoleTailored clients; depending on the type of work these users will perform, however, the development costs to create the forms may outweigh the licensing costs.

See also

- ▸ Displaying NAV Data in SharePoint
- ▸ Consuming web services

Instant messaging using Office Communicator

Office Communicator is an instant messenger client for businesses, similar to AOL Instant Messenger or MSN Messenger. This recipe will show you how to integrate with Office Communicator and send a message to someone through NAV.

Getting ready

Office Communicator must be installed and configured on the client machine.

How to do it...

1. Create a new C# Class Library project from Visual Studio.

2. Add the following code to the project:

```
using System;

using CommunicatorAPI;
using System.Threading;
using System.Runtime.InteropServices;

namespace NAVCommunicator
```

```csharp
{
  [ClassInterface(ClassInterfaceType.AutoDual)]
  [ProgId("NAVCommunicator")]
  [ComVisible(true)]
  public class NAVCommunicator
  {
    CommunicatorAPI.MessengerClass communicator;
    bool connected = false;

    public NAVCommunicator()
    {
      connected = false;
    }

    public bool IsConnected()
    {
      return connected;
    }

    public void Signin()
    {
      if (connected)
        return;

      if (communicator == null)
      {
        communicator = new
                       CommunicatorAPI.MessengerClass();
        communicator.OnSignin += new
                 DMessengerEvents_OnSigninEventHandler(
                                 communicator_OnSignin);
      }
      communicator.AutoSignin();
    }

    void communicator_OnSignin(int hr)
    {
      if (hr != 0)
      {
        throw new Exception("Unable to sign in!");
      }

      connected = true;
    }

    public void SendIM(string sendTo)
    {
      object[] sipUris = new object[1];
      sipUris[0] = sendTo;

      long windowHandle;
      CommunicatorAPI.IMessengerAdvanced msgrAdv =
              communicator as CommunicatorAPI.IMessengerAdvanced;
```

```
    if (msgrAdv != null)
    {
      try
      {
        object obj = msgrAdv.StartConversation(
                CONVERSATION_TYPE.CONVERSATION_TYPE_IM,
                sipUris,null,"Testing","1",null);
        windowHandle = long.Parse(obj.ToString());
      }
      catch (Exception ex)
      {
        throw new Exception(
                "Unable to launch Communicator Window!");
      }
    }
  }
}
```

3. Save, compile, and close the project.

4. Create a new form using the Form Generation Wizard based on the User Setup table.

5. Add the **User ID** and **E-Mail** fields to the form.

6. Add a button to the form and set the following properties:

Property	Value
Caption	Send IM
HorzGlue	Right
VertGlue	Bottom

7. Your form should look like the one shown in the following screenshot:

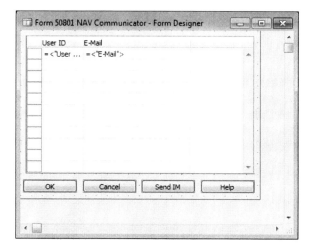

8. Add the following local variables to the OnPush trigger for the new button:

Name	Type	Subtype
NAVCommunicator	Automation	'NAVCommunicator'.NAVCommunicator
I	Integer	

9. Add the following code to the OnPush trigger:

```
IF ISCLEAR(NAVCommunicator) THEN
    CREATE(NAVCommunicator);

NAVCommunicator.Signin();
i := 0;
WHILE( (i < 10) AND (NOT NAVCommunicator.IsConnected()) )
                                                    DO BEGIN
    i+=1;
    SLEEP(1000);
END;
NAVCommunicator.SendIM("E-Mail");
```

10. Save and close the form.

How it works...

Our .NET Class is composed of three main functions. The first is named Signin, and as you might guess, handles the authentication part between our client and Office Communicator. It does so by calling the AutoSignin method in the Communicator automation. We also add a delegate to our main Communicator variable which will be triggered every time we sign in. This method, communicator_OnSignin, sets our connected variable when we successfully connect to the server.

Once we know that we are connected, we can call our third function, SendIM. This function relies on a method called StartConversation to start the instant message (although it can also start phone calls, meetings, and other conversation types).

So how can this be used in NAV? Well, Communicator works off of an e-mail address, which is frequently stored in the User Setup table. As long as we can establish a link between a piece of data, like Salesperson Code, we can determine whom to send the message to. Our SendIM function creates an instance of our .NET Class, waits to make sure we connect successfully, and opens a message window with the selected user as shown in the following screenshot:

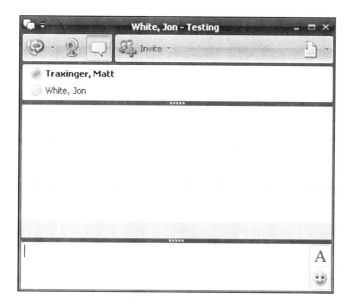

There's more...

For more information on the Office Communicator Object Model you can visit the following MSDN site:

`http://msdn.microsoft.com/en-us/library/bb758727.aspx`

See also

▸   Using the Form Generation Wizard

▸   Writing your own automation using C#

Creating charts with Visio

Microsoft Visio is a product used for creating charts and diagrams. Here we will show an example of how to create a simple flowchart with two connected shapes.

Getting ready

Microsoft Visio must be installed on the client machine.

 You may also need to download the Microsoft Office Interop Assemblies from Microsoft here:

```
http://www.microsoft.com/downloads/details.
aspx?FamilyID=59daebaa-bed4-4282-a28c-
b864d8bfa513&displaylang=en
```

How to do it...

1. Create a new C# Class Library project in Visual Studio.
2. Add the following code to the project:

```csharp
using System;
using System.Collections.Generic;

using System.Runtime.InteropServices;

using Microsoft.Office.Interop.Visio;

namespace VisioSample
{
  [ClassInterface(ClassInterfaceType.AutoDual)]
  [ProgId("VisioNAV")]
  [ComVisible(true)]
  public class VisioNAV
  {
    Application VisioApp;
    Documents VisioDocs;
    Document visioStencil;
    List<Shape> shapes;

    public VisioNAV()
    {
      try
      {
        shapes = new List<Shape>();
        VisioApp = new Application();
        VisioDocs = VisioApp.Documents;
      }
      catch (Exception e)
      {
        throw new Exception("Unable to open Visio!");
      }
    }

    public void CreateFile()
```

```
  {
    try
    {
      VisioApp.Documents.Add("");
    }
    catch (Exception e)
    {
      throw new Exception("Unable to create Visio file!");
    }
  }

public void OpenTemplate(String templateName)
{
    visioStencil = VisioDocs.OpenEx(templateName,
                    (short) VisOpenSaveArgs.visOpenDocked);
}

public void AddTable(float x, float y, String text)
{
    Page visioPage = VisioApp.ActivePage;
    Master visioMaster =
                  visioStencil.Masters.get_ItemU(@"Class");
    Shape visioShape = visioPage.Drop(visioMaster, x, y);
    visioShape.Text = @text;

    shapes.Add(visioShape);
}

public void ConnectShapes(int s1, int s2)
{
    Page visioPage = VisioApp.ActivePage;
    Master visioMaster =
                    visioStencil.Masters.get_ItemU(@"Link");
    Shape connector = visioPage.Drop(visioMaster, 1f, 1f);
    Shape shape1 = shapes[s1];
    Shape shape2 = shapes[s2];

    Cell beginXCell = connector.get_CellsSRC(
          (short)VisSectionIndices.visSectionObject,
          (short)VisRowIndices.visRowXForm1D,
          (short)VisCellIndices.vis1DBeginX);

    beginXCell.GlueTo(shape1.get_CellsSRC(
          (short)VisSectionIndices.visSectionObject,
          (short)VisRowIndices.visRowXFormOut,
          (short)VisCellIndices.visXFormPinX));

    Cell endXCell = connector.get_CellsSRC(
          (short)VisSectionIndices.visSectionObject,
          (short)VisRowIndices.visRowXForm1D,
          (short)VisCellIndices.vis1DEndX);
```

```
          endXCell.GlueTo(shape2.get_CellsSRC(
                  (short)VisSectionIndices.visSectionObject,
                  (short)VisRowIndices.visRowXFormOut,
                  (short)VisCellIndices.visXFormPinX));
      }

      public void Zoom(double zoomFactor)
      {
          VisioApp.ActiveWindow.Zoom = zoomFactor;
      }
    }
}
```

3. Save, compile, and close the project.

4. Create a new codeunit from **Object Designer**.

5. Add the following global variable:

Name	Type	Subtype
VisioNAV	Automation	'VisioNAV'.VisioNAV

6. Add the following code to the `OnRun` trigger:

```
IF ISCLEAR(VisioNAV) THEN
  CREATE(VisioNAV);

VisioNAV.CreateFile();
VisioNAV.OpenTemplate('UML Static Structure.vss');
VisioNAV.AddTable(4.25, 5.5, 'G/L Entry');
VisioNAV.AddTable(2.25, 5.5, 'G/L Register');
VisioNAV.ConnectShapes(0, 1);
VisioNAV.Zoom(1.5);
```

7. Save and close the codeunit.

How it works...

Our C# project has several important functions that we will go through. The first is the `CreateFile` method. This adds a blank document to the `VisioApp` variable, which was instantiated in the constructor. If for some reason the system is unable to create a file, it will display an error message for the user.

Next is the `OpenTemplate` function. This opens the available shapes for a given template. When viewing a Visio document you will find them on the left-hand side of the application.

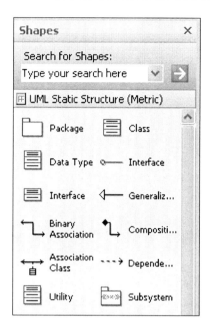

The `AddTable` function could just have easily been called `AddShape` and accepted a third parameter to tell Visio which shape it should add. In this case, we add a **Class** shape to our diagram. By retrieving the active page from the document, and the current template or stencil that is open on that page, we can drop a selected shape into the document at a specified position.

Our final C# function, `ConnectShapes`, places a link or connector between two shapes on the page. A connector is just a specialized shape so we add it to the page the same way. We can then set the start and end points for the link and attach it to the desired shapes.

In NAV we use each of the functions in the order described. First we create a new Visio document and open the UML Static Structure template. We then add two tables to the open document and connect them. Finally, we zoom in on the document so you have a better idea of what we have actually done. The following output is shown.

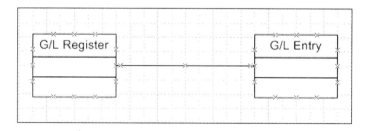

There's more...

To learn more about the Microsoft Visio Object Model you can visit the following MSDN site:

`http://msdn.microsoft.com/en-us/library/cc160740.aspx`

See also

▶   Using code coverage

▶   Using Client Monitor to diagnose problems

9
OS Interaction

In this chapter, we will cover:

- ▸ Using `HYPERLINK` to open external files
- ▸ Working with environment variables
- ▸ Using `SHELL` to run external applications
- ▸ Browsing for a file
- ▸ Browsing for a folder
- ▸ Checking file and folder access permissions
- ▸ Querying the registry
- ▸ Zipping folders and files within NAV

Introduction

If you have programmed with Windows or used a Windows-based operating system for any length of time you will see that it is really an all-encompassing OS. Unlike with other types of software development, we don't need to interact with device drivers or create three dimensional graphics for our users. Most of what we need to do involves integrating with the file system; that is searching for files or folders and running external applications.

Occasionally, we may need to go a little deeper than that. There may be instances where we need to check the user's environment, query the registry, or check for specific administrator permissions. These can all be performed within NAV, although many require a little outside help from a built-in or custom automation control.

As Windows is such a large piece of software, it already contains ways for us to do these things. As a result, the recipes in this chapter are not very lengthy or complicated, but that does not make them any less useful. They explore the basics of what you can do with the OS and it is up to you to decide when and how to make the best use of them.

 It is important to note that many of these recipes will require additional coding to make them work with the RoleTailored client. This is because the code is actually executing on a server, not your own computer as it does with the Classic client.

Using HYPERLINK to open external files

Many times you may need to open files external to the NAV program. NAV has a built-in function that interacts with the file system to open the file with the appropriate application.

How to do it...

1. Create a new codeunit from **Object Designer**.

2. Add the following global variable:

Name	Type
Selection	Integer

3. Add the following code to the OnRun trigger:

```
Selection := STRMENU('Image,Website');
IF Selection = 1 THEN
   HYPERLINK('C:\Users\Public\
     Pictures\Sample Pictures\Penguins.jpg')
ELSE
   HYPERLINK('HTTP://www.mibuso.com');
```

4. Save and close the codeunit.

How it works...

When you run the codeunit you will be presented with a simple selection menu that asks you to choose between an image and a website. Depending on your choice we will use the HYPERLINK command to load a specific file. This command takes in a single string which points to a location and loads that pointer using the default program on the current machine.

If you choose **Image** then the Penguins image that ships with Microsoft Windows 7 will load in the default program you have set to open pictures, usually **Windows Photo Viewer**.

If you choose **Website** then the Mibuso website will open in your default internet browser, typically Internet Explorer.

There's more...

With the RoleTailored client, it is best to use HYPERLINK with shared drives and folders. This is because the actual HYPERLINK command is running on the NAV service tier, not on the local computer or client. It has no idea about the user's system. This example is for the Classic client (thus the link to a file on the C: drive), but changing the parameter to a shared file on your network should work just fine.

See also

- Using SHELL to run external applications
- Browsing for a file
- Checking file and folder access permissions

Working with environment variables

Environment variables are a set of named values that can affect the way processes and applications run on a computer. NAV has a built-in function to reference these variables and lets you change the way it functions.

How to do it...

1. Create a new codeunit from **Object Designer**.
2. Add the following code to the OnRun trigger:

```
MESSAGE(' OS: %1\Temp: %2\WinDir: %3', ENVIRON('OS'),
        ENVIRON('TEMP'), ENVIRON('WINDIR'));
```

3. Save and close the codeunit.

How it works...

The ENVIRON function takes in a single string and returns a string. Our codeunit uses the ENVIRON function to return three common environment variables: the name of the operating system, the path to the temporary folder for the current user, and the path to the Windows installation directory.

In Windows 7, in order to see all of the options available to the ENVIRON command, simply right-click on **My Computer** and go to **Properties**.

Click on **Advanced system settings**, the **Advanced** tab, and then on the **Environment Variables** button. You will find them in the **System variables** section of the window.

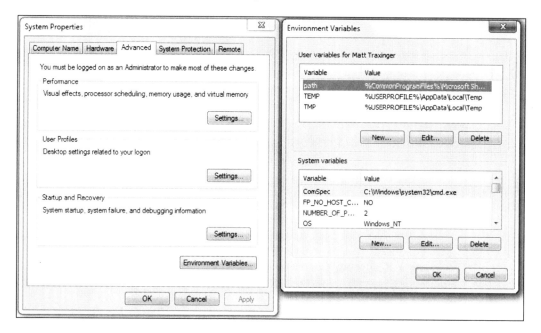

There's more...

This recipe is not compatible with the RoleTailored client. The code running on the NAV service tier does not know anything about the client operating system. There is, however, a way around this. We need a way to force code to be executed on the client-side instead of the server-side.

ENVIRON for the RoleTailored client

We can force our code to execute on the client-side by creating an Automation. Start by creating a new project in Visual Studio with the following code.

```
using System.Management;
using System.Runtime.InteropServices;

namespace RemoteSystemInfo
{
  [ClassInterface(ClassInterfaceType.AutoDual)]
  [ProgId("RemoteSystemInfo")]
  [ComVisible(true)]
  public class RemoteSystemInfo
  {
```

```csharp
public string GetSysInfo(string domain, string machine,
        string username, string password, string variable)
{
  ManagementObjectSearcher query = null;
  ManagementObjectCollection queryCollection = null;

  ConnectionOptions opt = new ConnectionOptions();
  opt.Impersonation = ImpersonationLevel.Impersonate;
  opt.EnablePrivileges = true;
  opt.Username = username;
  opt.Password = password;

  try
  {
    ManagementPath p = new ManagementPath(@"\\" +
                            machine + @"\root\cimv2");
    ManagementScope msc = new ManagementScope(p, opt);
    SelectQuery q = new SelectQuery("Win32_Environment");
    query = new ManagementObjectSearcher(msc, q, null);
    queryCollection = query.Get();

    foreach (ManagementBaseObject envVar in queryCollection)
    {
      if (envVar["Name"].ToString() == variable)
      {
        return envVar["VariableValue"].ToString();
      }
    }
  }
  catch (ManagementException e)
  {
    throw new ManagementException("Management Exception:
                                    " + e.Message);
  }
  catch (System.UnauthorizedAccessException e)
  {
    throw new ManagementException("Access Exception:
                                    " + e.Message);
  }
  return "";
}
}
}
```

Set the properties of the program according to the *Creating your own Automation using C#* recipe from *chapter 10, Integration*. When using the Automation in your NAV objects you must do the following:

```
CREATE(MyAutomation, FALSE, TRUE);
```

The third parameter tells the system to create the instance of the Automation on the client (TRUE) and not the server (FALSE). As the code executes on the client machine it can query the environment variables and easily return the correct result. Just pass the appropriate values to the GetSysInfo function.

See also

▸ Using SHELL

Using SHELL to run external applications

Just as external files can be opened from within NAV, so can external programs. This recipe will show you how to launch one of such applications.

How to do it...

1. Create a new codeunit from **Object Designer**.
2. Add the following code to the OnRun trigger:
   ```
   SHELL(ENVIRON('WINDIR') + '\notepad.exe');
   ```
3. Save and close the codeunit.

How it works...

The SHELL command takes in a required string parameter representing the application to launch. There is an optional second parameter that will be passed as an argument to the application to be launched (not used here). This argument could represent a file to open or other flags incorporated into the program.

See also

▸ Querying the registry

Browsing for a file

You will perform many modifications that require input from a file on the Windows file system. Instead of requiring the user to remember the full path and name of the file, we will show you how to use an out-of-the-box codeunit to let them select the file using a dialog box.

How to do it...

1. Create a new codeunit from **Object Designer**.

2. Add the following global variables:

Name	Type	Subtype	Length
CommonDialogMgt	Codeunit	Common Dialog Management	
SelectedFile	Text		255

3. Add the following code to the OnRun trigger:

```
SelectedFile := CommonDialogMgt.OpenFile('NAV File Browser',
                                    SelectedFile,1,'Filter',0);

MESSAGE('You selected %1', SelectedFile);
```

4. Save and close the codeunit.

How it works...

NAV provides a codeunit, number 412, named **Common Dialog Management**. It uses an OCX that references to the **Microsoft Common Dialog Control**. This codeunit provides a function that allows you to open a simple dialog box in either **Open** or **Save** mode. This function, OpenFile, takes five parameters.

The first is the title of the dialog box or Window. Next is the default file name to look for. The third and fourth parameters work together. The third is the default file type. When this is set to **Custom** the function uses the filter string passed in parameter four. The final argument tells the dialog box which mode to open in, that is **Open** or **Save**.

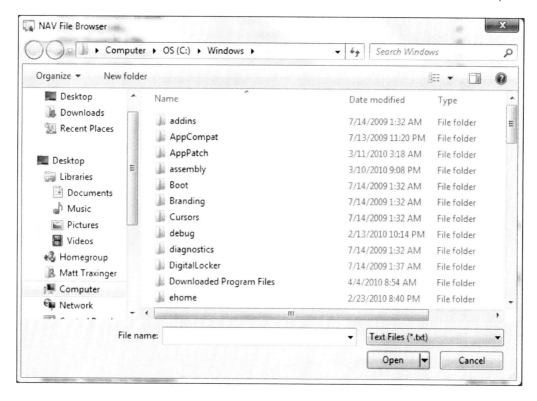

Should you choose to open the dialog box with a custom file type, you will have to enter a filter. You can see how these filters are formed by examining the global text constants, but we have also provided an example here:

Text Files (*.txt)|*.txt|All Files (*.*)|*.*

See also

▶ Using HYPERLINK to open external files
▶ Checking file and folder access permissions
▶ Browsing for a folder

Browsing for a folder

NAV provides us with a way to browse for a file right out-of-the-box, but it does not let us browse for a folder. This recipe will show you a work around using automation controls that should already be installed on your system.

How to do it...

1. Create a new codeunit from **Object Designer**.

2. Add the following global variables:

Name	Type	Subtype	Length
MSShell	Automation	'Microsoft Shell Controls And Automation'.Shell	
Folder	Automation	'Microsoft Shell Controls And Automation'.Folder3	
FilesInFolder	Automation	'Microsoft Shell Controls And Automation'.FolderItems3	
CurrentFile	Automation	'Microsoft Shell Controls And Automation'.FolderItem2	
SelectedFolder	Text		1024

3. Add the following code to the `OnRun` trigger:

```
CREATE(MSShell, FALSE, TRUE);
Folder := MSShell.BrowseForFolder(0, 'NAV Folder Browser', 0);
FilesInFolder := Folder.Items();
CurrentFile := FilesInFolder.Item();
SelectedFolder := FORMAT(CurrentFile.Path);

MESSAGE('Selected Folder: %1\Contains %2 files',
        SelectedFolder, FilesInFolder.Count());
```

4. Save and close the codeunit.

How it works...

This recipe depends entirely on the classes found in the Microsoft Shell Controls and Automation package.

 For a list of the objects found in this package you can search MSDN or go to `http://msdn.microsoft.com/en-us/library/bb776890%28VS.85%29.aspx`.

The code may seem like a lot just to get a folder name, but let's go through it line-by-line and explain why we are doing what we are doing. First we create or instantiate our `MSShell` variable, just as we do with every Automation variable. This one has a function called `BrowseForFolder` that launches the dialog box.

Unfortunately, this function returns a Folder object, which does not have text representation. So we have to take it a step further. We then retrieve a list of the files contained in that folder. This list is stored in our `FilesInFolder` variable. We can access the first item in this list. This file has a path and we can store that as our selected folder.

See also

▶ Browsing for a file

▶ Checking file and folder access permissions

Checking file and folder access permissions

Many systems have batch processes which read and write files to folders on the file system. In order to avoid some of the standard Windows error messages and prevent errors in the middle of the process you may want to check access permissions.

How to do it...

1. Create a new Class Library project in Visual Studio.

2. Create a new file with the following code:

    ```
    using System;
    using System.Security.Permissions;
    ```

```
using System.Runtime.InteropServices;

namespace FolderAccess
{
  [ClassInterface(ClassInterfaceType.AutoDual)]
  [ProgId("RegistryQuery")]
  [ComVisible(true)]
  public class FolderAccess
  {
    public bool TestFolderAccess(string folder, string access)
    {
      System.Security.Permissions.FileIOPermissionAccess
                                                accessLevel;
      switch (access.ToUpper())
      {
        case "NOACCESS": accessLevel =
                      FileIOPermissionAccess.NoAccess; break;
        case "READ": accessLevel =
                          FileIOPermissionAccess.Read; break;
        case "WRITE": accessLevel =
                         FileIOPermissionAccess.Write; break;
        case "APPEND": accessLevel =
                        FileIOPermissionAccess.Append; break;
        case "PATHDISCOVERY": accessLevel =
                 FileIOPermissionAccess.PathDiscovery; break;
        case "ALLACCESS": accessLevel =
                     FileIOPermissionAccess.AllAccess; break;
        default: return false;
      }

      FileIOPermission permission = new
                      FileIOPermission(accessLevel, folder);
      try
      {
        permission.Demand();
      }
      catch (Exception ex)
      {
        return false;
      }

      return true;
    }
  }
}
```

3. Set the properties of the program according to the *Creating your own Automation using C#* recipe from the integration chapter.

4. Save, compile, and close the project.

5. Create a new codeunit from **Object Designer**.

6. Add the following global variable:

Name	Type	Subtype
FolderAccess	Automation	'FolderAccess'.FolderAccess

7. Add the following code to the OnRun trigger:

```
CREATE(FolderAccess, FALSE, TRUE);

MESSAGE('Access: %1',
        FolderAccess.TestFolderAccess('C:\', 'WRITE'));
```

8. Save and close the codeunit.

How it works...

Our custom C# function, TestFolderAccess, takes in two parameters: the path or folder to check and the type of permission to check for. Using the FileIOPermission class we set these values and demand the access level. The Demand function will throw an exception if we do not currently have access to the folder. In that case we return false, but in all other cases we return true.

See also

▸ Browsing for a file

▸ Browsing for a folder

Querying the registry

You may never need to query the registry on the computer when creating a NAV modification, but you should consider it as an option.

How to do it...

1. Create a new Class Library project in Visual Studio.

2. Create a new file with the following code:

```
using System;
using System.Runtime.InteropServices;
using Microsoft.Win32;

namespace RegistryQuery
{
```

```csharp
[ClassInterface(ClassInterfaceType.AutoDual)]
[ProgId("RegistryQuery")]
[ComVisible(true)]
public class RegistryQuery
{
  public string GetKeyValue(string key, string name)
  {
    RegistryKey regKey = Registry.Users.OpenSubKey(key);
    if (regKey == null)
    {
      return "Key not found!";
    }
    else
    {
      object value = regKey.GetValue(name);
      if (value != null)
      {
        return value.ToString();
      }
      else
      {
        return "Name not found!";
      }
    }
  }
}
```

3. Set the properties of the program according to the *Creating your own Automation using C#* recipe from the integration chapter.

4. Save, compile, and close the project.

5. Create a new codeunit from **Object Designer**.

6. Add the following global variable:

Name	Type	Subtype
RegistryQuery	Automation	'RegistryQuery'.RegistryQuery

7. Add the following code to the OnRun trigger:

```
CREATE(RegistryQuery, FALSE, TRUE);

MESSAGE('%1', RegistryQuery.GetKeyValue('.DEFAULT\Environment',
                                        'TEMP'));
```

8. Save and close the codeunit.

How it works...

You may never have an instance where you need to examine registry values in your NAV code. In most instances, it will be easier to add a column to **User Setup** or store the information in a custom table. As a NAV developer, and less specifically, a business applications developer, you may encounter a situation that warrants this type of development. Let's take a look at the code.

Our C# code works for a specific root in the registry, HKEY_USERS. We access the subkey passed in the first parameter to our function using the Registry.Users.OpenSubKey function. If the key is not found, or null, we return an appropriate message. You could modify the code to access the other root folders by passing an additional parameter.

Next, we try to access the names stored in the key. Again, if we are unable to find the key equal to the second parameter of our function, we return null. If we do find it, we return its value.

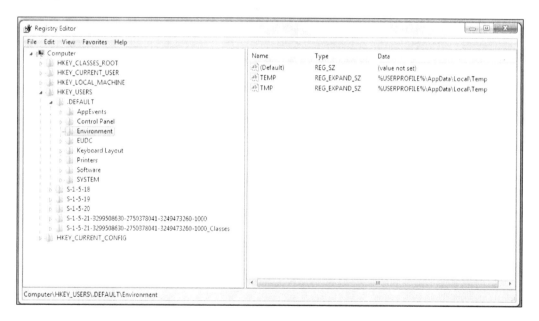

Our NAV code looks for the temporary folder assigned to the user, similar to what ENVIRON('TEMP') returns. Do not think that this is only limited to things that can also be found using the ENVIRON function, though. You can query any value in the registry.

There's more...

You can also perform other actions on the registry using the `CreateSubKey` and `DeleteSubKey` functions. Be warned, though. You should not play with the registry unless you know what you are doing. You can easily corrupt the entire system if you are not careful.

 For more information about the registry you can view this MSDN article: `http://msdn.microsoft.com/en-us/library/h5e7chcf.aspx`

See also

▸ Working with environment variables

Zipping folders and files within NAV

This might not be a common task, but creating files and e-mailing them from within NAV is. You can combine this with those recipes to send large groups of files at once.

How to do it...

1. Create a new codeunit from **Object Designer**.
2. Add the following global variables:

Name	Type	Subtype
ZipFile	File	
MSShell	Automation	'Microsoft Shell Controls And Automation'.Shell
ZipFolder	Automation	'Microsoft Shell Controls And Automation'.Folder

3. Add the following code to the `OnRun` trigger:

```
ZipFile.CREATE(
        'C:\Users\Public\Pictures\Sample Pictures\Pictures.zip');

CREATE(MSShell, FALSE, TRUE);
ZipFolder := MSShell.NameSpace(
        'C:\Users\Public\Pictures\Sample Pictures\Pictures.zip');
ZipFolder.CopyHere(
        'C:\Users\Public\Pictures\Sample Pictures\Desert.jpg');
```

4. Save and close the codeunit.

How it works...

A ZIP file is really just a folder that happens to have its contents compressed. We can create this file or folder just as we would create a text file, using the `CREATE` command.

Next, we assign the namespace of our `MSShell` object to this ZIP file. This means that whatever we do with our `MSShell` variable we will be doing to this file.

As the ZIP file is really just a folder, we can perform any file system action on it. In this case, we want to copy files into the folder. We achieve this by using the `CopyHere` function where the "Here" refers to our namespace and the parameter passed tells the function which file to copy.

See also

- Sending an e-mail from NAV through Outlook

10
Integration

In this chapter, we will cover:

- ▶ Flat file exchange using dataports
- ▶ Sharing information using XMLports
- ▶ Manually writing to and reading from files
- ▶ Creating a web service
- ▶ Consuming web services
- ▶ Sending data through FTP
- ▶ Printing reports to PDF
- ▶ Creating a custom NAS handler
- ▶ Writing your own automation using C#
- ▶ Using ADO to access outside data

Introduction

Microsoft Dynamics NAV does a lot of things really well. It has areas for sales, purchases, inventory, manufacturing, and financials just to name a few. It has the ability to do just about anything a company needs it to do, but that doesn't mean it will.

Businesses rely on multiple applications to run their operations. In the past, most of these applications have been housed on-site on the company's own servers. Integration between them was limited to flat file exchange or talking directly to the other database. Over the past few years there has been a major paradigm shift from the traditional client-server architecture towards a hosted model, often referred to as The Cloud. With the introduction of Web Services in NAV 2009, Microsoft has made sure that Dynamics NAV will continue to meet its customers' integration needs for this new type of infrastructure.

In this chapter, we will go over the old and the new. We will discuss how to do simple integrations using text and XML files and how to send those files to other locations using e-mail and FTP. We will also talk about ways to make our database talk to other applications and write our own code outside of NAV to integrate our systems. These recipes will serve as the foundation for all of your future integration efforts.

Flat file exchange using dataports

Although dataports have been dropped in favor of the more useful XMLport, there are still plenty of customers that are on versions where XMLports are not available. This recipe will show you how to create a basic dataport for importing and exporting data.

How to do it...

1. Create a new dataport from **Object Designer**.
2. Add a data item for the **Customer** table.
3. With the **Customer Data Item** selected, click on **View | Dataport Fields** (*Alt + V, D*).
4. Add the following fields to the **Field Designer** window.

Enabled	SourceExpr	StartPos	Width
Yes	"No."	0	0
Yes	Name	0	0

5. Your dataport should look similar to the following screenshot:

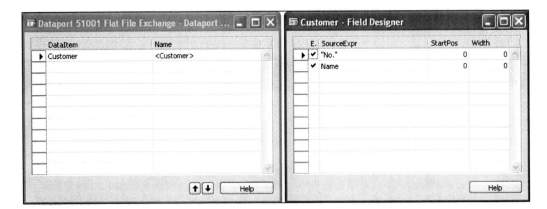

6. With a new, blank line selected in the dataport click on **View | Properties** (*Shift + F4*).

7. Set the following properties for the dataport:

Property	Value
FieldStartDelimeter	\<None\>
FieldEndDelimeter	\<None\>
FieldSeparator	\<TAB\>

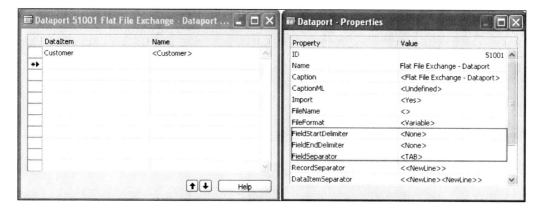

8. Save and close the dataport.

How it works...

In many programming languages you have to manually write code to export data from the system. NAV allows you to do this, but it also provides a much simpler way using a dataport.

First we tell the dataport which table we want to export from by creating a DataItem for the **Customer** table. Next, we tell it which fields we need by adding them to the **Dataport Fields** area.

As far as development goes this is all we have to do, but we can also change the format of the output file. We can tell the dataport to add characters to the beginning and end of a field as well as which character to use to separate fields. By default, fields are surrounded by double quotes and a comma is used to separate them. Unfortunately, double quotes and commas are often typed as data into fields which can throw off the dataport. Here we choose to separate the fields with a *Tab* character and to not surround them with any special characters.

When running the dataport you will be presented with two tabs.

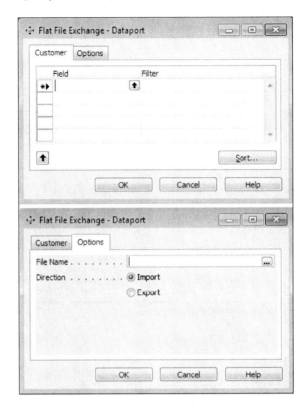

The first will let you specify any filters you want to apply to your data. The second allows you to choose the name of the file and whether or not you are importing or exporting data. When you click **OK** a progress bar will appear showing you how much of the file has been processed.

There's more...

Just like other objects you can add variables and code to dataports. One of the downsides, though, is that they cannot be run from the NAV Application Server (NAS). In these instances it is best to do your own file output using **Output Streams**.

See also

- ▸ Browsing for a file
- ▸ Sharing information using XMLports
- ▸ Sending data through FTP

Sharing information through XMLports

XML stands for **Extensible Markup Language** and is a text format for creating structured computer documents. NAV provides objects called XMLports that allow you to create these types of documents.

How to do it...

1. Create a new XMLport from **Object Designer**.
2. Add the following lines to the **XMLport Designer**:

Node Name	Node Type	Source Type	Data Source
Root	Element	Text	<Root>
Customer	Element	Table	<Customer>(Customer)
No	Element	Field	<Customer>::No.
Name	Element	Field	<Customer>::Name

3. Your XMLport should look like this:

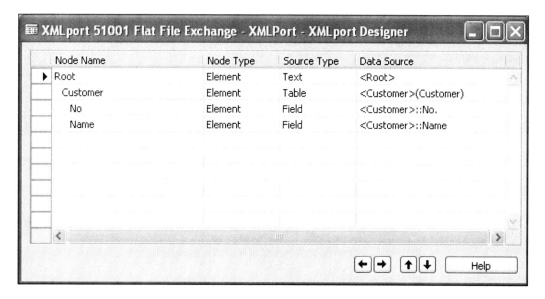

4. Save and close the XMLport.
5. Create a new codeunit from **Object Designer**.

6. Add the following global variables:

Name	DataType	Length
OutputFile	File	
OutputStream	OutStream	
FileName	Text	255

7. Add the following code to the `OnRun` trigger:

```
FileName := ENVIRON('TEMP') + 'Customers.xml';
OutputFile.CREATE(FileName);
OutputFile.CREATEOUTSTREAM(OutputStream);
XMLPORT.EXPORT(51001, OutputStream);
OutputFile.CLOSE;

HYPERLINK(FileName);
```

8. Save and close the codeunit.

How it works...

XMLports are similar to dataports, but their structure and creation is done a little differently. Understanding what XML output looks like can help you to better understand how to create these types of objects. A portion of the output from this XMLport is shown in the following image:

```
<?xml version="1.0" encoding="UTF-16" standalone="no" ?>
- <Root>
  - <Customer>
      <No>10000</No>
      <Name>The Cannon Group PLC</Name>
    </Customer>
  - <Customer>
      <No>20000</No>
      <Name>Selangorian Ltd.</Name>
    </Customer>
  - <Customer>
      <No>30000</No>
      <Name>John Haddock Insurance Co.</Name>
    </Customer>
  - <Customer>
      <No>40000</No>
      <Name>Deerfield Graphics Company</Name>
    </Customer>
  - <Customer>
      <No>50000</No>
      <Name>Guildford Water Department</Name>
    </Customer>
```

XML is a tree-like structure made of nodes. Every file has to start with some sort of parent node which is usually called the Root node. Once we have created the Root node we can tell the XMLport which table we want to use (in this case the **Customer** table). Next, we tell it which fields we want to use from that table. Notice in the output how each value is surrounded by a node with the name of that field, and each collection of fields is surrounded by a Customer node.

XMLports cannot be run directly from **Object Designer**. Instead, you have to create a codeunit to run them. Our codeunit creates a new export file along with an OutStream object that will be used to write the XML to that file. From here we run our XMLport and pass the OutStream object to it. While this may seem annoying, it has its benefits. This allows XMLports to be run through web services or run as scheduled tasks within NAV.

When developing XMLports for use with the RoleTailored client there is no need to create these codeunits to run them; they will run perfectly well from the RTC on their own.

There's more...

In NAV2009, XMLports have replaced dataports. But that does not mean you can only export data in XML. You can replicate this single line type of output by changing the Format property of the XMLport to Fixed Text or Variable Text. It also has the same FieldStartDelimiter, FieldEndDelimiter, and FieldSeparator properties as the dataport.

 For a complete explanation on XMLports, read *Chapter 9* of the book *Programming Microsoft Dynamics NAV 2009*, by David Studebaker,.

See also

- ▸ Browsing for a file
- ▸ Flat file exchange using dataports
- ▸ Sending data through FTP

Manually writing to and reading from files

Apart from the built-in object types for creating text files and XML files, you can also create them manually. This recipe will show you how to write your own code to do this.

How to do it...

1. Create a new codeunit from **Object Designer**.

2. Add the following global variables:

Name	DataType
StreamOut	OutStream
FileOut	File
StreamIn	InStream
FileIn	File

3. Add the following code to the OnRun trigger:

```
IF NOT FileOut.CREATE('C:\NAVFile.txt') THEN
   IF NOT FileOut.OPEN('C:\NAVFile.txt') THEN
      ERROR('Unable to write to file!');

FileOut.CREATEOUTSTREAM(StreamOut);
StreamOut.WRITETEXT('Line 1');
StreamOut.WRITETEXT();
StreamOut.WRITETEXT('Line 2');
StreamOut.WRITETEXT();
FileOut.CLOSE;

IF NOT FileIn.OPEN('C:\NAVFile.txt') THEN
   ERROR('Unable to read file!');

FileIn.CREATEINSTREAM(StreamIn);
WHILE NOT StreamIn.EOS DO BEGIN
   StreamIn.READTEXT(TextLine);
   MESSAGE('%1', TextLine);
END;
FileIn.CLOSE;
```

4. Save and close the codeunit.

How it works...

First we try to create a new file using the CREATE function with the File data type. If we are unable to create that file, we try to open a file of the same name. If that does not work we throw an error because we do not have a file to work with.

From there we have to create a stream to the file. In this case, we use an `OutStream` because we are writing data to the file. The stream object has a function called `WRITETEXT` that actually sends the data to the file. Unfortunately it does not send a carriage return, so to create a new line we have to use the `WRITETEXT` method with an empty parameter. Once we are done with writing text to the file we need to close it.

We follow a similar process for reading information from the file. Instead of using an `OutStream` variable we use an `InStream` variable. This stream has a function called `EOS` which stands for End of Stream. It returns the value `TRUE` when we reach the end of the file. As long as we have not reached the end of that file we can use the `READTEXT` function to retrieve a line of text from the file. It takes a text variable as a parameter and stores that line of text there. Our code displays it in a message window.

There's more...

This example creates a simple text file, but you can also create XML files. NAV provides functions for this in **Codeunit 6224, XML DOM Management**. Here is a short example:

Add the following global variables to a codeunit:

Name	DataType	SubType
XMLMgt	Codeunit	XML DOM Management
XMLDoc	Automation	'Microsoft XML, v6.0'.DOMDocument
XMLNode	Automation	'Microsoft XML, v6.0'.IXMLDOMNode
XMLNode2	Automation	'Microsoft XML, v6.0'.IXMLDOMNode
XMLNode3	Automation	'Microsoft XML, v6.0'.IXMLDOMNode

Add the following code:

```
CREATE(XMLDoc);
XMLDoc.async := FALSE;
XMLMgt.SetNormalCase;
XMLNode := XMLDoc.createNode('1','Root','');
XMLDoc.appendChild(XMLNode);
XMLMgt.AddElement(XMLNode,'Tag1','1','',XMLNode2);
XMLMgt.AddElement(XMLNode,'Tag2','2','',XMLNode2);
XMLMgt.AddElement(XMLNode,'Tag3','','',XMLNode2);
XMLMgt.AddElement(XMLNode2,'Tag3.1','3.1','',XMLNode3);
XMLDoc.save('C:\NAVXML.txt');
```

In order to start the document, you must create a node and append it to the document. This root node will be used throughout the file creation. The AddElement function takes in several parameters. The first is the parent node of the node being added. The tag name and value are also passed. The last parameter will hold the node that is being added. A sample output from this code is shown:

```
<Root>
   <Tag1>1</Tag1>
   <Tag2>2</Tag2>
   <Tag3>
      <Tag3.1>3.1</Tag3.1>
   </Tag3>
</Root>
```

See also

▸ Flat file exchange using dataports

▸ Sharing information through XMLports

Creating a web service

Web services are a standardized way of integrating applications that share business logic and data. With NAV 2009 you can easily create a web service in a matter of minutes.

How to do it...

1. Create a new page as described in the *Creating a list page* recipe in *Chapter 12, RoleTailored Client.*

2. From **Object Designer** run form 810, **Web Services**.

3. Add the following record to the table:

Object Type	Object ID	Service Name	Published
Page	51003 (or the ID of your Page object)	Web Service Example	Yes

4. Close the form.

How it works...

With NAV 2009, creating a web service is easy. Any code exposed through a page or codeunit object can be exposed as a web service. There is no need to create your own .NET class or write code outside NAV to access the database. All that is required is to add the object to the web service table and check the **Published** field.

► Creating an InfoPath form with NAV data

► Consuming a web service

Consuming web services

It is great that you can create web services in NAV, but you should be able to use them in outside applications. This recipe will show you how to create a basic program to use these web services.

How to do it...

1. Create a new codeunit from **Object Designer**.

2. Add a function named `GetCustomer`.

3. The function should take in the following parameter:

Name	DataType	Length
CustNo	Code	20

4. Add the following local variable to the function:

Name	DataType	SubType
Customer	Record	Customer

5. The function should return a text variable of length 50.

6. Add the following code to the function:

    ```
    IF Customer.GET(CustNo) THEN
      EXIT(Customer.Name)
    ELSE
      EXIT('Not Found!');
    ```

7. Save and close the codeunit.

8. Add the codeunit as a web service as described in the *Creating a web service* recipe.

9. Create a new **Console Application** project in Visual Studio.

10. Right-click the **References** link and click on **Add Web Reference**.

11. Enter `http://localhost:7047/DynamicsNAV/WS/Cronus_International_ Ltd/Services` (this may be different depending on the web server, service name, and NAV company name).

12. Select the web service corresponding to our codeunit and click on **Add Service**.

13. Add the following code to the program:

```
using System;
using System.Text;

using localhost;

namespace ConsumeWebService
{
  public class ConsumeWebService
  {
    public static void Main(string[] args)
    {
      ConsumeWS service = new ConsumeWS();
      ws.UseDefaultCredentials = true;
      Console.WriteLine(ws.GetCustomer("10000"));
      Console.ReadLine();
    }
  }
}
```

14. Compile, save, and close the program.

How it works...

In this example, we have created a simple codeunit that returns the name of a customer or the text as "Not Found". This codeunit has been published as a web service as is available to be used by our .NET program.

In order to use the web service in the application we have to add it as a reference. In our code we tell this class that it can use the functions from the web service by adding the `using localhost` line. We then create an instance of our service and tell it to use the default credentials to connect. From there we can call any of the available functions in our page or codeunit.

For a more in depth example you can read *Chapter 9* of *Programming Microsoft Dynamics NAV 2009*, by David Studebaker, or *Chapter 7* of *Implementing Microsoft Dynamics NAV 2009*, by David Roys and Vjekoslav Babic. The latter is available from Packt here for free:

```
http://www.packtpub.com/article/extending-
application-using-microsoft-dynamics-nav-2009-part1
```

See also

- ▸ Creating an InfoPath form with NAV data
- ▸ Creating a web service

Sending data through FTP

Many external applications still accept files and submissions through FTP. Windows has a built-in FTP client that we can leverage to perform this type of transmission.

Getting ready

You will need a working FTP server and valid logon credentials in order to run this recipe.

How to do it...

1. Create a new codeunit from **Object Designer**.
2. Add a function named `FTP` that takes in the following parameters:

Name	DataType	Length
UserName	Text	50
Password	Text	50
ServerName	Text	50
FileToMove	Text	255

3. Add the following local variables to the function:

Name	DataType	Length
BatchFileName	Text	250
BatchFile	File	
BatchFileStream	OutStream	
BatchFileData	Text	250

4. Add the following code to the function:

```
BatchFileData := 'c:\navFTP.dat';
BatchFileName := 'c:\navFTP.bat';
BatchFile.CREATE(BatchFileName);
BatchFile.CREATEOUTSTREAM(BatchFileStream);

BatchFileStream.WRITETEXT('@echo off');
```

```
BatchFileStream.WRITETEXT;
BatchFileStream.WRITETEXT('echo user ' +
                    UserName + ' >> ' + BatchFileData);
BatchFileStream.WRITETEXT;
BatchFileStream.WRITETEXT('echo ' +
                    Password + ' >> ' + BatchFileData);
BatchFileStream.WRITETEXT;
BatchFileStream.WRITETEXT('echo bin >> ' +
                                    BatchFileData);
BatchFileStream.WRITETEXT;
BatchFileStream.WRITETEXT('echo put ' +
                    FileToMove + ' >> ' + BatchFileData);
BatchFileStream.WRITETEXT;
BatchFileStream.WRITETEXT('echo quit >> ' +
                                    BatchFileData);
BatchFileStream.WRITETEXT;
BatchFileStream.WRITETEXT('FTP -n -s:' +
                    BatchFileData + ' ' + ServerName);
BatchFileStream.WRITETEXT;
BatchFileStream.WRITETEXT('del ' + BatchFileData);
BatchFileStream.WRITETEXT;
BatchFile.CLOSE;

SHELL(BatchFileName);
```

5. Add the following code to the `OnRun` trigger:

    ```
    FTP('YourUserName', 'YourPassword', 'YourServer', 'YourFile');
    ```

6. Save and close the codeunit.

How it works...

FTP stands for **File Transfer Protocol** and is a method for sending files from one file system to another. Although very basic, the Windows OS comes with a built-in FTP program. It is a simple command-line utility (no graphical interface), so it is not the easiest program to use, but for integration it works great.

 For a list of the available options or parameters that can be used with the FTP program type `ftp ?` at a command prompt.

Our program works by creating two files: a batch file and a data file. The data file will be used within the batch file to tell the FTP program how to act. Let's examine each line of the batch file.

The first line, @echo off, is for security purposes. By turning off the echo command we prevent the commands in our batch file from being displayed on the screen. This is extremely important to prevent the users of this program from learning the username and password that are echoed on the next two lines. You will notice that each of these lines ends with a >> BatchFileData. This tells the batch file to send the text to an actual file on the file system. Next we tell the FTP program to set the transfer-type to binary and to put, or send, a specific file. Finally, we quit and return to the command prompt.

Now we actually need to connect to the FTP program. We do this by adding the FTP command to our batch file followed by two parameters. The first, -n, tells the system not to automatically log in. The second, -s, tells it to issue the commands in the specified file when the program starts. Lastly, we must tell it the server to which we want to connect.

Once the file has been uploaded we delete the data file so that our credentials are not saved anywhere on the machine.

There's more...

This is a basic example that only uploads a single file, but you could easily script it so that it issues multiple PUT commands. This would most likely be used with some type of NAS Scheduler along with an XMLport to send and retrieve information.

See also

▶ Flat file exchange using dataports

▶ Sharing information through XMLports

Printing reports to PDF

Printing reports to PDF is extremely valuable for many companies. These documents can easily be saved and e-mailed for a variety of tasks like electronic invoicing. This recipe will show you how to develop this functionality.

Getting ready

PDFCreator must be installed on the system on which the code will be run. You can download it here:

http://sourceforge.net/projects/pdfcreator/

When installing, be sure not to install the ad-ware / spy-ware toolbar that comes with it. You may also want to turn-off the automatic updates for PDFCreator so that users do not end up on different versions of the software.

How to do it...

1. Create a new codeunit from **Object Designer**.

2. Add the following global variables:

Name	DataType	SubType	Length
PDFCreator	Automation	'PDFCreator'.clsPDFCreator	
PDFCreatorError	Automation	'PDFCreator'.clsPDFCreatorError	
PDFCreatorOption	Automation	'PDFCreator'.clsPDFCreatorOptions	
DefaultPrinter	Text		100

3. Add a function named `SetupPDFCreator`. This function should take in the following parameters:

Name	DataType	Length
FileDir	Text	1024
FileName	Text	1024

4. Add the following code to the function:

```
IF ISCLEAR(PDFCreator) THEN
  CREATE(PDFCreator, TRUE, TRUE);

IF ISCLEAR(PDFCreatorError) THEN
  CREATE(PDFCreatorError, TRUE, TRUE);

PDFCreatorError := PDFCreator.cError;

IF PDFCreator.cStart('/NoProcessingAtStartup', TRUE) = FALSE
                                                      THEN
  ERROR('Status: Error[' + FORMAT(PDFCreatorError.Number) + ']:
                        ' + PDFCreatorError.Description);

PDFCreatorOption := PDFCreator.cOptions;
PDFCreatorOption.UseAutosave := 1;
PDFCreatorOption.UseAutosaveDirectory := 1;
PDFCreatorOption.AutosaveDirectory := FileDir;
PDFCreatorOption.AutosaveFormat := 0;
PDFCreatorOption.AutosaveFilename := FileName;

PDFCreator.cOptions := PDFCreatorOption;
PDFCreator.cClearCache();
DefaultPrinter := PDFCreator.cDefaultPrinter;
PDFCreator.cDefaultPrinter := 'PDFCreator';
PDFCreator.cPrinterStop := FALSE;
```

5. Add a function named `WaitUntilFileExists`. It should take in the following parameter:

Name	DataType	Length
FileName	Text	1024

6. The function should return a Boolean value.

7. Add the following local variables to the function:

Name	DataType
i	Integer
maxi	Integer
FileFound	Boolean

8. Add the following code to the function:

```
i := 0;
maxi := 10;

WHILE (i < maxi) DO BEGIN
  IF FILE.EXISTS(FileName) THEN BEGIN
    i := maxi;
    FileFound := TRUE;
  END ELSE BEGIN
    i += 1;
    SLEEP(1000);
  END;
END;

EXIT(FileFound);
```

9. Add a function named `ClearPDFCreator` with the following code:

```
PDFCreator.cDefaultPrinter := DefaultPrinter;
CLEAR(PDFCreatorError);
CLEAR(PDFCreator);
```

10. Add the following code to the `OnRun` trigger:

```
SetupPDFCreator(ENVIRON('TEMP'), 'Test.pdf');
REPORT.RUNMODAL(REPORT::"Customer Listing", FALSE, FALSE);
IF WaitUntilFileExists(ENVIRON('Temp') + '\Test.pdf') THEN
  HYPERLINK(ENVIRON('Temp') + '\Test.pdf');
ClearPDFCreator;
```

11. Save and close the codeunit.

How it works...

Our code depends on several libraries that come with the PDFCreator software. We can reference these libraries using Automation variables in NAV.

Let's start by examining our first function, `SetupPDFCreator`. This function should be called right before you print your document. We start by instantiating our Automation variables. Once we know that we can start the PDFCreator application, we set some options. Specifically, we want to automatically save our file without prompting the user, so we set the path, filename, and file type (PDFCreator can save in more formats than just PDF). The last part of the function determines the current default printer and saves it to a `temp` variable. This is because we are going to set the default printer to PDFCreator and we want to be able to reset it after we finish printing the reports.

Our next function is called `WaitUntilFileExists`. This file checks once per second for ten seconds to make sure the PDF file has been created. Sometimes it takes some time for it to register with the file system and even though PDFCreator has completed working on the report, the file is not yet available.

The final function, `ClearPDFCreator`, clears up our variables and resets the default printer.

As long as you have run the `SetupPDFCreator` function, any report you run will be printed to PDF. When you do run the report, though, you will want to pass a `FALSE` value to the `UseDefaultPrinter` and `ShowRequestForm` parameters.

There's more...

In the RoleTailored client you can use the `SAVEASPDF` function. You can then use the `DOWNLOAD` command to move that PDF file to the client computer and display it. These functions should always be surrounded with a conditional that determines which client you are using, in the following manner:

```
IF ISSERVICETIER THEN BEGIN
  Report.SAVEASPDF;
  DOWNLOAD('Report.pdf','Download File',
                'C:\','PDF file(*.pdf)|*.pdf',ToFile);
END;
```

See also

▸ Display page X of Y

▸ Adding a watermark to a report

▸ Sending an e-mail from NAV through Outlook

Creating a custom NAS handler

The NAV Application Server is essentially a NAV client without a graphical interface. It can be used to automate exports or run any sort of code you might need for integration with software outside of the NAV system. This recipe will show you how to write the code to handle a custom application server.

Getting ready

You must have the NAV Application Server installed either on your machine or another server on your network.

How to do it...

1. Create a new codeunit from **Object Designer**.

2. Set the following properties on the codeunit:

Property	Value
SingleInstance	Yes

3. Add the following global variables to the codeunit:

Name	DataType	SubType
Timer	Automation	'Navision Timer 1.0'.Timer
Seconds	Integer	

4. Add the following code to the OnRun trigger:

   ```
   IF ISCLEAR(Timer) THEN
     CREATE(Timer);

   Seconds := 60;
   Timer.Enabled := FALSE;
   Timer.Interval := Seconds * 1000;
   Timer.Enabled := TRUE;
   ```

5. Add the following code to the Timer::Timer event:

   ```
   MESSAGE('Processed');
   ```

6. Save and close the codeunit.

7. Design codeunit 1, **Application Management**, from **Object Designer**.

8. Add the following global variable:

Name	DataType	SubType
CustomNASHandler	Codeunit	Custom NAS Handler (or the name of the Codeunit you just created)

9. Find the `NasHandler` function.

10. Towards the end, you should see this line of code:

```
IF CGNASStartedinLoop = FALSE THEN
```

11. Directly above that line add the following code:

```
IF COPYSTR(Parameter,1,6) = 'CUSTOM' THEN BEGIN
  CustomNASHandler.RUN;
END;
```

12. Save and close the codeunit.

13. Start the **Application Server Manager** from the server where the NAV Application Server is installed.

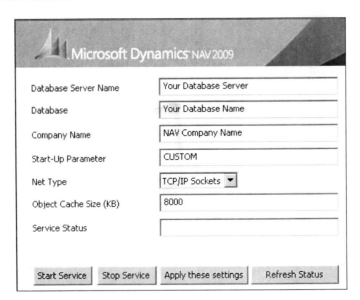

14. Set the start-up parameter of a new or existing application server to CUSTOM.

15. Restart the NAV Application Service.

How it works...

First we create a single-instance codeunit. We add an instance of the Navision timer Automation to our program. This DLL file is shipped with the Navision product and you should be able to find it in the installation directory. We set our timer to run once in a minute. This will fire the `Timer::Timer` event so we place a simple `MESSAGE` command here. You could add a call to another codeunit or any other code you want to use. Just be aware that you can't use any request forms or confirmation dialogs because there is no user to click anything.

Now that we have the codeunit to run we need to tell the application server how to access it. This is done in codeunit 1, specifically by the `NASHandler` function. Here we check the startup parameter and call the appropriate code, in this case, our custom codeunit.

See also

- Ending an idle session
- Automatically adding users to NAV
- Sending an e-mail in NAV through Outlook

Writing your own automation using C#

C/AL is a solid programming language, and NAV is a great system, but it cannot always exactly do what we want it to. Luckily, we can write our own code in .NET and use it in NAV. This recipe will show you how to set up a Visual Studio project so that it can be seen from within the NAV client.

How to do it...

1. Create a new Class Library Project in Visual Studio.
2. Add the following code to the project:

```
using System.Runtime.InteropServices;

namespace NAVAdd
{
  [ClassInterface(ClassInterfaceType.AutoDual)]
  [ProgId("NAVAdd")]
  [ComVisible(true)]
  public class NAVAdd
  {
    public int Add(int a, int b)
    {
      return a + b;
    }
  }
}
```

3. View the **Properties** for the project.

4. On the **Application** tab set the **Assembly name** to **NAVAdd**.

5. On the **Build** tab set the **Register for COM interop** property to true (checked).

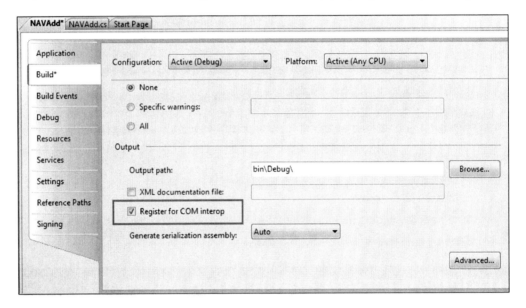

6. Save and compile your objects.

7. Create a new codeunit in **Object Designer**.

8. Add the following global variable:

Name	DataType	SubType
NAVAdd	Automation	'NAVAdd'.NAVAdd

9. Add the following code to the OnRun trigger:

```
CREATE(NAVAdd);
MESSAGE('%1', NAVAdd.Add(2, 3));
```

10. Save and close the codeunit.

How it works...

Let's examine the attributes of our class. The first attribute is called ClassInterface. By setting the value to ClassInterfaceType.AutoDual we tell the program to automatically register itself on the system, if we choose to register it at all (which we will later). The second attribute is called ProgId and is the name that our program will be referenced by. The last is called COMVisible and tells the system that this class can be registered on the computer.

For more information on the libraries and attributes you can go to `msdn.microsoft.com`.

In order to actually register the class as an Automation you must check the **Register for COM interop** option in the **Project Properties** window. Once you compile the program it will be available in the list of available Automation variables in NAV.

See also

- ▸ Display page X of Y
- ▸ Adding a watermark to a report
- ▸ Implementing `Try` / `Catch` / `Finally`
- ▸ Automatically adding users to NAV
- ▸ Instant messaging with Office Communicator
- ▸ Querying the registry

Using ADO to access outside data

ADO stands for **ActiveX Data Object** and is used to access data regardless of its structure. Here we will show how you can use an ADO Automation in NAV to access data from an outer database.

How to do it...

1. Create a new codeunit in **Object Designer**.
2. Add a function named `CreateConnectionString` that takes in the following parameters:

Name	DataType	Length
ServerName	Text	50
DatabaseName	Text	50
UserName	Text	50
Password	Text	50

3. The function should return a text value of length 1024.

4. Add the following code to the function:

```
EXIT(
    'Driver={SQL Server};' + 'Server=' + ServerName + ';' +
        'Database=' + DatabaseName + ';' + 'Uid=' + UserName +
                            ';' + 'Pwd=' + Password + ';');
```

5. Add the following local variables to the OnRun trigger:

Name	DataType	SubType
ADOConnection	Automation	'Microsoft ActiveX Data Objects 6.0 Library'.Connection
ActiveADOConnection	Variant	
ADOCommand	Automation	'Microsoft ActiveX Data Objects 6.0 Library'.Command
ADORecordSet	Automation	'Microsoft ActiveX Data Objects 6.0 Library'.Recordset

6. Add the following code to the trigger:

```
CREATE(ADOConnection);
ADOConnection.ConnectionString := CreateConnectionString(
        'MyServer', 'MyDatabase', 'MyUserID', 'MyPassword');
ADOConnection.Open;

CREATE(ADOCommand);
ActiveADOConnection := ADOConnection;
ADOCommand.ActiveConnection := ActiveADOConnection;

ADOCommand.CommandText := 'SELECT [Name] FROM
        [Company$Customer] WHERE [No_] = ''10000''';
ADOCommand.Execute;

CREATE(ADORecordSet);
ADORecordSet.ActiveConnection := ActiveADOConnection;
ADORecordSet.Open(ADOCommand);
WHILE NOT ADORecordSet.EOF DO BEGIN
  MESSAGE(FORMAT(ADORecordSet.Fields.Item('No_').Value));
END;

ADOConnection.Close;
```

7. Save and close the codeunit.

How it works...

First we need to connect to the database we need information from. We do this by setting up a new connection string and assigning the value to our ADO connection variable.

Once we open our connection we are ready to issue queries or commands against the external database. In this example, we want to select a customer from the **Customer** table in another NAV database.

In order to view the results of the query, we have to open the `RecordSet` that was returned by the command. We add a simple `WHILE` loop to process until we get to the end of the set. Each field can be accessed with the `.Fields.Item(FieldName)` syntax.

There's more...

This is a basic example, but it opens up a lot of possibilities. Everything that you can do using SQL you can now do in NAV. That includes executing stored procedures, creating views, and setting up SQL security. Your options are only limited by your knowledge of T-SQL.

11
Working with SQL Server

In this chapter, we will cover:

- ▸ Creating a basic SQL query
- ▸ Adding the $xp\_$ stored procedures
- ▸ Understanding SIFT tables
- ▸ Using SQL Profiler
- ▸ Displaying data from a SQL view in NAV
- ▸ Figuring out who is blocking whom
- ▸ Setting up a backup plan
- ▸ Scheduling NAV tasks from SQL server

Introduction

When Navision was introduced, the database option was a proprietary engine. Everything was stored in an **FDB** (**Financial Database**) file. The newer versions of the product added a second option: SQL Server. Unfortunately for some of these older customers, NAV 2009 is the last version to support the proprietary database; in the next version, SQL Server will be the only option.

SQL Server is becoming an integral part of the software. NAV partners must be certified in **SQL Server Implementation and Maintenance** to maintain their partnership. Even the NAV Installation and Configuration exams ask many questions about Windows and database servers. As NAV evolves, so must the people who work with it.

In this chapter, we will explore everything from writing a basic SQL query to some of the inner-workings of the NAV client. For those developers who have been resistant to change, or those who don't know from where to start, the recipes in this chapter will help "bring you out of your NAV shell" so to speak. For those of you who have been involved with SQL for some time, there are several recipes for you as well.

Creating a basic SQL query

It all starts with a query. This recipe will show you how to retrieve data from tables in the database.

How to do it...

1. Open **SQL Server Management Studio** and connect to the server that holds your NAV database.

2. Click on the **New Query** button.

3. Select your NAV database in the database dropdown.

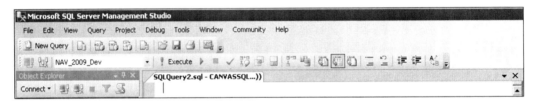

4. Enter the following code in the window:

```
SELECT [No_], [Name], [Address], [City], [County], [Post Code]
    FROM [CRONUS USA, Inc_$Customer]
    WHERE [No_] = '10000'
```

5. Press *F5* to run the query.

6. You should see the following results:

	No_	Name	Address	City	County	Post Code
1	10000	The Cannon Group PLC	192 Market Square	Atlanta	GA	31772

How it works...

This is a basic SQL query made up of three basic parts. The first is the SELECT line, which tells the system the names of the fields we want to retrieve. We surround the field names with brackets, [ ], because a lot of times the name of the field is also a reserved keyword or a space. The brackets are not mandatory for every field, but it makes it simpler to add them every time. Notice also that in NAV the customer number is stored in a field named "No.", but in SQL Server we reference it by "No_".

The second line tells the table where we want to get the fields from, in this case the Customer table. Here you can see that we do not just enter FROM [Customer]. In SQL Server, the tables are actually named in a format like Company$Table. There are exceptions to this, though. Any table that has the DataPerCompany property set to No will not contain the Company$ prefix on the table name.

Last is the WHERE clause. This is the same as filtering in NAV. In this case, we only want to retrieve customer number 10000.

This query would be equivalent to the following NAV code:

```
CustomerRec.SETRANGE("No.", '10000');
IF CustomerRec.FINDFIRST THEN;
```

> The book, The *NAV/SQL Performance Field Guide*, by Jörg A. Stryk contains a great list of translations between C/AL code and SQL statements in the *Querying SQL Server* section.

There's more...

SQL queries can be much more complicated. They can perform calculations, query multiple tables at the same time, and manipulate data in just about any way imaginable. Not only can you retrieve data through a SQL query, you can also insert, modify, and delete data.

> Entire books have been written on the subject of SQL. A great place to start is *Beginning SQL Queries: From Novice to Professional* by Clare Churcher.

Other Types of SQL queries

The following SQL queries are commonly used:

Adding data:

```
INSERT INTO [CRONUS USA, Inc_$Customer]
    ([No_],[Name],[Address],[City],[Post Code],[County])
      VALUES ('101382','Matt Traxinger','123 Main Street',
                  'Atlanta','30324','GA')
```

Editing data:

```
UPDATE [CRONUS USA, Inc_$Customer]
    SET [Name] = 'Matt Traxinger'
    WHERE [No_] = '10000'
```

Deleting Data:

```
DELETE [CRONUS USA, Inc_$Customer]
    WHERE [No_] = '10000'
```

Please note that you should not use SQL to do things that can be done within NAV or to correct issues that can be corrected on the NAV frontend. SQL does not execute business logic that is built into NAV. There is almost always a way to accomplish what you are trying to do using existing NAV functionality or NAV code.

See also

▶   Creating transactions to alter data

▶   Retrieving a single record from the database

▶   Using advanced filtering

▶   Retrieving data using FIND

▶   Displaying data from a SQL view in NAV

Adding the xp_ stored procedures

In order to enable **Single Sign-On (SSO)** through Windows logins, you must install two extended stored procedures on the SQL Server. This recipe will show you how to do that.

How to do it...

1.   Copy the file named xp_ndo_x64.dll from the SQL_esp\x64 folder on the product CD (if you are using a 64 bit server). The default location to move it to is C:\Program Files (x86)\Microsoft Dynamics NAV\60\Database on the SQL Server, but you can copy it to any location.

2. Open **SQL Server Management Studio** and connect to your server. In the **Object Explorer** pane on the left-hand side, expand the tree to **Databases**, **System Databases**, **master**, **Programmability**, **Extended Stored Procedures**.

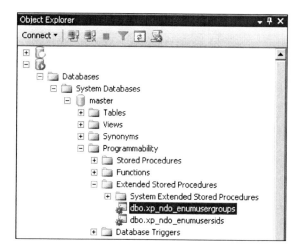

3. Right-click the **Extended Stored Procedures** folder and select **New Extended Stored Procedure**.

4. Enter `xp_ndo_enumusergroups` for the name and point it to the `xp_ndo_x64.dll` file you copied to the server.

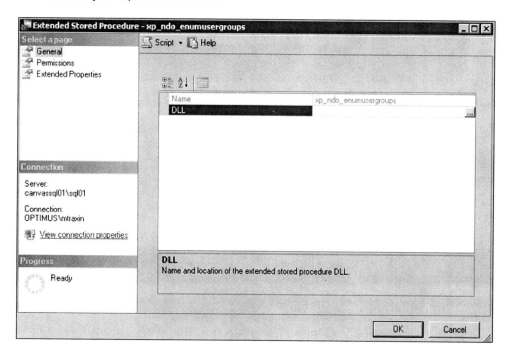

5. Go to the **Permissions** page from the left-hand pane.

6. Click the **Add** button.

7. Add the public account and grant it the **Execute** permission.

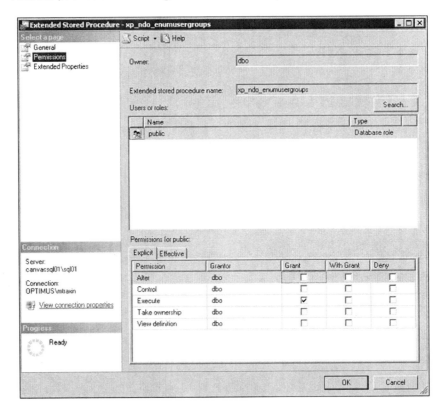

8. Click **OK**.

9. Repeat the same steps for the `xp_ndo_enumusersids` extended stored procedure.

See also

▶ Setting up a backup plan

▶ Scheduling NAV tasks from SQL Server

Understanding SIFT tables

SIFT stands for **Sum Index Field Technology** and is used by NAV to keep track of data to quickly perform complex calculations. This recipe will show you how they work.

How to do it...

1. Design **Table 379**, **Detailed Cust. Ledg. Entry**.
2. Click on **View | Keys** from the menu.

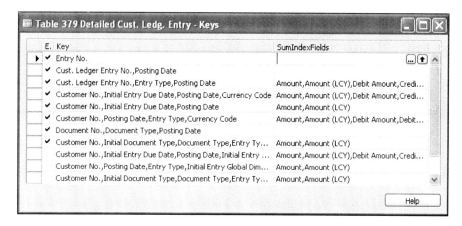

3. View the **Properties** for some of the enabled keys. You will notice one property called `MaintainSIFTIndex`. This is the property that tells SQL Server to store the totals of the **SumIndexFields**.

How it works...

Prior to NAV 5.0 SP1, SIFT values were stored in actual tables. In later versions, they earned the nickname **VSIFT** because they are stored as views. This explanation will focus on VSIFT, but for a deeper description of SIFT and how it works, check out Jörg A. Stryk's book, The NAV/ SQL Performance Field Guide.

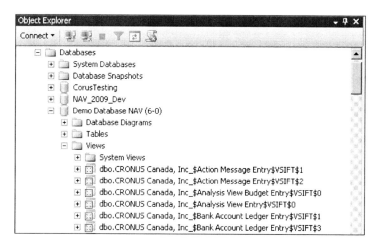

We will take a look at the key **Customer No.**, **Initial Entry Due Date**, **Posting Date**. This is the fourth key in the list (if you start with 0 as the first key). The view that will be created for this key will be in the format of `Company$Table$VSIFT$Key_Number`. Right-click on the `dbo. CRONUS USA, Inc_$Detailed Cust_ Ledg_ Entry$VSIFT$4` view and go to **Script View As | CREATE To | New Query Editor Window**. You will see the following code:

```
CREATE VIEW [CRONUS USA, Inc_$Detailed Cust_ Ledg_ Entry$VSIFT$4]
WITH SCHEMABINDING AS
    SELECT "Customer No_","Initial Entry Due Date","Posting Date",
                COUNT_BIG(*) "$Cnt",SUM("Amount") "SUM$Amount",
                        SUM("Amount (LCY)") "SUM$Amount (LCY)"
    FROM "CRONUS USA, Inc_$Detailed Cust_ Ledg_ Entry"
    GROUP BY "Customer No_","Initial Entry Due Date","Posting Date"
```

A **view** is just a `SELECT` statement that is linked to specific tables. If any one of those tables gets updated, the view is also updated. Do not be confused by this, though. Views do not store any data. In the older versions of NAV, SIFT tables were updated through triggers. These triggers slowed down functions like posting routines. The views, however, are optimized by SQL Server in order to provide faster transactions and better user experience.

As you can see, in this `SELECT` statement we are retrieving the same fields that are found in our key; that is **Customer No.**, **Initial Entry Due Date**, and **Posting Date**. We are also retrieving the sum of the fields in our **SumIndexFields** along with the number of records that make up that sum.

You can retrieve records from the view just like you would from a table. If you select the records from this view you would see the following table:

	Customer No_	Initial Entry Due Date	Posting Date	$Cnt	SUM$Amount	SUM$Amount (LCY)
1	01445544	2010-02-23 00:00:00.000	2010-01-25 00:00:00.000	1	2461.00000000000000000000	2461.00000000000000000000
2	01454545	2010-01-31 00:00:00.000	2009-12-31 00:00:00.000	1	0.00000000000000000000	0.00000000000000000000
3	10000	2010-01-01 00:00:00.000	2009-12-31 00:00:00.000	1	39127.27000000000000000000	39127.27000000000000000000
4	10000	2010-01-01 00:00:00.000	2010-01-17 00:00:00.000	1	-39127.27000000000000000000	-39127.27000000000000000000
5	10000	2010-01-07 00:00:00.000	2009-12-31 00:00:00.000	1	78254.54000000000000000000	78254.54000000000000000000
6	10000	2010-01-07 00:00:00.000	2010-01-17 00:00:00.000	1	-78254.54000000000000000000	-78254.54000000000000000000
7	10000	2010-01-11 00:00:00.000	2009-12-31 00:00:00.000	1	104339.38000000000000000000	104339.38000000000000000000
8	10000	2010-01-11 00:00:00.000	2010-01-17 00:00:00.000	1	-104339.38000000000000000000	-104339.38000000000000000000
9	10000	2010-01-17 00:00:00.000	2010-01-17 00:00:00.000	7	-382.86000000000000000000	-382.86000000000000000000
10	10000	2010-01-31 00:00:00.000	2009-12-31 00:00:00.000	3	228242.39000000000000000000	228242.39000000000000000000
11	10000	2010-02-07 00:00:00.000	2010-01-10 00:00:00.000	1	10806.72000000000000000000	10806.72000000000000000000
12	10000	2010-02-20 00:00:00.000	2010-01-20 00:00:00.000	1	5254.05000000000000000000	5254.05000000000000000000

Let us take a look at row number ten and the values from the detailed **Cust_ Ledg_ Entry** table. If you execute the following query you can see the records that make up this entry in the view.

```
SELECT [Customer No_],[Initial Entry Due Date],[Posting Date],
                                    [Amount],[Amount (LCY)]
    FROM [CRONUS USA, Inc_$Detailed Cust_ Ledg_ Entry]
```

```
WHERE [Customer No_] = '10000' AND
            [Initial Entry Due Date] = '2010-01-31' AND
                    [Posting Date] = '2009-12-31'
```

This produces the following results:

	Customer No_	Initial Entry Due Date	Posting Date	Amount	Amount (LCY)
1	10000	2010-01-31 00:00:00.000	2009-12-31 00:00:00.000	97818.17000000000000000000	97818.17000000000000000000
2	10000	2010-01-31 00:00:00.000	2009-12-31 00:00:00.000	52169.68000000000000000000	52169.68000000000000000000
3	10000	2010-01-31 00:00:00.000	2009-12-31 00:00:00.000	78254.54000000000000000000	78254.54000000000000000000

We have three records which match the count from the view. They all have the same **Customer No.**, **Initial Entry Due Date**, and **Posting Date**. If we sum the **Amount** or **Amount (LCY)** fields from the three records we get the same total found in the view.

We can run the following code to calculate the sum of the **Amount** field from NAV:

```
DtlCustLedgEntry.SETCURRENTKEY(
    "Customer No.", "Initial Entry Due Date", "Posting Date");
DtlCustLedgEntry.SETRANGE("Customer No.", '10000');
DtlCustLedgEntry.SETRANGE("Initial Entry Due Date", 013110D);
DtlCustLedgEntry.SETRANGE("Posting Date", 123109D);
DtlCustLedgEntry.CALCSUMS(Amount);
```

If we run Client Monitor while executing this code we can see that it actually queries the view we have been talking about instead of going record-by-record and adding up the value.

Entry No.	Function Name	Parameter	Data
20	CALCSUMS	Table	Detailed Cust. Ledg. Entry
20	CALCSUMS	SumIndexFields	Amount
20	CALCSUMS	Order	Customer No.,Initial Entry Due Date,Posting Date,Currency Code,Entry No.
20	CALCSUMS	Filter	Customer No.:10000, Initial Entry Due Date:01/31/10, Posting Date:12/31/09
20	CALCSUMS	Source Object	Codeunit 50001 CALCSUMS Example
20	CALCSUMS	Source Trigger/Function	OnRun()
20	CALCSUMS	Source Line No.	
20	CALCSUMS	Source Text	DtlCustLedgEntry. CALCSUMS(Amount);
20	CALCSUMS	SQL Statement	SELECT SUM("SUM$Amount") FROM dbo."CRONUS USA, Inc_$Detailed Cust_ Ledg_ Entry$VSIFT$4"

Entry No.	Function Name	Parameter	Data
20	CALCSUMS	Sum	228,242.39
20	CALCSUMS	Elapsed Time (ms)	

See also

▸ Adding a FlowField to a table

▸ Creating a SumIndex field

▸ Displaying data from a SQL view in NAV

Using SQL Profiler

SQL Profiler is a tool similar to the Client Monitor in NAV. It allows you to create a trace of the T-SQL commands between NAV and SQL issued by a specific user. This recipe will show you the basics of setting up a SQL trace and what to do with the data afterwards.

How to do it...

1. Go to **Start** | **All Programs** | **Microsoft SQL Server 2008** | **Performance Tools** | **SQL Server Profiler**.

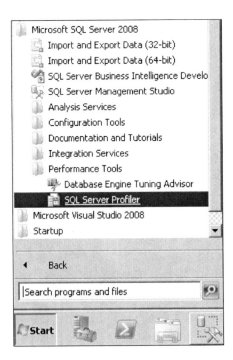

2. Click on **File | New Trace**. This will prompt you to connect to a SQL Server.

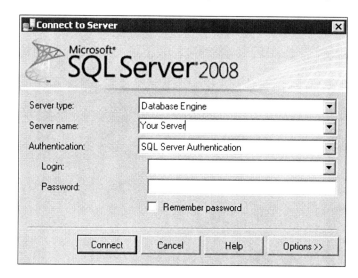

3. Once you have connected to the server, you will be presented with the **Trace Properties** screen.

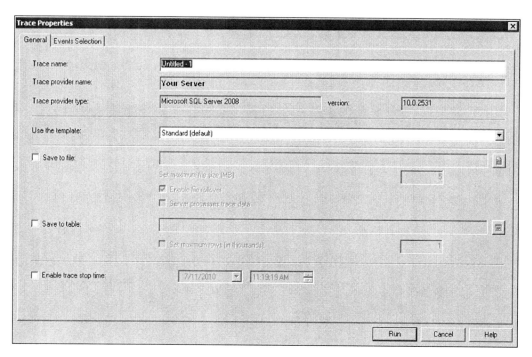

4. Here you can set the name of the trace and how you would like to save it. You can also click on the **Events Selection** tab to choose exactly what types of events and fields you want to record.

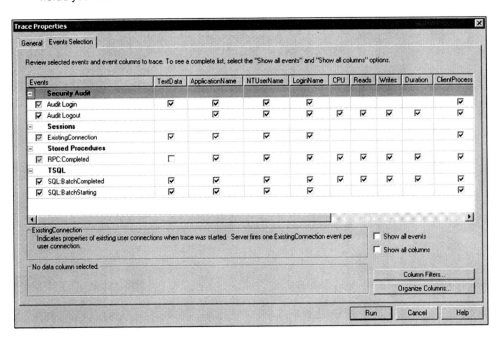

5. When you are satisfied with the setup you can click the **Run** button. This will begin the trace and you will see an output similar to the following:

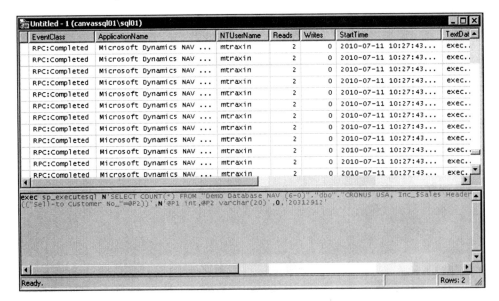

6. You can see the username, reads and writes on the database, execution time, and even the actual query being run. In this case, we were selecting the count of the total number of records in the **Sales Header** table.

How it works...

So what do you do with all of this data?

You can find processes that are taking too long to run using the Duration column. An example might be a posting routine or load time on a form. You could order the data by the number of reads and writes. This would tell you if you were maintaining too many indexes on a key during an insert or if you had a particularly CPU-intensive process.

What you do with it is really up to you. As you become more proficient in SQL Server and understand the basics, I highly recommend that you pick up some advanced books like *SQL Server 2008 Query Performance Tuning Distilled* by Grant Fritchey and Sajal Dam. These advanced discussions on the inner working of SQL Server are beyond the scope of this book, but I have no doubt that you will find them useful as you dive deeper into this area of NAV.

See also

▸ Using Client Monitor to diagnose problems
▸ Figuring out who is blocking whom

Displaying data from a SQL view in NAV

Most of the data in NAV is stored in tables, but you can also display data from other sources. This recipe will explain how to show data from a SQL View in NAV.

How to do it...

1. Open **SQL Server Management Studio**.
2. Select your database and open a new query window.
3. Execute the following code:

```
CREATE VIEW [Customer Ledger View] AS
    SELECT "Customer No_","Initial Entry Due Date","Posting Date",
                COUNT_BIG(*) "$Cnt", SUM("Amount") "SUM$Amount",
                    SUM("Amount (LCY)") "SUM$Amount (LCY)"
    FROM "CRONUS USA, Inc_$Detailed Cust_ Ledg_ Entry"
    GROUP BY "Customer No_", "Initial Entry Due Date",
        "Posting Date"
```

4. Create a new table from **Object Designer**.

5. Add the following fields to the table:

Field Name	Data Type	Length
Customer No_	Code	20
Initial Entry Due Date	Date	
Posting Date	Date	
$Cnt	BigInteger	
SUM$Amount	Decimal	
SUM$Amount (LCY)		

6. Set the following properties on the table.

Property	Value
DataPerCompany	No
LinkedObject	Yes
LinkedInTransaction	No

7. Save the table as **Customer Ledger View**.

8. When you run the table you will see the following data:

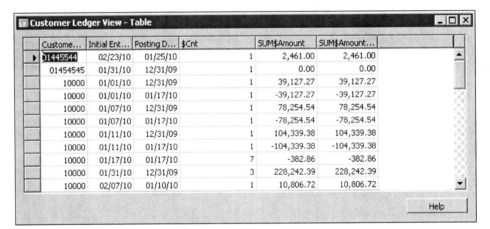

How it works...

First we create a view that we want to display in NAV. This view is actually a copy of a VSIFT view from the **Customer Ledger Entry** table.

Next we create a table in NAV with the exact same name and the exact same field names.

At this point, we have two separate objects with the same structure, a table and a view. Now we need to link the two together. The table has a property called `LinkedObject` that we need to set to `Yes`. This makes the `LinkedInTransaction` property available which should be set to `No`. We also need to set the `DataPerCompany` property to `No`. With these properties set, the server knows that these objects refer to each other because they have the same name.

There's more...

Be careful when displaying this data in a NAV form or page. You can inadvertently allow users to modify or delete records that they do not have permission to. The View is not the same as the table. That means a user could have no permissions to do anything with the G/L Entry table, but could do anything they wanted with a view on that data. NAV permissions do not apply to linked objects.

See also

- ▸ Creating a table
- ▸ Creating a basic SQL query

Figuring out who is blocking whom

Deadlocking can be a common occurrence in NAV. Unfortunately, users cannot work in the system when their actions are being blocked by another user. This recipe will show you how to determine who is blocking other users and resolve the situation.

How to do it...

1. Open **SQL Server Management Studio**.
2. Open a new query window.
3. Execute the following code:

   ```
   sp_who
   ```

4. You will see results similar to this:

	spid	ecid	status	loginame	hostname	blk	dbname	cmd	request_id
1	1	0	background	sa		0	NULL	RESOURCE MONITOR	0
2	2	0	background	sa		0	NULL	XE TIMER	0
3	3	0	background	sa		0	NULL	XE DISPATCHER	0
4	4	0	background	sa		0	NULL	LAZY WRITER	0
5	5	0	background	sa		0	NULL	LOG WRITER	0
6	6	0	background	sa		0	NULL	LOCK MONITOR	0
7	7	0	background	sa		0	master	SIGNAL HANDLER	0
8	8	0	sleeping	sa		0	master	TASK MANAGER	0
9	9	0	background	sa		0	master	TRACE QUEUE TASK	0
10	10	0	sleeping	sa		0	master	TASK MANAGER	0
11	11	0	background	sa		0	master	BRKR TASK	0

How it works...

The `sp_who` command queries the `sys.sysprocesses` system table in SQL. It returns a list of all connections to the server and if they are being blocked by anyone, the column labeled **blk** will be filled in with the **spid** of the user doing the blocking.

This provides similar information to what can be found in NAV. If you go to **File | Database | Information**, and drill down into the **Current Sessions** number, you can see the users who are being blocked.

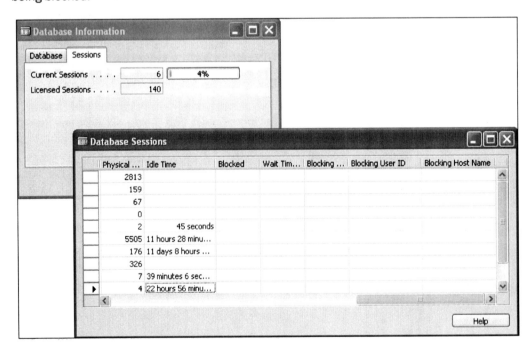

There's more...

You can also write your own query to find the deadlocks.

Another way to find deadlocks

The following query will pull all of the user IDs that are blocked as well as the root cause of the block.

```
SELECT
  SP.[spid] AS [SPID],
  CASE WHEN SP.[blocked] > 0 THEN 'Yes' ELSE '' END AS [Blocked],
  SP.[blocked] AS [Blocked by SPID],
  SP.[nt_username] AS [User ID],
  SD.[name] AS [Database],
  SP.[waittime],
  SP.[status] as [Current Status],
  SP.cmd AS [Current Command]

  FROM
    [master].[dbo].[sysprocesses] AS SP JOIN
    [master].[dbo].[sysdatabases] AS SD ON
        (SP.dbid = SD.dbid) LEFT OUTER JOIN
    [master].[dbo].[sysprocesses] AS SP2 ON (SP.[blocked] =
                                            SP2.[spid])

  WHERE SP.[program_name] Like '%Dynamics NAV%'
  ORDER BY SP.[waittime] DESC, SP.cmd DESC
```

From there you can issue a KILL spid command where spid is the ID of the user doing the blocking.

See also

▶   Using SQL Profiler

Setting up a backup plan

Not all customers have an IT department, much less a full-time DBA on staff. It is extremely important that you know how to set up an automatic backup plan for your customers' databases.

How to do it...

1. Open **SQL Server Management Studio** and connect to your server. In the **Object Explorer** pane on the left-hand side, expand the tree to **Management**, **Maintenance Plans**.

2. Right-click on the **Maintenance Plans** folder and select **Maintenance Plan Wizard**.

3. Click **Next**.

4. In the following window, you can set the name of your backup plan as well as the basic schedule.

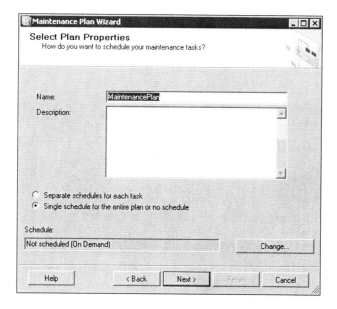

5. Click the **Change...** button.

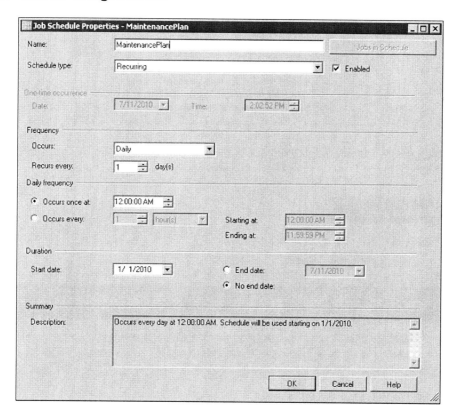

6. Here we have chosen to run our backup every midnight.

7. Click **Next**.

8. Check the **Database Backup** (Full) checkbox.

9. Click **Next**.

10. Click **Next** again.

11. Select the database(s) that you want to backup.

12. Keep clicking **Next** until you finish the wizard.

How it works...

When you have completed the Wizard you will see new items in the **Object Explorer** tree.

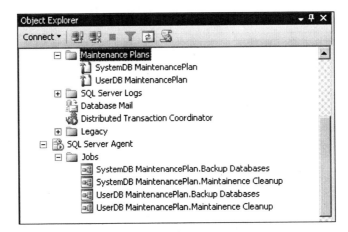

Here we can see two separate maintenance plans and the **Jobs** that they have created. These jobs will execute at the time we specified in the wizard and backup our database.

See also

▶ Adding the xp_ stored procedures

▶ Scheduling NAV tasks from SQL Server

Scheduling NAV tasks from SQL Server

You cannot call NAV code directly from outside the database, but you can create a .NET program that can be used by SQL to issue commands through a NAV web service. This recipe will show you exactly what to do.

How to do it...

1. Create a new SQL CLR project in Visual Studio. When creating this project you will have to add a reference to your NAV database.

2. Right-click on your project in **Solution Explorer** and add a new stored procedure named NAVJobScheduler.

3. Add the following code to the project:

```
using System;
using System.Net;
using System.IO;
using System.Xml;

public partial class StoredProcedures
{
  [Microsoft.SqlServer.Server.SqlProcedure]
  public static void NAVJobScheduler(
      string ObjectType, int ObjectID, string Login,
      string Password,string Domain,string WebServiceURL)
  {
    string Body =
        @"<soapenv:Envelope xmlns:soapenv=
        ""http://schemas.xmlsoap.org/soap/envelope/""xmlns:run=
        ""urn:microsoft-dynamics-schemas/codeunit/RunObject"">"
        + "<soapenv:Header/>" + "<soapenv:Body>" + "<run:RunJob>"
        + "<run:objectType>" + ObjectType + "</run:objectType>" +
        "<run:objectID>" + ObjectID + "</run:objectID>" +
        "</run:RunJob>" + "</soapenv:Body>" +
        "</soapenv:Envelope>";

    WebRequest request = HttpWebRequest.Create(WebServiceURL);
    request.Headers.Add("SOAPAction", @"""urn:microsoft-
                dynamics-schemas/codeunit/RunObject:RunJob""");
    request.ContentType = "application/xml; charset=utf-8";
    request.ContentLength = Body.Length;
    request.Method = "POST";

    System.Net.CredentialCache myCredentials = new
                                System.Net.CredentialCache();
    NetworkCredential netCred = new NetworkCredential(
                                Login, Password, Domain);
    myCredentials.Add(new Uri(WebServiceURL), "NTLM", netCred);
    request.Credentials = myCredentials;
    Stream strWrite = request.GetRequestStream();
    StreamWriter sw = new StreamWriter(strWrite);
```

```
sw.Write(Body.ToString());
sw.Close();

WebResponse wr = request.GetResponse();
HttpWebResponse httpRes = (HttpWebResponse)wr;
Stream s = httpRes.GetResponseStream();
StreamReader sr = new StreamReader(s);
XmlDocument xmlDoc = new XmlDocument();
xmlDoc.Load(sr);

if (xmlDoc.FirstChild.FirstChild.FirstChild.FirstChild.
                      FirstChild.Value != "SUCCESS")
{
  throw new Exception(
  "ObjectType " + ObjectType + " ObjectID " +
       ObjectID.ToString() + " failed with Error: " +
       xmlDoc.FirstChild.FirstChild.FirstChild.
       FirstChild.FirstChild.Value);
}
  }
};
```

4. Save, compile, and close the project.

5. Create a new codeunit in **Object Designer**.

6. Add a function named `RunObject`. This function should return a text value.

7. Add the following code to the function:
   ```
   EXIT('SUCCESS');
   //EXIT(GETLASTERRORTEXT);
   ```

8. Compile and save the object.

9. Run **Form 810, Web Services**.

10. Add the codeunit and check the **Published** column.

11. Open **SQL Server Management Studio**.

12. Expand the **SQL Server Agent, Jobs** folder from **Object Explorer**.

13. Right-click the **Jobs** folder and select **New Job**.

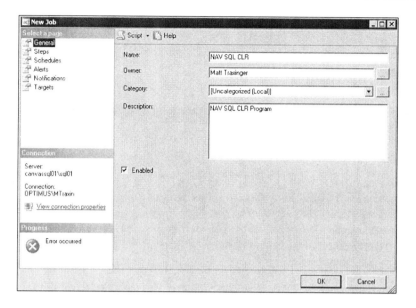

14. Click on the **Steps** option on the left-hand side.

15. Click **New**.

16. Enter the information as shown in the following screenshot:

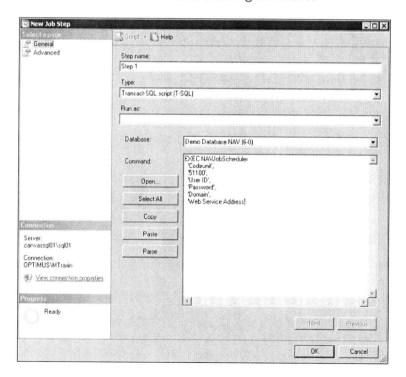

17. Click **OK**.

18. Save the job.

How it works...

First off, let me give credit where credit is due. This recipe is based on a blog entry by Rashed Amini, or ara3n as you may know him from the forums. It can be found here:

```
http://mibuso.com/blogs/ara3n/2009/11/14/replacing-nas-with-sql-jobs-
and-nav-web-service/
```

This program is built on **SQLCLR**, or **SQL Common Language Runtime**. . It allows .NET code to be executed within the SQL Server environment. Our function takes in six parameters. The first two are the object type and object ID of the object that should be run in NAV. The next three are the login information that is used to connect to the database. The last is the web service address that is published by NAV.

Our code starts by creating a SOAP message. **SOAP** stands for **Simple Object Access Protocol** and is a way to exchange information across web services. This message is stored in our string variable named Body.

Next, we need to initiate a request to our web service. We create our credentials using the domain, login ID, and password that we passed to the function. The value stored in the body variable, the SOAP message, is then sent to the Request Stream of the web service. Once the web service is done processing our request we retrieve the response that it sends back to us. This response is sent back to us in the form of an XML document. We can parse that document to find a Success error message, or possibly the error message generated by NAV.

For more information about creating your own CLR code have a look at the following website: `http://www.codeproject.com/KB/cs/CLR_Stored_Procedure.aspx`

Our NAV codeunit is extremely simple. It always returns the word SUCCESS. You are most likely to execute your own code and return this value if it completed, otherwise you would return the last error message generated.

This codeunit must be published as a web service so that external applications can access it. This is easily accomplished with NAV 2009 through the Web Serviced form.

Finally, we create a SQL job to call our .NET code. You could just as easily execute that code in a query window.

For more on creating SQL jobs check out MSDN here: `http://msdn.microsoft.com/en-us/library/ms187910.aspx`

There's more...

With this type of program, you can get rid of the NAV Application Server. As NAV moves completely to SQL Server for database management, as well as for converting all C/AL code to be managed .NET code in NAV 2009, this type of coding will become more common. C/AL will not be going away any time soon, but NAV cannot reach its full potential with C/AL alone.

See also

- ▶ Creating a web service
- ▶ Consuming a web service
- ▶ Creating a custom NAS handler
- ▶ Writing your own Automation using C#
- ▶ Using ADO to access outside data
- ▶ Adding the xp_ stored procedures
- ▶ Setting up a backup plan

12

The RoleTailored Client

In this chapter, we will cover:

- ▸ Creating a page using the Page Generation Wizard
- ▸ Building a Role Center
- ▸ Changing default filter columns
- ▸ Building the report layout
- ▸ Interactive sorting for reports
- ▸ Displaying a graph on a report
- ▸ Displaying a .NET add-in on a page

Introduction

The RoleTailored client represents a major paradigm shift for NAV developers. It was introduced with NAV 2009 as a new way for users to access the data they use in their day-to-day tasks. This version of NAV represents the transition phase between the Classic and RoleTailored approaches to the system; NAV 2009 is the last version where the Classic client is available and the first where the RoleTailored client is available.

As a developer you will find yourself performing the same types of tasks, but in different ways. For example, you are will still be building on ways to show data to the user, but where forms had a visual design component, pages will now be designed primarily through an interface similar to XMLports. You still build reports in C/AL, but they have to be converted for use with the RoleTailored client. This chapter will show you how to perform some of the basic tasks associated with developing for this new interface style.

Creating a page using the Page Generation Wizard

Pages are the objects that display data in the RoleTailored client. They are similar to forms in the Classic client. This recipe will show you how to design a basic page.

How to do it...

1. Create a new page from **Object Designer**.
2. Enter **Customer** for **Table**.
3. Select **Create a page using a wizard**.
4. Select **Card**.

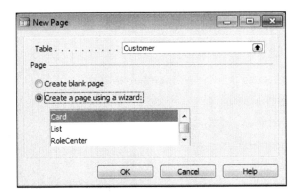

5. Click **OK**.
6. Add a line for a new FastTab called **Communication**.

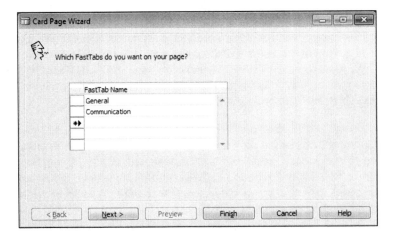

7. Click on **Next**.

8. Add the **No.**, **Name**, **Address**, **City**, and **County** fields to the **General** tab.

9. Add the **Phone No.** and **E-mail** fields to the **Communication** tab.

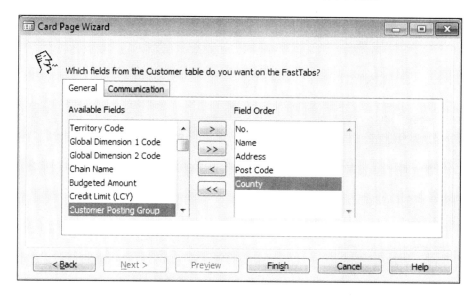

10. Click **Finish**.

11. The source of your page will look like the following screenshot:

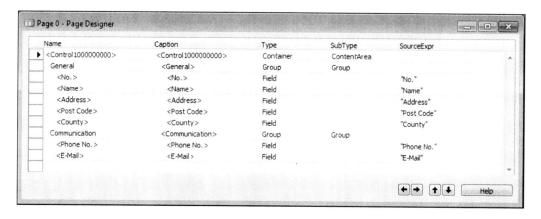

12. Compile, save, and close the page.

13. In NAV 2009 SP1 you can run the page directly from Object Designer. It will look like the following screenshot:

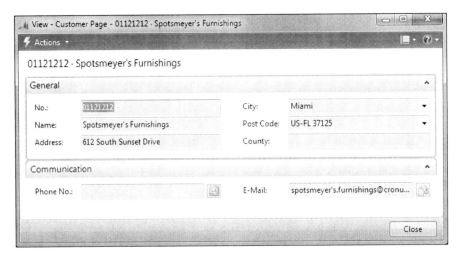

How it works...

Pages are the way the new RoleTailored client displays data. They are similar to forms in functionality, but different in their design. Currently, there is no visual page designer. Until one becomes available, the quickest way to build a page is by using the wizard.

The Page Generation Wizard is very similar to the Form Generation Wizard. We start by selecting the table to which the page will be bound along with the type of page to create.

In the NAV Classic client, the tabs were spaced horizontally across the screen. In the RoleTailored client they are called **FastTabs** and are spaced vertically. These tabs can be minimized on the screen or expanded to show all the data at once. Just as we do in the Form Generation Wizard, here we specify the names of our tabs: **General** and **Communication**.

Now we must choose the fields that will be displayed within each tab. This is exactly the same as the Form Generation Wizard. The fields can be selected in the panel on the left-hand side and moved to the panel on the right-hand side to add them.

When you click on **Finish** you may be surprised at what you see. It is not at all like the Form Designer you may be used to, but instead it is a list of page elements. Let's take a look at each of these lines and how they relate to what we have just done.

Every page begins with a container element. In this case, our container is a **ContentArea**. All of the lines indented beneath this container will be displayed within it. This container has two group elements that represent the FastTabs. Each group is made up of multiple field elements, similar to the textboxes on forms.

It is difficult to visualize how the page will look like in this form, so you may find yourself previewing it much more often than you would when designing a form object.

There's more...

For a more comprehensive look at pages and how to build them, I encourage you to read *Programming Microsoft Dynamics NAV 2009*, by David Studebaker. You will find examples of how one can position elements on the page, add elements to the toolbar, and many others.

See also

- ▶ Using the Form Generation Wizard
- ▶ Changing default filter columns
- ▶ Displaying a .NET control on a page

Building a Role Center

The Role Center is like a dashboard that displays data and functionality related to a specific user role. This recipe will show you how to create a Role Center page for the new RoleTailored client.

How to do it...

1. Create a new page from **Object Designer**.
2. Set the properties of the page as follows:

Property	Value
Caption	Activities
PageType	CardPart
SourceTable	Sales Cue

3. Add the following lines in the **Page Designer**:

Name	Caption	Type	SubType	SourceExpr
MainContainer	<Main Container>	Container	ContentArea	
ForReleaseGroup	For Release	Group	CueGroup	
OpenQuotes	Open Sales Quotes	Field		"Sales Quotes – Open"
OpenOrders	Open Sales Orders	Field		"Sales Orders – Open"

4. Set the following property on the **OpenQuotes** line:

Property	Value
DrillDownFormID	Sales Quotes

5. Set the following property on the **OpenOrders** line:

Property	Value
DrillDownFormID	Sales List

6. It should look like the following screenshot:

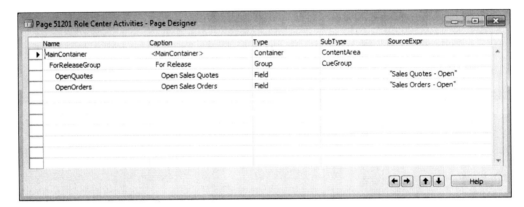

7. With your cursor on the **ForReleaseGroup** line click on **View | Actions**.

8. Add the following lines:

Name	Caption	Type
Action1	New Sales Quote	Action
Action2	New Sales Order	Action

9. Set the following property on the **New Sales Quote** line:

Property	Value
RunObject	Page Sales Quote

10. Set the following property on the **New Sales Order** line:

Property	Value
RunObject	Page Sales Order

11. Compile, save, and close the page.

12. Create a new page from **Object Designer** with the following lines.

Name	Caption	Type	SubType
Content	<Content>	Container	RoleCenterArea
LeftSide	<LeftSide>	Group	Group
Activities	<Activities>	Part	
Outlook	<Outlook>	Part	
RightSide	<RightSide>	Group	Group
MyCustomers	<MyCustomers>	Part	
MyItems	<MyItems>	Part	
MyNotes	<MyNotes>	Part	

13. They should be indented as shown in the following screenshot:

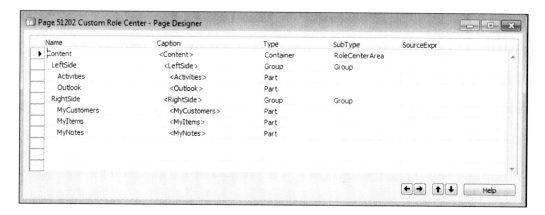

14. Set the following property on the **Activities** line:

Property	Value
PartType	Page
PagePartID	The ID of the activities page that we just created

15. Set the following property on the **Outlook** line:

Property	Value
PartType	System
SystemPartID	Outlook

16. Set the following property on the **MyCustomers** line:

Property	Value
PartType	Page
PagePartID	My Customers

17. Set the following property on the **MyItems** line:

Property	Value
PartType	Page
PagePartID	My Items

18. Set the following property on the **MyNotes** line:

Property	Value
PartType	System
SystemPartID	Notes

19. Compile, save, and close the page. The resulting Role Center should look like the one shown in the following screenshot:

How it works...

The Role Center works as a one-stop shop for the user's most important tasks. It displays tasks that the user needs to perform along with data that relates specifically to them.

The first part of the Role Center is known as **Activities**. This is where the user looks to know what actions they need to do. The activities are built on top of special tables known as **Cues**. These Cue tables are made mostly of FlowFields and FlowFilters. We are going to build our activities part on the **Sales Cue** table. It should display any Open Sales documents we are working on.

By adding the **Group** line to our page and specifying the SubType as a `CueGroup`, we tell the RoleTailored client to display the fields indented beneath it in a specific way. Activities are displayed as stacks of paper that grow and shrink based on the numbers returned by the FlowFields in the Cue table. Additionally, in order to provide the same type of data access that you would gain on a form, we specify the `DrillDownFormID` for each of the fields or activities. We can also define actions on our group lines. In this example, we have created simple links to create new sales quotes and sales orders.

This is just a part of the Role Center, though. Now we need to build the actual page that will display the activities part. Like all pages, we begin with a container, but this time we set the SubType to `RoleCenterArea`. This essentially divides the page vertically into a left and right section. We add groups for each of these sections and then choose what to display.

Deciding what to display is fairly straightforward. Instead of adding fields to our group, we add **Parts**. First we choose what type of part will be shown. For our activities, this will be a `Page` object, so we set the `PartType` property to `Page` and the `PagePartID` to the object ID of the page. Directly beneath that part, we are displaying the built-in Outlook part. For this we set the `PartType` to `System`, because it comes with NAV, and the `SystemPartID` to `Outlook`. The right-hand side is made up of similar parts.

There's more...

Role Centers are not easy to build from scratch. One easy way to build them is to design an existing one and then save it under a new ID. From there you can edit it to fit to your needs.

For a more comprehensive look at Role Centers you should check out *Programming Microsoft Dynamics NAV 2009*, by David Studebaker or *Chapter 3* of *Implementing Microsoft Dynamics NAV*, by David Roys and Vjekoslav Babic.

See also

▸ Creating a table

▸ Adding a FlowField to a table

▸ Using the Form Generation Wizard

▸ Creating a page using the Page Generation Wizard

▸ Displaying a .NET control on a page

Changing default filter columns

Some fields in the RoleTailored client allow filter-as-you-type functionality, meaning that as you type into the textbox a drop-down menu will display all the available options. This recipe will show you how to customize such a drop-down menu.

How to do it...

1. Design the **Customer** table from **Object Designer**.

2. Select the last line in the table and click on **View | Field Groups**.

3. Enter (or replace) the following line in the window:

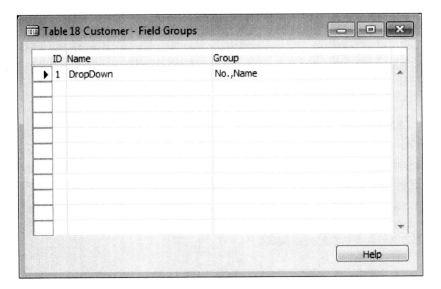

4. When you begin to type in any field with a table relation to the **Customer** table you will see a drop-down menu as shown in the following screenshot:

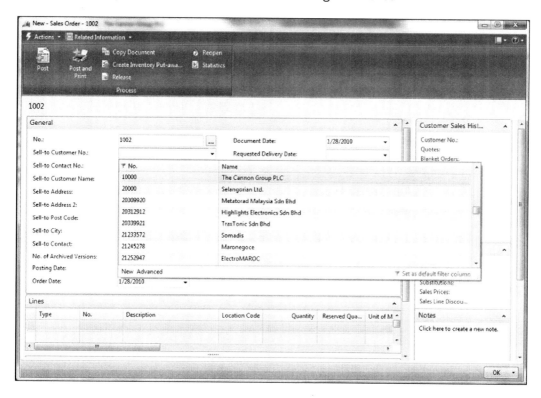

5. As you type, the list will automatically filter with the possible values.

How it works...

In the RoleTailored client, some data is displayed as you type in the field. This keeps the user from having to open a list and finding the record. All the information needed is provided in one place.

Fortunately, this is easy to customize. NAV provides a functionality called **Field Groups**. Specifically, a Field Group called **DropDown**, controls which fields are displayed in the view. When the system sees a group with this name it shows the fields specified in the **Group** column.

There's more...

If you want to learn more about Field Groups you can search the NAV C/SIDE help or read NAV Development course books.

See also

- ▶ Creating a page using the Page Generation Wizard
- ▶ Creating a table
- ▶ Using advanced filtering

Building the report layout

In the RoleTailored client reports are based on **SQL Reporting Services**. These reports are still built within NAV, but they are translated into a layout that can be read by Visual Studio. This recipe will show you how to build and change this layout.

How to do it...

1. Create a report as described in the *Using the report generation wizard* recipe.

2. Click on **Tools | Create Layout Suggestion**.

3. After a few seconds it will open in Visual Studio.

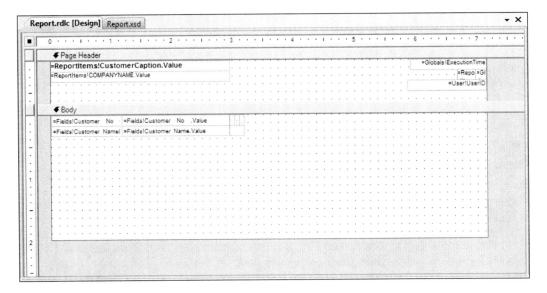

4. We could change things around here, but we will leave it as is. Compile, save, and close the report layout.

5. When running the report you will be presented with the request page.

6. After you click on **Preview** you will see the report generate. It should look similar to the one shown in the following screenshot:

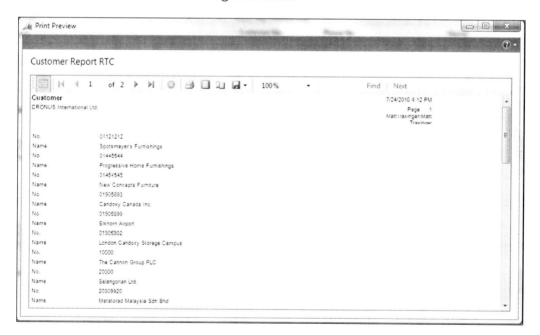

How it works...

NAV will do its best to automatically translate your report layout to one that is compatible with SQL Reporting Services and Visual Studio. This is done using the **Create Layout Suggestion** command under the **Tools** menu.

From Visual Studio you can click on **View | Toolbox** to see the available controls you can add to your report.

There's more...

In NAV 2009, you have to think about data items a little differently. In the older versions of the product, data items were indented to show the relationship between the two. For example, you would indent a Customer Ledger Entry data item under a Customer data item and link them with the customer number. You can probably visualize it with the following structure:

- Customer No. 1
    - Ledger Entry 1
    - Ledger Entry 2

- Customer No. 2
    - Ledger Entry 3

In SQL Reporting Services, the data is flattened out using a SQL JOIN statement. In other words, each combination of Customer and Customer Ledger Entry is combined into a single record like this:

Customer No. 1 : Ledger Entry 1

Customer No. 1 : Ledger Entry 2

Customer No. 2: Ledger Entry 3

It may not make a difference to how you design your reports, but it is important to know what is happening in the background.

See also

- Using the Report Generation Wizard
- Interactive sorting for reports
- Displaying a graph on a report

Interactive sorting for reports

With the NAV Classic client you can sort data only based on keys that currently exist in the database. The RoleTailored client allows you to sort on any column that is displayed on the report.

How to do it...

1. Build the report layout as described in the *Building the report layout* recipe.

2. Click on **View | Layout**.

3. Change the layout so that the data is presented in columns. You can do this by deleting the existing table and dragging a new one from the toolbox to the **Body** section.

4. The result should look similar to the following screenshot:

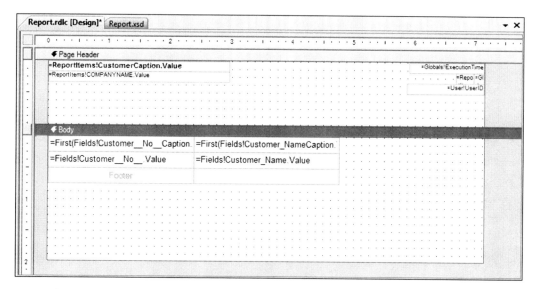

5. Right-click on the **Table Header** cell for the **Customer No.** field and go to **Properties**.

6. Click on the **Interactive Sort** tab.

7. Check the box for **Add an interactive sort action to this textbox**.

8. In the **Sort expression:** select the **Customer No.** field.

9. The properties should be set as follows:

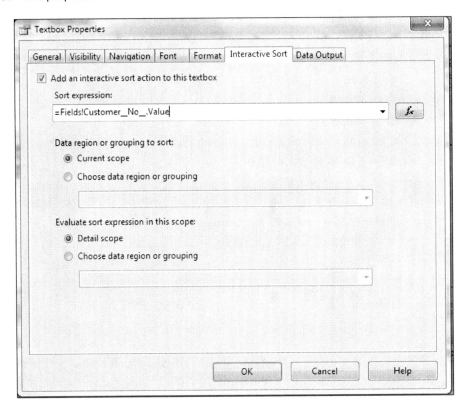

10. Repeat for the **Customer Name** textbox.

11. Compile, save, and close the report layout.

12. Compile, save, and close the report.

13. When you run the report you will notice two small arrows next to the column headers:

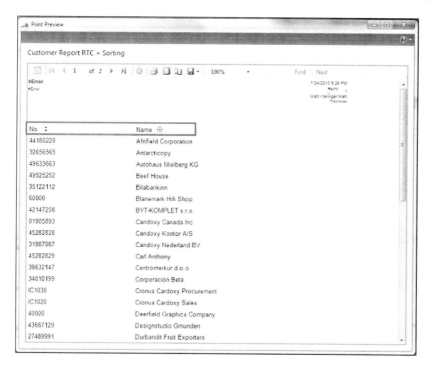

14. You can use them to sort the data.

How it works...

SQL Reporting Services allows for a lot of functionality that were just not possible in base NAV reporting. One of them is interactive sorting of columns. You can set columns to be sortable by setting a property on the textbox in Visual Studio. On the **Interactive Sort** tab for the properties of the textbox, you simply check a box to allow sorting and then tell it how you want to sort.

The next time you run the report you will see small arrows next to each column header. An arrow in a circle means that the report is currently sorted by that column, while two small arrows mean that it is a sortable column.

There's more...

I recommend reading the book *Programming Microsoft Dynamics NAV 2009*, by David Studebaker or the *NAV 2009 Development Courseware/Application Designer's Guide* that ships with the product.

See also

▸ Building the report layout

▸ Displaying a graph on a report

Displaying a graph on a report

Graphs and other data visualization techniques make for more interesting and sometimes more useful reports. Until NAV 2009, these types of reports were missing. This recipe will show you how to leverage these options in the RoleTailored client.

How to do it...

1. Create a new Tabular style report using the Report Generation Wizard. It should be based on the **Customer** table and display the **No.**, **Name**, and **Location Code** fields.

2. Click on **Tools | Suggest Report Layout**. After a few seconds the report will open in Visual Studio.

3. In Visual Studio, click on **View | Toolbox**.

4. Drag a Chart Report Item to the body of the report.

5. Right-click on the chart and go to **Properties**.

6. On the **General** tab change the Title to **Customers by Location**.

7. Change the **Chart type** to a **Pie chart**.

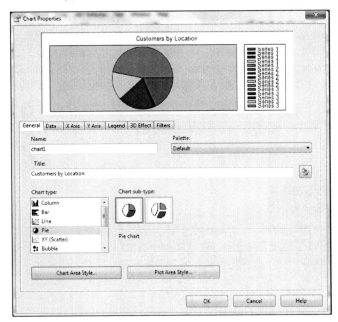

8. On the **Data** tab click on the **Add** button in the **Values** area.

9. Clear the **Series label** textbox.

10. In the **Value** textbox enter the following formula: `=Count(Fields!Customer__Location_Code_.Value)`

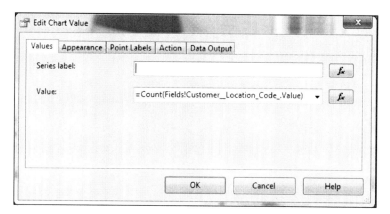

11. Click **OK**.

12. Click **OK** to close the **Chart Properties** window. Your layout should now look like the following screenshot:

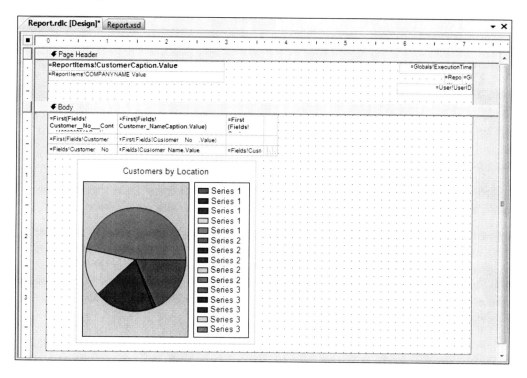

13. Compile, save, and close the layout.

14. Compile, save, and close your NAV report.

15. When you run the report you should see a graph on the last page similar to the following screenshot:

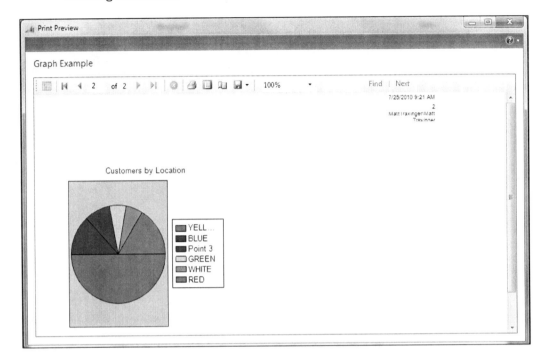

How it works...

With NAV 2009, we are no longer bound to the boring black and white reports of the past. Not only can you display your text in beautiful, vibrant color, but you can also show data visualizations in the form of built-in graphs.

To start, we drag a graph control from the Visual Studio toolbox to the **Body** section of the report. We have a variety of graphs to choose from, but in this case we will show a pie chart.

Setting up the data for the graph is very similar to setting up a graph or chart in Microsoft Excel. The **Data** tab on the graph properties allows you to set up the Series names as well as the actual values to display. Here we are displaying the total number of customers by location code. Just as we would in a NAV FlowField, we enter a COUNT formula. Notice how the series name in the legend defaults to the value "Point" and the index number if the display name is blank.

That is all there is to it. There are of course many more options, but as you can see, adding graphs to a report requires only a few clicks.

There's more...

For more information about reporting in NAV 2009 you can search the NAV C/SIDE Help or MSDN.

See also

- ▸ Building the report layout
- ▸ Interactive sorting for reports

Displaying a .NET add-in on a page

The NAV Page Designer is limited in what it can do and what data it can display. By creating a visual .NET add-in and adding it to a page, you can display your data in the same formats available in .NET Windows Forms.

Getting ready

Download and install the client add-in tool from Christian Abeln.

```
http://www.cooldudette.net/BlogFiles/AddInImporter.zip
```

How to do it...

1. Create a new class library project in Visual Studio.
2. Add the following references to the project:

   ```
   System.Windows.Forms
   Microsoft.Dynamics.Framework.UI.Extensibility
   ```

3. The latter can be found in the NAV installation directory under the `RoleTailored client` folder.
4. Add the following code to the program:

   ```
   using System.Xml;
   using System.Data;
   using System.Windows.Forms;
   using Microsoft.Dynamics.Framework.UI.Extensibility;
   using Microsoft.Dynamics.Framework.UI.Extensibility.WinForms;

   namespace RSSReader
   {
     [ControlAddInExport("NAV_RSS")]
     public class RSSReaderAddIn : WinFormsControlAddInBase
   ```

```csharp
{
  private DataGridView grid;

  public void LoadRSS(string URL)
  {
    System.Net.WebRequest myRequest =
                      System.Net.WebRequest.Create(URL);
    System.Net.WebResponse myResponse = myRequest.GetResponse();
    System.IO.Stream rssStream = myResponse.GetResponseStream();
    System.Xml.XmlDocument rssDoc = new
                                  System.Xml.XmlDocument();
    rssDoc.Load(rssStream);
    System.Xml.XmlNodeList rssItems =
                      rssDoc.SelectNodes("rss/channel/item");

    XmlNode attribute;
    int i = 0;

    foreach (XmlNode node in rssItems)
    {
      attribute = node.SelectSingleNode("title");
      string[] rowArray = new string[] { attribute.InnerText };
      grid.Rows.Add(rowArray);
      i++;
    }
  }

  public override bool AllowCaptionControl
  {
    get
    {
      return false;
    }
  }

  protected override Control CreateControl()
  {
    grid = new DataGridView();
    grid.Columns.Add("Title", "Title");
    grid.Columns["Title"].Width = 600;
    grid.Height = 500;
    LoadRSS(
        "http://mibuso.com/forum/smartfeed.php?u=
7776&e=dGmFiU150Nty0rhD8WG9KPwqlx38DiyvBH0tybeha8xNIA6Pr4x6EA..&
lastvisit=1&filter_foes=1&forum=32&limit=NO_LIMIT&count_limit=10&
sort_by=postdate_desc&feed_type=RSS2.0&feed_style=HTML");
    return grid;
  }
}
}
```

5. Go to the project properties and click on the **Signing** tab. Check the **Sign the assembly** checkbox.

6. Compile, save, and close the project.

7. Copy the NAV_RSS.dll file from your default project folder, usually under C:\ Users\Your Username\Documents\Visual Studio 2008\Projects\ RSSReader\RSSReader\bin\Debug to the Add-Ins folder for the RoleTailored client, usually under C:\Program Files (x86)\Microsoft Dynamics NAV\60\ RoleTailored Client\Add-ins.

8. Run form 100000, **Client Add-In**, from **Object Designer** in the Classic client. This object is found in the Client Add-In tool referenced in the *Getting started* section.

9. Click on **Register Add-Ins** and navigate to the NAV_RSS.dll file.

10. Click **Open**.

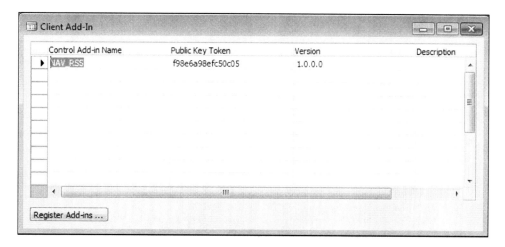

11. The add-in should be registered.

12. Create a new page from **Object Designer**.

13. Add the following lines:

Name	Caption	Type	SubType
MainContainer	<MainContainer>	Container	ContentArea
NAV_RSS	<NAV_RSS>	Field	

14. Set the following property on the **NAV_RSS** line:

Property	Value
ControlAddIn	NAV_RSS;PublicKeyToken=f98e6a98efc50c05

15. Your value may not be exactly the same. Use the lookup arrow to select the add-in. Your page should look similar to the following screenshot:

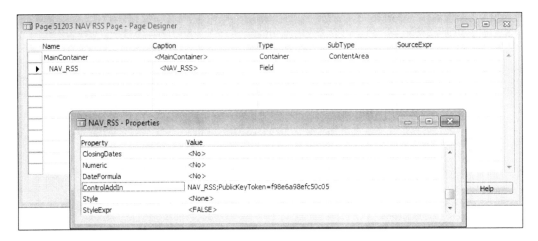

16. When you run the page it should similar to the following screenshot:

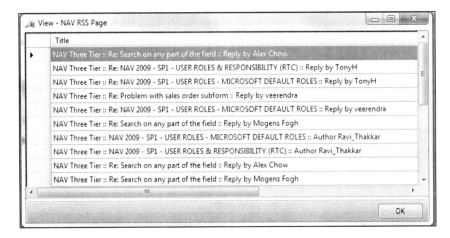

How it works...

In NAV 2009 SP1 you can create your own .NET objects to display in RoleTailored client pages. This is done by using the functionality in the `Microsoft.Dynamics.Framework.UI.Extensibility` dll.

For a complete list of Control classes you can search MSDN, but here we will display a simple GridView that contains the last 10 posts from the NAV 2009 Forum on one of my favorite websites, `www.Mibuso.com`.

The `LoadRSS` function is the bulk of our class, but it is not important to the recipe, so we will only discuss it in brief. Many sites publish data from their site in a format called **RSS**, or **Really Simple Syndication**. This RSS format is just a form of XML which can be parsed and used for our own use, in this case to fill in our **GridView**.

We have two functions that allow us to control the way we interact with pages in NAV 2009. The first is `AllowCaptionControl`. By overriding the function in the extensibility DLL file, we can force our control not to display a label.

The second function is the most important: `CreateControl`. It returns a control object which tells the RoleTailored client what to display. Our function sets up a simple grid with one column called **Title**. We then call our `LoadRSS` function to fill in the actual data.

In order to use this new DLL in NAV 2009 we also have to make sure it is a signed assembly.

With the Client Add-in tool, registering the new control in NAV is easy. When we select the file to register, it automatically determines the Public Key Token which is used to identify the DLL.

Finally, it is time to use our control in a page. We create a new page and add a field line. There is a property on field lines called `ControlAddIn` which we can point to our newly registered add-in.

Although it may not be the prettiest add-in, that is all there is to it. Our control is now ready to be used anywhere in the RoleTailored client.

See also

- ▸ Writing your own automation using C#
- ▸ Creating a page using the Page Generation Wizard
- ▸ Building a Role Center

Index

Thank you for buying
Microsoft Dynamics NAV 2009 Programming Cookbook

About Packt Publishing

Packt, pronounced 'packed', published its first book "*Mastering phpMyAdmin for Effective MySQL Management*" in April 2004 and subsequently continued to specialize in publishing highly focused books on specific technologies and solutions.

Our books and publications share the experiences of your fellow IT professionals in adapting and customizing today's systems, applications, and frameworks. Our solution-based books give you the knowledge and power to customize the software and technologies you're using to get the job done. Packt books are more specific and less general than the IT books you have seen in the past. Our unique business model allows us to bring you more focused information, giving you more of what you need to know, and less of what you don't.

Packt is a modern, yet unique publishing company, which focuses on producing quality, cutting-edge books for communities of developers, administrators, and newbies alike. For more information, please visit our website: www.PacktPub.com.

About Packt Enterprise

In 2010, Packt launched two new brands, Packt Enterprise and Packt Open Source, in order to continue its focus on specialization. This book is part of the Packt Enterprise brand, home to books published on enterprise software – software created by major vendors, including (but not limited to) IBM, Microsoft and Oracle, often for use in other corporations. Its titles will offer information relevant to a range of users of this software, including administrators, developers, architects, and end users.

Writing for Packt

We welcome all inquiries from people who are interested in authoring. Book proposals should be sent to author@packtpub.com. If your book idea is still at an early stage and you would like to discuss it first before writing a formal book proposal, contact us; one of our commissioning editors will get in touch with you.

We're not just looking for published authors; if you have strong technical skills but no writing experience, our experienced editors can help you develop a writing career, or simply get some additional reward for your expertise.

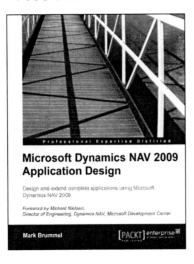

Microsoft Dynamics NAV 2009 Application Design

ISBN: 978-1-849680-96-7   Paperback: 496 pages

A focused tutorial for Microsoft Dynamics NAV application development

1. Learn how Dynamics NAV ERP suite is set up and customized for various industries

2. Integrate numerous parts of a company's operations including financial reporting, sales, order management, inventory, and forecasting

3. Develop complete applications and not just skeleton systems

4. Covers the design and implementation of two new add-on services: The Squash application and the Storage & Logistics application

Implementing Microsoft Dynamics NAV 2009

ISBN: 978-1-847195-82-1   Paperback: 552 pages

Explore the new features of Microsoft Dynamics NAV 2009, and implement the solution your business needs

1. First book to show you how to implement Microsoft Dynamics NAV 2009 in your business

2. Meet the new features in Dynamics NAV 2009 that give your business the flexibility to adapt to new opportunities and growth

3. Easy-to-read style, packed with hard-won practical advice

4. Real-world examples with step-by-step explanations

Please check **www.PacktPub.com** for information on our titles

Programming Microsoft Dynamics NAV 2009

ISBN: 978-1-847196-52-1   Paperback: 620 pages

Develop and maintain high performance NAV applications to meet changing business needs with improved agility and enhanced flexibility

1. Create, modify, and maintain smart NAV applications to meet your client's business needs

2. Thoroughly covers the new features of NAV 2009, including Service Pack 1

3. Focused on development for the three-tier environment and the Role Tailored Client

4. For experienced programmers with little or no previous knowledge of NAV development

Programming Microsoft® Dynamics™ NAV

ISBN: 978-1-904811-74-9   Paperback: 480 pages

Create, modify, and maintain applications in NAV 5.0, the latest version of the ERP application formerly known as Navision

1. For experienced programmers with little or no previous knowledge of NAV development

2. Learn as quickly as possible to create, modify, and maintain NAV applications

3. Written for version 5.0 of NAV; applicable for all versions

Please check **www.PacktPub.com** for information on our titles

LaVergne, TN USA
18 February 2011
217069LV00003B/21/P